*Culture and Entertainmer.*

# CULTURE AND ENTERTAINMENT IN WARTIME RUSSIA

Edited by
Richard Stites

*Indiana University Press*

*Bloomington and Indianapolis*

© 1995 by Indiana University Press

The paper used in this publication meets the minimum requirements of American
National Standard for Information Sciences—Permanence of Paper for Printed
Library Materials, ANSI Z39.48-1984.

Manufactured in the United States of America

**Library of Congress Cataloging-in-Publication Data**

Culture and entertainment in wartime Russia / edited by Richard
Stites.
p.  cm.
Includes index.
ISBN 0-253-35403-X (alk. paper).—ISBN 0-253-20949-8 (pbk.)
1. Soviet Union—Intellectual life—1917–1970.   2. Soviet Union—
Popular culture.   3. World War, 1939–1945—Soviet Union.
I. Stites, Richard.
DK273.R78   1995
947.084'2—dc20   94-27315

1  2  3  4  5  00  99  98  97  96  95

# Contents

# Contents

*Culture and Entertainment in Wartime Russia*

# 1

# Introduction

## Russia's Holy War

### Richard Stites

O N JUNE 22, 1941, without prior declaration of war, about 150 divisions of German and Axis satellite troops poured across the Soviet frontier, fanning out in three major frontal directions: Army Group North toward Leningrad, the city of Peter the Great; Army Group South toward Kiev, the ancient capital of old Rus; and Army Group Center—headed straight toward Moscow, the Soviet capital and the original seat of the Muscovite Tsars. In spite of previous warnings from Western sources and Soviet agents, the nation was stunned and its inhabitants thrown into agonizing panic and confusion. Joseph Stalin was among those shaken by this sudden attack that threatened to bring Soviet history to a violent conclusion after two and a half decades of Communist rule. The dictator disappeared from the public scene for two weeks and then came back to address his people on the radio. The picture was one of utter blackness: whole cities laid flat by bombers, airfields and their planes torn up; huge armies gobbled up in German pincer movement, hundreds of thousands of casualties, and prisoners destined to a terrible end in German camps. Citizens shivered in terror of the bombers that hovered over cities with their dreadful cargo. When Kiev fell to the invader, its Jewish population was rounded up and put to death brutally in the pits of Babi Yar. Leningrad was subjected to a blockade unprecedented in the annals of modern war and a million or more of its citizens perished of cold, hunger, and enemy shells. But Moscow held on. After dozens more major defeats and catastrophes, the Red Army turned the tide at Stalingrad, the Germans began moving back westward, and the Soviet steamroller stormed into Europe. It was one of the miraculous turnabouts of the twentieth century.[1]

After the initial shock of invasion, the populace gradually began to hear news about the massive losses at the front. Later came the stories and newsreels of the occupation: executions, massacres of hostages, POWs systematically starved, peasants dragged off as slave laborers to German factories. The German occupation was a genuinely horrifying experience. No recitation of numbers massacred, tortured, or enslaved can possibly evoke the kind of emotional response suitable to the phenomenon. One need only summon up the image—if one can—of a small baby being burned alive in a Belorussian barn along with an entire village to recapture even partly the shocked sense of what people endured over and over again. When the Soviet forces began moving back into the formerly occupied areas, even hardened soldiers—some of whom had participated in atrocities of their own making—were sickened by the grisly evidence: hostages hanged, young girls raped, men, women, children, old folks machine-gunned or sometimes buried alive. It may be even more difficult to recover those feelings of numbing fear, agony, loss, and painful death today because it is happening again in other parts of the world—and indeed has happened continuously since the end of World War II. The peoples of the USSR—along with Poles, Yugoslavs, and the European Jews—perished in numbers so large and in ways so barbarous as to defy the imagination. In the case of the Soviet people, the numbers probably reached toward thirty million dead.

On the Soviet home front, social volcanoes began erupting. State policy, military operations, and popular reaction to the invasion took numerous forms. The government, party, and police mobilized the people, evacuated personnel and factories to the rear, moved whole segments of the population around on an immense scale, relocated government offices and cultural establishments—including film studios and theaters—and saw to the manufacture of weapons, the transport of troops, and the recruitment of ever fresh levees. Within six months, over 1,500 large-scale enterprises, including over 100 aircraft factories, were evacuated; all in all about one-eighth of the nation's industrial assets were dismantled, relocated, and reassembled in the Urals, Central Asia, and Siberia. High school graduates of both sexes and women of all ages enlisted. Villagers melted into the forest and became partisans. Youngsters organized urban spy rings to wreak sabotage on the German garrisons. A million women served in the armed forces, not only in traditional wartime roles of nurses, doctors, and antiaircraft gunners, but also as flyers, soldiers, tankers, and partisans. They also played a big part in the wartime offering of culture and entertainment both at the front and behind the lines.[2]

State officials, the propaganda machine of the Communist Party, the unions and mass organizations, carefully reading the psychology of the wartime masses, constructed new myths and legends and cultural icons designed to draw upon the deep wells of national pride, to substitute emotional themes about the beloved homeland for the drier and more bombastic official patriotism of the prewar period. For reasons both noble and ignoble, they reached out to find the heart of war in every Russian and to make it beat the rhythms of love, hate, anger, and ridicule—all directed to the smashing of the "fascist" enemy and the saving of Mother Russia. The enemy was smashed, after the battles of Stalingrad and Kursk, and expelled from Soviet soil; and Mother Russia, ruined and despoiled though it was, was saved. The Red Army poured across Eastern Europe into Germany and by May 1945, the war in Europe was over.

Less well-known to the general public inside and outside the country at the time and even now is the grim unholy war of Russian atrocities. This part of the war was largely hidden from the public; the final campaigns were couched in triumphalism and the rhetoric about heroic liberators of enslaved peoples and inmates of the Nazi death camps of Poland. The rhetoric was by no means false but it obscured the story. Between 1939 and 1941, while the USSR was an ally of Hitler, about a million and a half Poles, Ukrainians, Belorussians, Jews, Lithuanians, and others were forcibly deported to the arctic North, Siberia, and Central Asia. In the nightmare of nocturnal arrests and searches, looting, cattle cars, resettlements, and executions, almost 300,000 people perished.[3]

Nor did wartime harmony and public spirit reign universal inside the Soviet Union itself. Drunkenness, looting, food riots, arson, and panic were visible in the early days. Authorities persecuted anyone vaguely suspected of disloyalty, cowardice, or in some cases ineptitude—to say nothing of desertion and shirking. Executions and other atrocities were unleashed inside the camps, and punishment units were formed for onerous and dangerous frontline duties. Among the biggest Soviet atrocities was the harsh punishment of suspected collaborators: whole nations such as the Volga Germans, Crimean Tatars, and the Mountain Peoples of the Caucasus were uprooted and relocated under hideous conditions even though the vast majority did not collaborate.[4]

During the final campaigns in Eastern Europe in 1944 and 1945, Red Army soldiers and security forces repeated on a larger scale the cruel actions of the Hitler-Stalin Pact period. The Polish anti-German resistance Home Army was, by deliberate military decision, allowed to be butchered by the Germans in Warsaw in 1944. The rape of Germany was an orgy of vengeance, which one of its historians tries to explain (without justifying its sickening sadism) as a combination of revulsion at the sight of the liberated Nazi death camps with their mountains of corpses and living skeletons, plain military rage, and the ferocious bloodthirsty language of hate propaganda poured forth throughout the war. Ilya Ehrenburg, a voice of hope and Russian patriotism, was also the principal voice of vengeance, especially as Soviet troops entered German territory. Some consider Stalin' s greatest crime against the Soviet people his treatment of his own country's repatriated prisoners of war, who were routinely jailed for cowardice or desertion when they returned home; others consider it the execution of the Vlasov soldiers who had volunteered to fight on the side of Hitler for a Russia without Stalinism. But it was far from Stalin's last crime, as Soviet Jews and the political, cultural, and religious leaders of Eastern Europe were to learn in the next eight years.[5]


Previous works have told in great detail the history of diplomacy, military operations, economics, political collaboration, and statecraft in this war; newer ones have described the home front and the memory of struggle and survival.[6] Still relatively neglected in general accounts is the cultural life of the time. This volume attempts to correct this, at least for the Russian population. The cultural contributions and experiences of the non-Russian nationalities have yet to be be chronicled, although Jews, it will be noted throughout these essays, played a prominent role in the creation and dissemination of culture and entertainment as well as propaganda. Religion and literature, though never adequately treated, have at least have been discussed and for that reason are mostly omitted from this book, which addresses the expressive life of the wartime experience in communications, creativity, entertainment, the arts, hagiography and legend-making, and finally the colossally important memorialization of the war. Elements of propaganda will be found in all of this, but it is not especially novel or original to the time or the place. The main focus of this volume is the resurfacing into public life of emotional and even spiritual expression, recently suppressed or distorted in the media during the 1930s.

Two cultural-psychological currents were at large during this momentous struggle, coexisting and occasionally clashing. The first was the official style of nationalism, authoritarianism, and hierarchy—formal, impersonal, pompous, and unnervingly unemotional. It expressed itself in various terms: Stalinism, *partiinost* (high ideological consciousness and dedication to political business), socialist realism (the fantasy world of 1930s art that required folkloric structures and idealistic messages), heroicized traditional history, revolutionary glory, and proletarian robustness. Perhaps only the Soviet Russian adjectives *ofitsioznyi* and *kazënnyi* can convey the terms of expression that in English suggest words like official, state, declamatory, pompous, inflated, bureaucratic, impersonal, formal, heraldic, authoritarian, operatic, stylized, melodramatic, posed, monumental, utopian, and panegyric. The style was burdened with values of official boast and state talk, as illustrated in the radio voices of Yurii Levitan and other announcers, communiqués, *Pravda* headlines and editorials, and some of the films, songs, music, plays, graphics, and legends.

But it was the unofficial and semiofficial culture that rose to ascendance after the initial shock and best expressed the feelings of a people at war. In vivid contrast to the official style, it was emotional, personal, loose, relaxed, earthy, coarse, natural, spontaneous, free, autonomous, expressive, honest about death and suffering and heroism and hate. Wartime culture reflected the resurgence in Soviet public culture of personal life, intimate feelings, a deep emotional authenticity, and even quasi-religiosity that had been muted during the "optimistic" thirties. Coming from below, it was, in the words of Jeffrey Brooks, "more truthful and humane" than what came before. Nina Tumarkin speaks of the "terrible freedom wrought by the shock of war" and she quotes survivors saying that "those were our finest hours, the most brilliant time of our lives." For those people, the horrors recalled with equal vividness did not blot out the golden glow of that memory. Suffering and perhaps fear led to a passionate exaltation of Russian nature, its people, history, culture, and ancient religion. Art in every form could not fail to intersect with the changing mood. The journalist Alexander Werth recalled "the extraordinary emotional atmosphere that summer, for instance at any routine Tchaikovsky concert—as though all Russian civilization were now in deadly danger. I remember the countless tears produced on one of the worst days in July 1942 by the famous love theme in Tchaikovsky's *Romeo and Juliet* Overture."[7]

All sources attest to the relative loosening of intellectual and creative controls in the years of the German occupation and the life and death struggle for national and state survival. Sad and terrible as it is to say, the war seemed to unleash creativity and create a kind of relieved joy. "When war flared up," wrote Boris Pasternak, "its real horrors and real dangers, the threat of a real death, were a blessing compared to the inhuman reign of fantasy, and they brought relief by limiting the magic force of the dead letter."[8] And the composer Dmitrii Shostakovich recalled "that the war helped. The war brought great sorrow and made life very hard. Much sorrow and many tears. But it had been even harder before the war, because then everyone was alone in his sorrow."[9] A community of honest, deep, and shared sorrow as well as the near unanimity in the hatred of the enemy helped to reshape national consciousness—to an extent that the old revolutionary élan could never again dislodge.

The persistent recollection of the war in the minds of millions continued to configure cinema, songs, performance arts, and fiction in the decades after 1945. The wartime mood was a complex and changing blend of emotions: hate, fear, contempt, sorrow, disgust, and euphoric joy—to name a few. The loss of life in this war exceeded that of all the other allied and enemy belligerents combined. For decades, Soviet people were constantly barraged by the regime with these facts; but they knew it also through family memory. In the present book, Nina Tumarkin has shown eloquently how the solemnized memory sponsored by the government often converged with the actual recollection of it by the people. To this process popular and high culture contributed a major share.

The cultural community—as this volume describes—was enlisted to popularize the major wartime themes: heroism and love of country; hate and ridicule of the invader. Military valor was among the first themes celebrated in the media, as had been the case in World War I under the Tsar. But now a new kind of hero, the city, was exalted for endurance or resistance; Leningrad, Brest, Kiev, Odessa, Sevastopol, and Stalingrad were eventually named Hero Cities. Mythic cults of human heroes and martyrs arose around the partisans, the twenty-eight Panfilov men, the five sailors of Sevastopol, Dovator's cavalry, the Young Guard of Krasnodon, and Captain Gastello who plunged his burning plane into an enemy armored column. Most famous of all were Alexander Matrosov, who in February 1942 allegedly threw his body across a German machine-gun nest to block its fire; and the partisan high-school girl Zoia Kosmodem'ianskaia, who was allegedly tortured and hanged by the Germans early in the war. Rosalinde Sartorti offers in this volume a searching analysis of hagiography and myth-making in Russian life. She points out that the function of these myths during the fighting is as important historically as their truth or falsity—and perhaps in a social psychological sense even more important.

The news of German atrocities quickly evoked the theme of hatred in Soviet public life. Implacable loathing erupted from all levels of culture but especially in the printed word. "With these hands of mine," wrote the poet Alexei Surkov about the Germans, "I want to strangle every one of them." Konstantin Simonov's "Kill Him!" was the culmination of a frenzied rage: "Kill a German, kill him soon/ And every time you see one—kill him."[10] Hate was accompanied by gross ridicule. Hitler, his minions, and his troops were portrayed in the circus, frontline shows, and graphic art as doomed descendants of Napoleon, physical degenerates—brutish, sly and stupid, gross, fat or bony, effeminate, and evil. Argyrios K. Pisiotis has analyzed the various levels and modes of emotional content in the cartoons and posters of the wartime period.

Beneath the alternating styles and patriotism and anti-Axis sentiment ran the deepest and most comprehensive current of wartime sensibility: home and country. Popular songs, as Robert A. Rothstein reveals in his essay, evoked simplicity and family happiness (real or imagined) with occasional visions of a rustic cabin or a home-town street. The land, with its familiar and often poeticized forms—rivers, steppes, meadows, birch trees, and endless forests—was tightly woven into wartime culture. To it was added the special thematics of such sacred and endangered places as Moscow and Leningrad. The Motherland (*rodina*)—often represented in graphic art as a maternal figure—became an object of unabashed idolatry. Russian history, traditions, cultural treasures, and the very soil itself were sacralized in story, song, and picture. Great heroes of the tsarist past were refurbished, and a temporary truce was reached with the Orthodox Church.

Propaganda and official pomposity never disappeared. One finds it even in the genuinely popular and emotional films: in *She Defends the Motherland*, the heroine stands on the gallows from which she has just been rescued and recites a speech that mixes human feeling with clichés from the press as Soviet planes soar overhead; in *Zoia*, after the heroine is hanged, her smiling face is superimposed against rolling tanks and troops moving westward to victory. After Stalingrad bombastic motifs of victory and military might suffused the media; and after the even greater battle of Kursk, resolemnization ensued on a vast scale. On the great day of victory over the Germans the surgeons of official culture began to excise the great heart that had beat so spontaneously in the cauldron of battle. Wartime songs and films were, to be sure, repeated again and again for decades. But they were sanitized, passed through a filter of piety and self-congratulation which burnt out much of the original spirit of some wartime culture. The multipurpose myth of war and victory extended down the decades; but the heart had become a valentine for the state.

What did soldiers expect of the postwar period? Probably a return to the imagined joys of prewar peacetime life (every day will be like the movie *The Great Waltz*, wrote a campaigner to his wife in 1942).[11] It was not to be. A major backlash took place against satire, modernism, jazz, and "unpatriotic" or "rootless" elements (such as Jews). The purge of certain war novels (especially Fadeev's *Young Guard*) is well known. But the entire postwar cultural pogrom—sometimes called the *zhdanovshchina* after its principal witch-hunter—was as much a reaction against wartime spontaneity, intimacy, emotionalism, and displays of eclectic desire for *both* deep Russian and Western entertainment forms as it was a reaction to the Cold War. But the latter did add a strong element of paranoid xenophobia. The replacement of the holy war by the Cold War brought a flourish of Russian chauvinism and anti-cosmopolitanism, a re-tightening of ideological orthodoxy and control, an austerity program that was covered over with a glistening cultural smile, and the escalation of the Stalin cult to unprecedented heights. Consciousness reasserted itself over the spontaneity born of battle, hardship, heroism, and adventure. Life returned to a tedious round of "prosaic tasks."

This book offers the most recent scholarship on the Russian cultural offerings of the wartime period—in the rear areas, on the home front, on the battlefield, and over the airwaves, with coverage ranging from the Moscow press to frontline correspondents in the field, from entertainment brigades at the front to amateur and spontaneous composition of songs and poems by fighting men and women; from symphonic representations of a country facing extinction to literary classics revived, adapted, republished, and read over the radio; from the stages of Moscow to folk ensembles performing on the battlefield; from the politicized organization and censorship of entertainment to the reception of cultural outpourings in the hearts and souls of ordinary people at war.

## Notes

1. For recent scholarship on the campaign, see *Operation Barbarossa: The German Attack on the Soviet Union, June 22, 1941*, ed. Norman Naimark, Alexander Dallin, David Holloway, and Sasha Pursley (special issue of *Soviet Union*, 18/1–3 [1991]).

2. John Barber and Mark Harrison, *The Soviet Home Front, 1941–1945: A Social and Economic History of the USSR in World War II* (London, 1991), pp. 59–76, 127–32; Anne Griesse and Richard Stites, "Russia: War and Revolution," in Nancy Goldman, ed., *Female Soldiers—Combatants or Noncombatants?: Historical and Contemporary Perspectives* (Westport, 1982), pp. 61–84. On wider issues of the war and its historiography and legacy, see the excellent collection, Hans-Heinrich Nolte, ed., *Der Mensch gegen den Menschen: Überlegungen und Forschungen zum deutschen Überfall auf die Sowjetunion, 1941* (Hanover, 1992).

3. For one of many studies of these atrocities, see Jan Gross, *Revolution from Abroad: The Soviet Conquest of Poland's Western Ukraine and Western Belorussia* (Princeton, 1988).

4. Barber and Harrison, *Soviet Home Front*, pp. 59, 63–64; Robert Conquest, *The Nation Killers: The Soviet Deportation of Nationalities* (London, 1970); Alexander Nekrich, *The Punished Peoples: The Deportation and Fate of Soviet Minorities at the End of the Second World War* (New York, 1978).

5. On some of these events, see Christopher Duffy, *Red Storm on the Reich: The Soviet March on Germany, 1945* (New York, 1991).

6. For a review of the main scholarly works, see *Operation Barbarossa*; Barber and Harrison, *Soviet Home Front*; Helene Keyssar and Vladimir Pozner, *Remembering War: A U.S.-Soviet Dialogue* (New York, 1990).

7. Alexander Werth, *Russia at War, 1941–1945* (1964; New York, 1984), p. 410.

8. Pasternak quoted in Geoffrey Hosking, *A History of the Soviet Union* (London, 1985), p. 276.

9. Shostakovich and Solomon Volkov, ed., *Testimony: The Memoirs of Dmitri Shostakovich*, trans. Antonina Bouis (New York, 1979), p. 135.

10. Aleksei Surkov, *Sochineniia*, 2 vols. (Moscow, 1954), vol. 2 (especially the poems of 1941–43); Konstantin Simonov, *Sobranie sochinenii*, 12 vols. (Moscow, 1979–87), vol. 1, 105–107.

11. *Iskusstvo v boevom stroiu: Vospominaniia, dnevniki, ocherki* (Moscow, 1985), p. 235. *The Great Waltz* was a prewar Hollywood musical based on the life of the Strausses. This and other American movies were captured by Soviet troops at various stages of the war.

# 2

## *Pravda* Goes to War

### Jeffrey Brooks

PRAVDA WAS THE most authoritative printed word in the Soviet Union on the eve of World War II, and the center of an information system shielded from consumer demand and from the interests of most Soviet citizens.[1] Those who wrote for it spoke largely of the successes and shortcomings of the bureaucratic order to a "little public" of bosses, managers, activists, and party members. They represented people in the news as creatures of this order, motivated by commands from above.

The German invasion of June 1941 shattered this discourse. *Pravda* opened to new voices and new images of soldiers, partisans, civilians, and citizens. Discussions of bureaucratic tasks faded from the news. War imposed its own truths, which were often incompatible with the public language of the 1930s. War had little to do with the phony assignments and performance indicators of the Stalinist economy. Pompous directives from above often backfired, as did Stalin's famous May Day order of 1942 to destroy the Germans within the year. Under these conditions, an alternative story of the Soviet experience arose, one that allowed for a very different image of humanity. When the tide of war turned in 1943, Stalin and his supporters reinforced the old story, but their efforts were not entirely successful.

The chief characteristic of the leading central newspapers, and particularly *Pravda*, on the eve of the war was their association with the official Soviet project. The dominant narrative that unfolded from the late 1920s was the continuing story of the successes and failures of important officials and local cadres in carrying out their assignments.[2] Key words were task (*zadacha*) and job or assignment (*zadanie*).[3] The party, state, and Stalin assigned tasks, and people in the news carried them out. Stalin and his supporters used this composite fable to imbue Soviet society with a single meaning and purpose.[4] Public language atrophied. By 1940 newspaper writers motivated their protagonists, if at all, with orders and directives from above, but they frequently neglected to tell who gave the orders, except for Stalin.[5] The class consciousness and revolutionary idealism that had loomed large as public motivations after the October Revolution vanished from the press, as did explanations and rationalizations of policy.

A passive commentary ensued in which directives and occasions inspired actors, as if officials themselves were too lowly to take responsibility for society's progress. "Before party and city organizations stands a task [*zadacha*]," wrote a local official from Kalinin in the fall of 1940.[6] " 'The wise decision of the Party and Government,' said the award-winning kolkhoz member Ekaterina Rats, 'summons the Stakhanovite workers of the kolkhoz fields to work even better,' " observed a correspondent the following year.[7] "The shipbuilders of the Baltic Order-of-Lenin Factory named after Sergo Ordzhonikidze will fulfill their duty in the competition to honor the Seventeenth All-Union Conference," reads a January 10, 1941, report.

*Pravda*'s writers fit almost everything into this Stalinist story. The anonymous author of an article on education explained:

> The spring examination is a big event in the life of the higher school and in the life of each Soviet student. Why? The spring examination session ought to be a means to the resolution of the basic task [*zadacha*] posed before the higher educational institutions by the XVIII Congress of the VKP(b) [All Union Communist Party (Bolsheviks)]—raising the quality of higher education.[8]

"The masses" also belonged to this fantasy. The hearts of young people marching on Physical Culture Day in 1940 are "filled with gratitude toward the one to whose fatherly concern they owe their present happiness and their still more beautiful future, to the one who lovingly raises our youth, to Comrade Stalin."[9] Similarly, new Soviet citizens of Lithuania, only recently incorporated by force into the USSR, were reported to have written in a letter:

> Dear Iosif Vissarionovich! We understand very well that we have only taken the first steps. Before us stands an enormous task [*zadacha*]—to traverse the path traveled by the working people of the Soviet Union in the shortest time.[10]

On the eve of the war, commentators rarely explained policies or showed self-motivated public figures.[11] The people reported on in *Pravda* acted in the name of the party, the state, and official functions such as party conferences; or to please Stalin "personally."[12] At the core of such articles was a notion of agency and authority. People acted because of an order, an occasion, or the leader's wish. Other motivations were less common and personal ones, virtually nonexistent.[13] This behavioral logic may have been alien to most citizens, but not to the "little public," to whom obedience was familiar. Promoting this cramped vision of man, in which the Soviet people lost something of their humanity, Stalinists conjured up old traditions of servitude, patriarchal power, and of a nationality based on loyalty to the tsar and the state church. They also drew on the experience of early Bolsheviks, who helped collapse the image of the individual in the public mirror by promoting citizenship as state service and conspicuously disavowing the self, the family, and their own private lives.[14]

The war undercut this Stalinist universe, and those who wrote for *Pravda* and other central Soviet newspapers recast the language of Soviet power in order to confront it. The invasion could not be denied, and recognizing it challenged deep-seated habits of deception. But newspaper people did not stop lying because of the war. Even in the first year newspapers continued to cloak the workings of the police state, which now included imprisonment of newly persecuted nationalities, beginning with the Volga Germans; of soldiers who had been trapped in German encirclements; of so-called rumor mongers; and of many others.[15] *Pravda's* editors instead redirected their reportage to cover the German advance.[16] Although vigorously promoting the Stalin cult and other familiar features of the old order, they grudgingly allowed for new voices and new ways of thinking about the national polity, public authority, and the individual.[17]

One way to conceptualize variation in this medium is to see it as drama. After the invasion, the scene, actors, and actions on the Soviet public stage changed, and the dynamics of action shifted, particularly in terms of motive and agency in the sense of an overall logic of human actions.[18] What followed was a reshaping of the Soviet public imagination to suit the unyieldingly practical problems of fighting and surviving in wartime. The critic Vera Aleksandrova aptly described a parallel process in literature, when she wrote, "The future historian of Soviet letters will find that from the very first days the Soviet-German war brought about a change both in the themes and subject matter of Soviet literary works, and in their choice of heroes."[19] She herself observed a turn from Communist heroes to "ordinary, nonpartisan people of the masses—peasant women, children, townsmen, and villagers."[20] The process in *Pravda* was similar.

On June 22, 1941, *Pravda* was full of the usual news of the 1930s. The next day the paper announced the war with a small-type headline taken partly from Molotov's radio speech:

> Fascist Germany has made a bandit attack on the Soviet Union—our valiant army and fleet and the brave falcons of the Soviet air force are inflicting shattering blows on the aggressor. The government calls on all citizens of the Soviet Union to close ranks around our glorious Bolshevik Party, around the Soviet government, around our great leader—Comrade Stalin. Our cause is just. The enemy will be beaten. Victory will be ours.

Stalin's picture filled the upper left-hand quarter of page one; the text of Molotov's radio speech was on the right. Decrees on mobilization and public order appeared below. The rest of the paper contained reports of meetings denouncing the Germans and promising support for the war effort. Demonstrators were featured as peasants, workers, and *intelligenty*; and there were several signed statements, including one from the physicist P. L. Kapitsa. Such distinctions were soon to be uncommon.

Producing this first wartime issue, the editors affirmed continuities of the Stalinist order—the cult of the leader and the charismatic legitimation of the government, compulsory unanimity, and an idea of citizenship based on enthusiastic involvement in

Soviet institutions. Meetings denouncing "fascist reptiles" echoed those of the previous decade and even the 1920s, when commentators regaled readers with reports of citizens' calls for the execution of political opponents. Only in Molotov's appeal to all citizens did there seem to be a new note, suggesting a less exclusive polity.

Changes followed, however. The war was a problem of veracity for the Soviet press, as it was in all belligerent countries where patriotic reporters and governments that watched them wished to put a good face on war news. Yet the Soviets, as had the French a year earlier, had to deal with defeat. The first report from the Soviet military on June 23, 1941, when even Stalin had little idea what was happening, read in part, "After bitter fighting, the enemy was beaten off with large losses."[21] Although the true story was soon known to leaders, claims of victory were repeated.

Stalin in his first war speech (in *Pravda* on July 3) followed Molotov's lead and appealed to "Comrades! Citizens Brothers and Sisters! Fighters of our army and fleet" (see fig. 1). He also set the tone for the half truths that characterized the first months:

> Despite the heroic opposition of the Red Army, despite the fact that the best divisions of the enemy and the best part of his air force are already destroyed and have found a grave on the field of battle, the enemy continues to move ahead, throwing new forces into the front.[22]

Overstatement of enemy losses was common on all sides, but this was something more. Soviet journalists covered startling losses in the first four months of the war, and they often fudged the story. Minsk fell on July 9—the first big town—but the Soviet Information Bureau reported successful operations even while Soviet defenders were doomed to capture. The bureau announced on June 29 that "In the direction of Minsk [a euphemism of Soviet war reporting] Red Army troops continue their successful struggle with the tanks of the enemy, opposing his movement to the east." On July 2 the bureau claimed the army was holding firm, inflicting "significant defeats." On July 3 air victories were reported and on the fourth "significant [enemy] losses" claimed. "The enemy cannot bear the bayonet thrusts of our troops," reads that report.[23] On July 5 the bureau denied German claims of "a fantastic number of prisoners," but said nothing more about Minsk's defenders. So Minsk vanished from *Pravda*, and readers surmised what happened from reports of battles "in the direction of Mogilëv-Podolskii," well to the east.

As cities fell and soldiers were trapped, reporters ceased to mention specific battlefields. By mid-July they avoided cities and referred only to northwestern, western and southwestern "directions." Reportage gradually became more truthful, however, following the unreported loss of the "Smolensk pocket," with twenty-five Russian divisions in August. "After a stubborn struggle our troops left Novgorod," wrote a commentator at the end of the month.[24] "After a bitter struggle our troops evacuated the city of Tallin," wrote another on September 3. "After a stubborn battle our troops left the city of Chernigov," wrote a third on September 13.

Kiev's capture on September 27 was ignored, but Moscow's peril could not be. *Pravda* sounded impassioned battle calls but expressed little alarm as Germans neared the city. "After many days of bitter battle, in which the enemy suffered enormous casualties in people and weapons, our troops left Viazma [the last major town before the capital]," wrote a *Red Star* correspondent in *Pravda* on October 14. "The bloody Hitlerite hordes are reaching for Moscow and thrusting into the Donbass," the editors wrote on October 15. Two days later the paper prepared readers for Odessa's fall by portraying heroic and still unbeaten defenders, when the garrison had begun to withdraw.[25] The paper noted the loss the next day, but claimed a successful evacuation.[26]

Coverage of the Moscow crisis of October and early November, weeks that included the evacuation of the city and the public celebration of the November 7 anniversary of the revolution with a parade in Red Square, showed the tension between considering people "cogs in the wheel" or self-directed patriots.[27] *Pravda* ignored the panic flight of cadres and officials on October 16, later called "the big skedaddle" (*bolshoi drap*) according to the British journalist Alexander Werth.[28] Several days later, a reassuringly confident picture of General Georgii Zhukov, "Commander of the Western Front," a single star on his chest, graced page two, as the radio announced that Stalin was still in the city.[29] The editors thus headed their report of the evacuation on October 25: "We Will Defend Our Moscow [*rodnuiu Moskvu!*]" and alluded to Stalin's presence. "The front approaches Moscow," they wrote. "The State Committee of Defense with its head, Comrade Stalin, is located in Moscow and carrying out all work for the country's defense."[30] "This announcement inspires Moscow's defenders to glorious new feats," they wrote. Although images of a country in arms momentarily displaced the little bureaucratic public, the system's consummate logic persisted in privileging Stalin's presence over patriotism or self-interest in motivating defenders.

Stalin spoke to both country and cadres in two speeches for the anniversary. He told the faithful at the Moscow City Council on November 6 (published on the seventh) that after successes at "peaceful construction" they should embrace the task (*zadacha*) of winning the war. He admitted that the enemy "threatens our glorious capital Moscow," but claimed improbable German casualties of 4.5 million compared with Russian losses of 378,000 and 1.2 million wounded.[31] The next day at the parade he appealed to defenders, from soldiers to "brothers and sisters in the rear of our enemy," but the message in *Pravda* flanked by his quarter-page picture substantiated his dictatorial authority.[32]

The war's impact on public values was more apparent in the daily news. David Joravsky writes of "a Russian Communist dream world of meaningful unity" counterpoised to a "real world of modern culture disorder."[33] During the war the real world broke through. War correspondents, even important ones, illuminated a different kind of public authority and motivation, as did local reporters. What comes to the fore in these accounts is not a simple Stalinist narrative of orders fulfilled for state, party, and leader, but another story of individuals with dignity. This other telling of the Russian experience had powerful antecedents in late imperial culture—in the intense individualism of the literary tradition, in the expanded sense of citizenship expressed in large-circulation newspapers, and in the new self-directed heroes and heroines of popular commercial fiction and film.[34]

Soviet journalists openly acknowledged this counter narrative in the 1920s and 1930s when addressing nonbelievers. Editors who portrayed America as an inferno of crime and exploitation, for example, often used argumentative captions, such as "Life in Rich America," "In the Democratic Heaven," or "In the Country of Freedom," as if to say—we know you think America is rich and free, but here is contrary evidence.[35] Printing such accounts, the managers of *Pravda* and other central newspapers recognized, however unwillingly, not only opinions and lives of people outside "the little public," but also the counterweight of another Russian imagination.

The wartime counter narrative was less conspicuous than that of the 1920s, but potentially more subversive. There were few open arguments with doubters, but commentators broke with the recent past when they showed individuals motivated by patriotism, anger, or simply their own initiative in the face of adversity, rather than orders from above. The notion of individual authority seems paradoxical when applied to an army, but once the main public drama became the war, old styles of reportage ceased to work. The war was important to everyone, not only the "little public." Wartime tasks could not be handed out like peacetime assignments, and results could not be predetermined from above. So war became an occasion for the expression of more truthful and humane notions of agency and individual worth.

*Pravda* authors alternated between two understandings of human behavior. In one, Stalin, the party, and the state moved people. In the other, people acted from a mix of motives, ranging from patriotism to self-interest, revenge, and protection of dear ones. The balance swung most heavily against *homo sovieticus*, the particularly Soviet type of subservient person represented in the media during 1941 and 1942, years when the authorities' resolve was most shaken.[36] During this time particularly, *Pravda* authors enhanced the public image of the individual citizen with a new sense of agency and motive in four situations: the battle, the individual military feat, the home front, and the scene of atrocity. What was contested in these accounts was patriotism and national identity. On the one hand was a nation that found its character in loyalty to the leader and the administrative organs; on the other, citizens with an active sense of themselves and their wishes.

The Soviet Information Bureau produced several battle reports a day for the newspapers, and *Pravda* usually carried a morning and afternoon report on page one. These were generally a pastiche of short paragraphs on local actions, prefaced by a few brief sentences about the main theaters of action. In addition, there were separate reports from local reporters attached to the army, as well as features by more prestigious correspondents. These longer articles often appeared at the bottom of page two in the format of the pre-invasion feuilletons. This is how occasional articles from writers such as Ilya Ehrenburg and Boris Polevoi were often featured. The Information Bureau's regular battle reports were remarkable for what was left out, particularly in the first months, when there was little attention to ideology. During these days the authors showed soldiers fighting without any inspiration from without. An entry in the regular bureau report from the first weeks of the war reads in its entirety:

> The other day N unit attacked superior enemy forces. The battle ended with the enemy's defeat. On the battlefield 267 killed and 130 wounded German soldiers remained. During the battle, a soldier, Comrade Dovzhikov, burst into a group of German officers and bayoneted three as the others fled. Junior political officer Comrade Petrov nailed six fascist soldiers in a few minutes.[37]

Another complete entry on May 3, 1942, was limited to a few lines:

> A group of enemy bombers tried to bomb the military formations of one of our infantry units. Sergeant Poliakov's machine-gun crew opened fire on the enemy and with a few salvos shot down two German bombers.

These reports may seem too mundane to mention, but compared to the alternative, the difference is significant. Major General Golubev, who claimed on January 4, 1942, to be "fulfilling the instructions of Comrade Stalin about destroying the German fascist occupiers," concluded his entry with the observation that even though the front had neared Moscow,

> Comrade Stalin's practical plan establishes a basis for the more grandiose defeat of the enemy. The Maloiaroslavets operation is only part of the brilliant commander's general plan.

A report from early 1942, when hopes were high, was captioned "Red Army soldiers swear to fulfill the leader's order."[38] In it a soldier is quoted, "We give a solemn oath to fulfill the order of the leader: in 1942 we will finally destroy the German fascist troops." An editorialist reiterated the story on November 11, 1941:

> At a meeting of fighters of Lieutenant Pushkin's regiment, Red Army soldier Kuzin said: "My heart was overjoyed when I heard Comrade Stalin's voice and exciting words. His speech bolstered my certainty of our own victory. I want to say in the name of all my comrades, be sure, Comrade Stalin, that we will defend our Motherland persistently, that our hand will not tremble. We are ready to give our lives for freedom."

The fact that such statements were absent from most reports at the outset of the war is significant. Authors of battle reports tended to stress other aspects of the fighting men's behavior, such as skill, courage, or the desire for revenge. Each of these traits, when presented in print, tended to broaden the public image of the individual and citizen.

One aspect of the Stalinist idea was a stress on ideological motivations, "a faith in the miraculous world," in the words of L. Gozman and A. Etkind.[39] Yet belief in the power of spirit in military matters had a lineage in Europe, as well as Russia. In France, it was popularized before World War I as a mystical cult of the offensive. In Russia, according to William C. Fuller, generals divided over this issue into "magicians," who stressed the Russian soldiers' superior spirit and "technologists," who doubted their efficacy.[40] The same dichotomy surfaced in 1941 between those who stressed devotion to party, state, and leader and those who emphasized knowledge, training, and technology. The first affirmed the Stalinist master narrative, the second, an alternative view of man and society.

The issue was sometimes one of emphasis. Tension between a stress on skill or technology and an emphasis on spirit was expressed in 1942 by the Ukrainian dramatist Aleksandr Korneichuk, whose play *Front* appeared in *Pravda* from August 24 through August 27.[41] The publication of a large piece, which filled a full page in each issue of *Pravda*, was an event. The drama was simple but revealing. The hero, Major General Ognёv, opposes an old Civil War general, who "learned to fight in battles, not in academies." The old warrior sputters: "The main thing for a commander is spirit. . . . I am not used to sitting a long time in an office breaking my head over maps." He mocks a local commander who stresses wireless communications. "We will beat any enemy and not with wireless communications, but with heroism, valor." But his brother, head of an airplane factory, warns, "It is necessary to learn how to fight in a contemporary way." Although Korneichuk used an off-stage Stalin to validate his practical soldier, he also showed the importance of the knowledgeable individual.

The emphasis on skill and experience in battle rather than ideology grew throughout the war, and the result was often to enhance the public actors' persona. Editorialists stressed military skill under headings such as "Ceaselessly Improve the Art of Fighting on Skis."[42] "Persistently Study Military Affairs" is the caption of another editorial beginning:

> The know-how of Soviet fighters and commanders, flyers, and tank crews, artillery crews and machine gunners, infantrymen and cavalry troops, sniper-avengers and sailors has grown and continues to grow day by day in the fire of the Soviet people's great liberation war against the Hitlerite invaders.[43]

"When they ask me how we succeeded," observed a worker, "I answer this way: coordination and thoroughness at work, conscientiousness and technical literacy."[44]

This meant an image of fighting men who acted on their own rather than waiting for orders. "The Baltic sailors know well that in contemporary battle it is important to seize the initiative," reads a report from July 8, 1941. The emphasis on skill rather than spirit or ideology later in the war led to the portrayal of battles almost as a game of skill, as in a report from 1943:

> In the region of Voronezh our troops carry on a selfless struggle with the German fascist troops. In separate regions the initiative passed into the hands of Soviet units, and the Hitlerites were compelled to go over to the defense. Moving ahead, one of our units met a powerful antitank defense from the enemy. With a swift blow our fighters broke the first line of the defense and destroyed at this time more than one hundred antitank weapons. Then the second line of the German defense was broken.[45]

One way in which Soviet correspondents promoted the dignity of Soviet soldiers in battle reports was—in a reversal of clichés—to stress their cleanliness and orderliness in contrast to slovenly Germans. The author of an article captioned simply "Notes from the Front" in September 1941, a low point in the war, compared a German prisoner who "has not shaved or washed for a long time" to Russians who build a bath house near the front line.

> People make war, sit in trenches, go into the attack, but they do not forget to take a bath, shave, and change their underwear. This is order. And without order there can be no victory.[46]

War correspondents who described heroes also stressed dignity and skill rather than ideological commitment, particularly early in the war. Boris Polevoi portrayed a pilot in a feuilleton captioned, "This Is the Way the Guards Fly":

> Thickset and quiet, Captain Meshcheriakov seems sluggish on the ground. But see him in the air! The regimental staff once heard that fifteen "Junkers" were coming to bomb the airfield. Berkal [the regimental commander and commissar] sent five fighters, led by Meshcheriakov, to greet the uninvited guests. The captain dueled with one "Junker" and shot him down. He chased another, closed on him, . . . and chopped his tail assembly with his propeller. The German fell like a stone, but Meshcheriakov landed safely at our airfield. By ramming the enemy, he saved his machine with only light damage to the propeller. So, this stocky youth, serious beyond his years, has downed six planes during his combat career.[47]

What difference does it make if the heroes are identified as Communists, Komsomols, or Commissars? The point is their humanity, personal authority, and stature as independent actors on the stage of history. There were many brief entries in Information Bureau reports similar to this one from September 13, 1942: "Heroism and bravery were demonstrated by the medical personnel Prolivko, O. P., and Iakimenko, M. K.; they carried from the battlefield, and gave first aid to, ninety wounded fighters and commanders."

Reporters also presented civilian heroes and heroines without reference to ideology. An Information Bureau report from March 16, 1942, reads:

> The names of many heroes are unknown. People who perform exploits stand humbly aside. This is the way a kolkhoz woman from the village of N. Starorusskii district acted. . . . Risking her life, the kolkhoz woman ran across a field strafed with fire from both sides and gave information to the commander.

Reporters praised those on the home front in the same way. "Each person feels himself a fighter, and does not spare his energy," wrote a reporter from Omsk.[48] Another observed on September 14, 1941:

> Patriots give themselves wholly to production. They quickly learn new skills and produce unprecedented output in the name of one general idea, which was formulated concisely by the Stakhanovite Beliaeva, the sister of two fighters and the wife of a Red Army fighter: "We are also soldiers, just like Red Army men, only not at the front but at the factory."

Initiative was a key word. "Let every worker, engineering technical personnel, and white collar employee at our factory," wrote employees of an automobile plant on July 8, 1941, "look to their sector for possibilities to increase the productivity of labor, to double up on jobs, to free extra labor, and so forth."

What was remarkable about many of these articles was the motivation attributed to the actors. Instead of party, state, or Stalin, inspiration came from the army, the country, or the people. The anonymous author of an article captioned "The Immortal Deed of the Sixteen Guards" portrays the doomed company commander gathering his fighters around him: " 'We are Komsomols,' said the commander. The country awarded us the high rank of guards.' "[49] An Information Bureau bulletin on January 4, 1942, reads simply: "The kolkhoz workers of Omsk Oblast, inspired by the successes of the Red Army, give the country additional agricultural products."

Many reporters expressed the idea that soldiers were fighting on behalf of "familiar" people. Typical was a war correspondent's report, "Behind Enemy Lines," on January 4, 1942, about a unit that entered a newly liberated village. "A village boy, having already managed to decorate his cap with a Red Army star, follows the fighters with joyful eyes," the author wrote. The boy runs to the unit commander, shouting, "That is our house, it's warm. And are you also coming to our house?" The colonel replies, "I am also coming to your place." Similar is a soldier's letter in the same issue:

> Respected Unknown [Correspondent], I received your package. Many thanks from a Red Army soldier. How pleasant it would be to shake your hand per-

sonally and say more, much more. . . . Do you know that here in the snow of
a frontline position your love and concern bring great joy to a fighter's heart.
I want even more than before to beat the enemy.

D. Zaslavskii, a regular columnist, forcefully expressed this notion of personal
links when he wrote on January 4, 1942, about New Year's visits of frontline soldiers
with Moscow families, under the heading "In One's Own Family." Just how strong the
link between soldier and citizen could be was apparent from a report on March 11,
1943, about a soldier who set out mines while under fire, "And his commander was
correct when, in response to the thanks of the liberated inhabitants of the village, he
answered: 'bow down to Zakharov, he is our hero.' "

Anger at discovering German atrocities was another motive for fighting. "Un-
heard-of Massacre of Wounded Fighters and of the Civilian Population of Kalinin" was
the caption of an article from July 19, 1942. "The Soviet people keep accounts of the
monstrous crimes of the Hitlerite cutthroats," wrote the author, "in order to take revenge for each burned village, for each tortured Soviet person." A major wrote on
September 12, 1943, of one of the most famous heroes of the Soviet Union, Aleksandr
Matrosov: "He and his fellows went to the front with one thought: to take revenge on
the enemy for all the crimes they committed on our native land." (See Sartorti, this
volume.) Ilya Ehrenburg wrote bitingly in November of the same year in a feuilleton
captioned "In the Fascist Menagerie": "They wanted to destroy the world, and now the
bloody dawn of retribution is breaking over them."[50]

Yet despite the threats, the new patriotism was not primarily about revenge but
about independent self-motivated citizens fighting in defense of families, friends, and
native land. This was an expression of humanistic values that recaptured something of
the individualism of the pre-revolutionary intelligentsia and of the public culture of
the late imperial era. In the Soviet context, such ideals had an almost insurrectionary
meaning. This humane turn, so apparent in the portrayals of Russian soldiers and civilians, had a curious counterpart in the presentation of excerpts from letters of dead
and captured Germans and prisoners' interviews in the first year and a half of the war.

*Pravda's* readers met many nasty Germans in reports from liberated villages and
articles by Ehrenburg and others, but quotations from Germans themselves in the Information Bureau bulletins were sometimes very different. In 1941 and 1942, before
advancing Soviet soldiers discovered most atrocities, excerpted letters showed a very
human enemy. A German soldier wrote his wife: "Among us many have already fallen
in the East; and how many more victims will there be?"[51] Another informed his father
of the death of friends: "It is very sad; where is the end; when will the war end?"[52] A
moving selection of letters in which Germans complain about atrocities they are told
to commit appeared in August 1942. The author of one letter described how German
officers forced villagers across a river: "Several girls and children drowned, but these

pigs have no pity."[53] Similarly, "A Letter from a Deserter from the 16th German Army," that appeared on March 16, 1942, lacked ideological appeal:

> Dear comrades! I voluntarily went over to the side of the Red Army. Follow my example, by this you will prepare for a quicker end of this hopeless war. You may still attain the joy of the homeland and family.

By 1943, however, Germans were mostly represented as eager to grab Russian land. "When you get this letter, you will know that Ordzhonikidze, an important city of the Caucasus, will be in our hands," wrote another German soldier to his wife.[54] *Pravda*'s commentator was pleased to point out that the letter never arrived and the city never fell. A German prisoner confessed in 1944 how he dreamed of an estate in Ukraine: "Then I was sure of a German victory."[55] Another explained in 1943 that many of his fellows "decided to go and 'master Russland.' "[56] As the war progressed, the idea of vengeance became more explicit.

Even in this almost peripheral way, however, the counter narrative to the official Stalinist story concerned an alternative sense of Russian nationality and citizenship. The humanizing of the most real and brutal of all enemies the Soviet Union ever faced, even if it did not last to the end of the war, was a way of situating Russians in a world of like peoples, and in that sense, it signified a rebuttal of the xenophobia preached by the Stalinist regime.[57] It was a way of saying that all people are similar and want to live peacefully at home with their families. Russianness in this context meant being part of the outer world and not divided from it by barricades or hostile classes. This vision fit the often reiterated liberating purpose of the war. It was reinforced by the coverage of visits of Allied dignitaries and journalists, of Allied military actions, and by the very occasional mention of lend-lease aid.

Also important were the frequent quotations from the Allied media about Soviet successes, particularly in the last two years of the war. By giving space to such reports, the editors of *Pravda* and other Soviet newspapers broke with a decade of enmity. "Radio San Francisco stressed the enormous expanse of the Soviet troops' attack," read one such comment.[58] "London radio communicated a summary of articles from English newspapers in which they comment on the progress and possibilities of the Soviet forces' attack in Ukraine," read another.[59] Editors who printed such comments granted foreigners a legitimacy and authority that clashed sharply with the xenophobia of the 1930s. In this respect as in others, the counter narrative had little to do with official commemorations of Muscovite and tsarist heroes, the glorification of the Russian past begun in the mid-1930s, or the use of pseudo-folkloric imagery.[60] Quantitatively such seemingly Russian rather than Soviet themes were a minor part of the larger discourse, and articles about "Holy Russia," which made a great impression on some foreign observers, were infrequent amidst the daily news of the war.[61] The conflict was not between "Holy Russia" and the "Soviet Union," as the correspondent Alexander Werth suggested after the war, but between one kind of Russia and another.[62]

The new patriotism featuring more active and humanized images of individual citizens had little to do with the idealized past Stalin and his followers had so assiduously promoted. Typical was a war correspondent's tribute to Crimean partisans, written after a flight over the occupied peninsula. "The plane goes lower; there she is, the land of the Crimea, tormented by the enemy but still unconquered, persistently fighting against the hated occupiers with the hands of the people's avengers."[63]

The Russianness of the official narrative was partly the Russianness of empire, and the nationalities figured importantly in this story as symbols of the "unity of the great family of peoples" and for their slavish devotion to Stalin, the party, and the state.[64] "The Uzbek people know that their fate will be resolved in Ukraine, on the fields of Belorussia, on the outskirts of Leningrad," wrote one commentator, who concluded, "Let our great leader, Comrade Stalin, be healthy for our happiness."[65] A Soviet Latvian leader wrote, "We are deeply certain that under the leadership of the great strategist Stalin, the German bandit imperialism will be finally destroyed in 1942 and all the Soviet land will be cleansed of the fascist vermin."[66]

The idea of the nationalities as separate peoples was largely absent from the stories of the counter narrative. As one author wrote simply in the spring of 1942, "Everyone for whom the word Motherland is a holy word took part in the struggle against the occupiers."[67] When these largely Russian war correspondents and newspaper people wrote about active citizens, they identified them simply as soldiers or civilians, not as Uzbeks, Ukrainians, or other peoples. The fact that independent, self-motivated people represented in the press were not identified with any nationality except sometimes with the Russian suggests that, at least in *Pravda*, the nationalities and therefore the empire itself were in some sense peripheral to the counter narrative, despite an emphasis on these regions and peoples as they were reconquered by advancing Soviet armies.[68] Also marginal in these accounts were women, who hardly figured in either the official narrative or its alternative.[69] The war as portrayed in *Pravda* was largely a male experience, despite the enormous role of women in the struggle.

The turning tide in favor of the Soviet Union after Stalingrad brought a second great shift in *Pravda*'s representation of Soviet society. Whereas the official story lost some credibility and coherence during the initial defeats and desperate battles of 1941 and 1942, the victories that followed brought attempts to buttress the old Stalinist creed. One aspect of this was the flood of medals, the public announcements of which filled page after page in *Pravda* during this period, often taking up a quarter of an issue or more. Another was the redesign of officers' uniforms, which was covered in great detail in the press. Both had much to do with hierarchy and the role of the state as a source of all rewards, honors, and status. The promotion of the Stalin cult was also part of this rallying of old forces, and Stalin presented himself with increasing pomp in the press during this period as the chief of the army and the architect of the victory. Finally, the official resurgence was characterized by the reappearance in *Pravda* of the old formulaic story of bureaucrats doing their jobs.

Alexander Werth described what happened to officers' dress after Stalingrad as a shift from the "thoroughly plebeian" to gold braid, epaulets, and other decorations.[70] The *Pravda* editors described the changes as an expression of the Party's concern for "discipline in the ranks."[71] The stature of the state was enhanced by these outward signs of rank, displayed as they were not only in newspaper illustrations of the decorations themselves, but also in the many pictures of officers that followed. The effect, together with the new military titles, was to give the army a more hierarchical public configuration. And this was clearly the intent. The idea of the preeminence of Stalinist authority was expressed in every situation. As one agricultural worker was quoted as saying, "For the Soviet people, the government's high evaluation of their work is the highest of all rewards."[72]

A heavy sprinkling of medals, awards, and commendations accompanied the introduction of the new uniforms. There were public announcements of rewards for heroes and families of those who perished even in 1941 and 1942; but in the last year of the European war these became a flood for civilians as well as soldiers. There were grand military orders for bygone military and naval heroes: Suvorov, Aleksandr Nevskii, and Kutuzov in 1942; Bogdan Khmelnitskii in 1943; Ushakov and Nakhimov in 1944. New orders of Glory and of Victory encrusted with diamonds came in 1943.[73] There were also medals for the liberation or capture of foreign cities, for partisans, and for civilian feats such as "labor valor" and "labor excellence."[74]

Some awards were publicly identified with monetary benefits. "The best masters of sharpshooting are awarded government medals and valuable gifts," reads one announcement from 1943.[75] The report of awards to the families of Major General Panfilov and the twenty-eight heroic guards who perished in the battle of Moscow with him, included a "one-time payment of 2,000 rubles," as well as a pension and the promise of living quarters in Alma Ata.[76] Sometimes the leaders spoke on the occasion of the awards. " 'I am certain,' said Comrade Kalinin, 'that these awards will serve as a new stimulus in the job of the further improvement of all the work of river transport.' "[77] The fact that the awards belonged to the state, and that their purpose was to reaffirm the bureaucratic order, was driven home on May 3, 1943, when the government published an order of the Supreme Soviet declaring illegal the sale, transfer, or giving of medals, awards, or insignia by recipients to other people. The medal given out to all participants in the Soviet armed forces "For Victory over Germany in the Great Patriotic War, 1941–45" bore Stalin's image.

The grotesque enlargement of the Stalin cult accompanied the promotion of medals, badges, and ribbons as bureaucratic emblems. Stalin appeared frequently in the last year and a half of the war as the author of proclamations and "orders" to the army. These were usually commendations in which the successful action of the previous day was summarized. Typical was the "Order of the Supreme Commander to Marshal of the Soviet Union General Konev" on March 22, 1944. After a summary of the engagement that made Stalin seem the master strategist, the text read: "For excellent military action I ANNOUNCE THANKS to all the leaders of your troops participating in the battle for the liberation of the city of Mogilëv-Podolskii." It was signed "Supreme Commander Marshal of the Soviet Union I. Stalin." Similar orders were published for Marshal Zhukov in the same issue and appeared almost every day until the end of the war.

To these military reports were added the most fawning personal testimonials, many of which were letters announcing sums of money gathered locally and sent to the central government for reconstruction. A district party secretary from the Bashkir Autonomous Republic wrote on January 1, 1944, to "Dear Iosif Vissarionovich," announcing that the Bashkirs had gathered 1.5 million rubles for reconstruction and concluding: "Live long years, our dearly beloved Comrade Stalin." Another such testimonial from the manager of a railroad read:

> Filled with burning thanks for Soviet soldiers, unlimited devotion to the Motherland, and selfless love for YOU, dear Iosif Vissarionovich, and wishing to speed the victory over the fascist monsters, the railroad workers of the Starobelskii section of the Northern Donets Railroad deposit from their personal savings 424,338 rubles into the country's account.[78]

Stalin answered these and other such declarations publicly in *Pravda* as he did one from Alma Ata, "I ask to give to the kolkhoz workers of the Altai Flora for their donation my brotherly greeting and the thanks of the Red Army."[79] Lest readers fail to understand that the purpose of these rites was to fix the meaning of patriotism, there were a number of editorials on this subject. As one editorialist put it, "Stalin is the wisdom of our people, its conscience, its genius; with his name are linked the main pages in the history of our young state."[80] Soviet patriotism in this version was something which diminished rather than enlarged the individual patriot.

The rise and ebb of the counter narrative can be tracked against the fortunes of the Communist Party, whose membership dropped by nearly a quarter during 1941, after having nearly quadrupled from January 1938 to January 1941. After 1941, membership again rose rapidly, nearly doubling the pre-invasion level by the end of the European war.[81] *Pravda* marked the return of the bureaucrats and "the little public" they represented with a bevy of articles about the reestablishment of Soviet power. "A Big Day in Iaroslavl" was the caption for an article about the return of Soviet authority, in which "The secretary of the oblast committee Comrade Larionov in his speech pointed out the immediate material tasks before the agricultural workers of Iaroslavl

Oblast."[82] The idea of the bureaucratic imperative was evident in many articles about orders to local populations. A kolkhoz chairman explained on May 3, 1943, the importance of meeting the plan. Under the heading "Siberians Respond to the Order of the Leader," he said, "It is good, comrades, but we cannot relax. We do not have the right. Comrade Stalin demands from us the application of all our strength." Similarly kolkhoz workers reacted to stringent state norms for the harvest:

> They say—the government and the party call on us to gather in the harvest according to wartime standards. It must be necessary to check over again, one more time, what we have done in order to really carry out the grain harvesting according to military standards.[83]

The authors of such articles were not only telling readers that the bureaucracy had its pride of place back, but that life would go on as it had before, with no concessions to the feelings and hopes aroused in the wartime experience. As one kolkhoz worker was quoted as joyfully exclaiming, "The free Russia of kolkhozes and workers existed and will exist."[84] The authorities greeted the end of the war in this fashion.

*Pravda* proclaimed victory in a blaze of official patriotism and of public "orders" by Stalin to his generals. Yet there was also emphasis on another theme—the idea of international human values, which had flickered off and on in the pages of the newspaper throughout the war. "The babies of the world can sleep peacefully in their cradles," wrote the novelist Leonid Leonov on May 7, 1945. "Soviet troops, and the troops of our Western friends . . . will not return home until the wind of the liberating hurricane makes Germany unfit for the fascist fiend." This common purpose crept even into editorials and proclamations. *Pravda* on May 10, 1945, carried a half-page picture of Stalin, with smaller pictures of Churchill, the new President Truman, and of the former "Big Three" (Churchill, Stalin, Roosevelt) at Teheran. Speeches by Churchill and Truman followed on page two. Although Ilya Ehrenburg concluded his essay of the day with thoughts of Stalin, he also wrote: "We have saved not only our Motherland, we have saved universal culture."

Many historians have argued that the war strengthened the Stalinist hold on Soviet culture and society.[85] Certainly, the laboriously crafted postwar reconstruction of the wartime experience was used to reinforce central myths that bound Soviet society. Yet *Pravda*'s treatment during the war of patriotism, citizenship, motivation, and what it means to be human was fundamentally subversive of the Stalinist ethos. The opening of the press to the feelings and experience of a wider public was part of a national resurgence that was partly, if not wholly, responsible for the Soviet victory. The humanistic values that came into play in *Pravda*'s telling of the wartime experience were real, and the crosscurrents of narrative and counter narrative paralleled actual changes in people's attitudes and feelings.

## Notes

1. I discuss the uniqueness of the Soviet press in "Popular and Public Values in the Soviet Press, 1921–28," *Slavic Review* 48, no. 1 (spring 1989): 16–35; "The Press and Its Message: Images of America in the 1920s and 1930s," in *Russia in the Era of NEP* (Bloomington, Ind. 1991), pp. 231–53; and "Official Xenophobia and Popular Cosmopolitanism in Early Soviet Russia," *American Historical Review* 97, no. 5 (December 1992): 1431–81.

2. I describe this change in "Revolutionary Lies/Revolutionary Truths: The Press in Revolutionary Russia," a paper for the Conference on Media and Revolution at the University of Kentucky, funded by the NEH, October 1992; see also my "Revolutionary Lives: Public Identities in *Pravda* during the 1920s," *New Directions in Soviet History*, ed. Stephen White (Cambridge, 1991), pp. 27–40.

3. The term *zadacha* is also a key word in Stalin's "Short Course," *Istoriia Vsesoiuznoi Kommunisticheskoi Partii (bol'shevikov): Kratkii kurs* (1937; Moscow, 1945).

4. This master narrative parallels, but differs markedly from, the master plot of Soviet socialist realist novels, described by Katerina Clark as based on "spontaneity" and "consciousness" in *The Soviet Novel* (Chicago, 1981).

5. These and other remarks about changes in the content of *Pravda* are based on a systematic analysis of a random sample of six issues per year from June 1940 to May 1945, chosen to be evenly distributed throughout a given year by month. A total of 627 articles on politics, society, economics, and the war were analyzed. Excluded were articles on culture, entertainment, and foreign affairs, including the war elsewhere in the world. I also read the newspaper generally to trace the coverage of particular events, but used this small sample to measure changes in the language.

6. *Pravda*, Sept. 9, 1940.

7. *Pravda*, Jan. 10, 1941.

8. *Pravda*, May 14, 1941.

9. *Pravda*, July 21, 1940.

10. *Pravda*, Nov. 11, 1940.

11. These and other statements about the quantitative balance of materials in the press are based largely on the analysis of the distribution of space and numbers of articles in a sample of wartime issues.

12. *Pravda*, May 14, 1941.

13. This notion of bureaucratic agency appears in 64 percent of the sample articles, which occupied 72 percent of the space allotted to the home front and domestic affairs in sample articles between June 1940 and May 1941.

14. See Brooks, "Revolutionary Lives," pp. 27–40.

15. Lev Kopelev, *Khranit Vechno* (Ann Arbor, Mich., 1975) provides one of the most powerful descriptions of these events; see also Mikhail Heller and Aleksandr M. Nekrich, *Utopia in Power: The History of the Soviet Union from 1917 to the Present* (New York, 1986), pp. 376–83.

16. *Pravda* was edited during the war by a member of the Central Committee, P. N. Pospelov; E. M. Iaroslavskii, another member of the Central Committee, sat on the editorial board. *Istoriia Kommunisticheskoi Partii Sovetskogo Soiuza*, vol. 5 (Moscow, 1970), p. 411.

17. Legitimation by reference to Stalin characterized roughly a quarter of the sample articles from the prewar period (June 1940–June 1941) to the end of the war; similarly Stalin figured as an authority in roughly a fifth of the articles over this period, with a peak of 28 percent in 1943 and a low of 16 percent in 1940–41.

18. I borrow the dramatic metaphor and some terminology from the works of Kenneth Burke, especially *A Grammar of Motives* (1945; Berkeley, Calif., 1969).

19. Vera Alexandrova, *A History of Soviet Literature*, trans. Mirra Ginsburg (New York, 1963), p. 233.

20. Ibid., p. 234.

21. Dimitrii Volkogonov, *Triumf i tragediia. I. V. Stalin*, Book 2, Part 1 (Moscow, 1989), p. 158.

22. *Pravda*, July 3, 1941.

23. *Pravda*, July 4, 1941.

24. *Pravda*, Aug. 26, 1941.

25. *Pravda*, Oct. 17, 1941.

26. *Pravda*, Oct. 18, 1941.

27. The phrase is from a speech by Stalin at the end of the war; see Mikhail Heller, *Cogs in the Wheel: The Formation of Soviet Man* (New York, 1988), p. 2.

28. Alexander Werth, *Russia at War 1941–1945* (New York, 1964), p. 232.

29. Werth, *Russia at War*, p. 240.

30. *Pravda*, Oct. 25, 1941.

31. See also *Pravda*, Oct. 30, 1941, for this kind of narrow appeal.

32. *Pravda*, Nov. 7, 1941.

33. David Joravsky, *Russian Psychology: a Critical History* (Oxford, 1989), p. 447.

34. See Louise McReynolds, *News under Russia's Old Regime: The Development of a Mass Circulation Press* (Princeton, 1991); Jeffrey Brooks, *When Russia Learned to Read: Literacy and Popular Literature, 1861–1917* (Princeton, 1985), pp. 166–213.

35. I discuss this in "Official Xenophobia," pp. 1431–48 and "The Press and Its Message," pp. 231–53. Headings are from *Rabochaia gazeta*, Aug. 16, 1922, Aug. 25, 1922, Dec. 28, 1927.

36. The percentages of articles with a bureaucratic agency dropped from 64 percent in sampled issues in June 1940 to May 1941 to 16 percent in June 1941 to December 1942. But in 1943 the percentage was 54 percent and in 1944–45, 53 percent. By space, articles of this type declined from 72 to 8 percent over the same period, but rose to 43 percent in 1943 and to 50 percent in 1944–45.

37. *Pravda*, July 9, 1941.

38. *Pravda*, May 3, 1942.

39. L. Gozman and A. Etkind, "Kult vlasti: struktura totalitarnogo soznaniia," in Kh. Kobo, ed., *Osmyslit kult Stalina* (Moscow, 1989), pp. 352–54.

40. William C. Fuller, *Strategy and Power in Russia, 1600–1914* (New York, 1992), pp. 303–05; he credits Peter von Wahlde, "Military Thought in Imperial Russia," Ph.D. dissertation, Indiana University, 1966, pp. 100–15 for a similar distinction.

41. On the importance of the play see Alexander Werth, *The Year of Stalingrad* (New York, 1947), pp. 289–90; Richard Stites, *Russian Popular Culture: Entertainment and Society since 1900* (Cambridge, 1992), p. 107; Segel, this volume.

42. *Pravda*, Jan. 4, 1942.

43. *Pravda*, May 3, 1942.

44. *Pravda*, Nov. 5, 1942.

45. *Pravda*, July 17, 1943.

46. *Pravda*, Sept. 14, 1941.

47. *Pravda*, Jan. 4, 1943.

48. *Pravda*, July 8, 1941.

49. *Pravda*, Sept. 13, 1942.

50. *Pravda*, Nov. 1, 1943.

51. *Pravda*, Nov. 11, 1941.

52. *Pravda*, Nov. 11, 1941.

53. *Pravda*, Aug. 24, 1942. This issue is not in my sample, but I include it as particularly noteworthy.

54. *Pravda*, Jan. 7, 1943.

55. *Pravda*, Jan. 22, 1944.

56. *Pravda*, Sept. 12, 1943.

57. I discuss this process in the 1920s in "Official Xenophobia," pp. 1437–42.

58. *Pravda*, Jan. 22, 1944.

59. *Pravda*, March 22, 1944.

60. On these topics see Clark, *The Soviet Novel*, pp. 138, 148 and Robert C. Tucker, *Stalin in Power* (New York, 1990), pp. 568–70.

61. Russian nationalism as distinct from a more Soviet nationalism accounts for less than five percent of the articles in my sample for the entire war, with a high of four percent in 1941–42.

62. Werth, *Russian at War*, pp. 741–42; but interestingly, this may have been a cold-war conceit, since Werth writes in his wartime diary, "There is no longer a dividing line between 'Soviet' and 'Russian' " (*Moscow War Diary* [New York, 1942], p. 102).

63. *Pravda*, Nov. 1, 1943.

64. *Pravda*, July 20, 1942.

65. *Pravda*, July 20, 1942.

66. *Pravda*, July 20, 1942.

67. *Pravda*, March 16, 1942.

68. Alexander Werth describes the nationalities' increased role in the official story beginning in late 1942 in *Year of Stalingrad*, pp. 295–97.

69. There were only six articles in my sample signed exclusively by women, and women figured as the sole agents in only six articles out of 627.

70. Werth, *Year of Stalingrad*, p. 289.

71. *Pravda*, Jan. 7, 1943.

72. *Pravda*, March 22, 1944.

73. V. A. Durov, *Russkie i sovetskie boevye nagrady* (Moscow, 1990), pp. 76–99.

74. *Pravda*, July 17, 1943.

75. *Pravda*, May 3, 1943.

76. *Pravda*, May 3, 1942.

77. *Pravda*, Sept. 12, 1943.

78. *Pravda*, March 22, 1944.

79. *Pravda*, March 22, 1944.

80. *Pravda*, Sept. 7, 1944.

81. Figures include members and candidate members: Institut Marksizma-Leninizma pri TsK KPSS, *Istoriia Kommunisticheskoi Partii Sovetskogo Soiuza*, vol. 5 (Moscow, 1970), pp. 27, 372.

82. *Pravda*, Jan. 22, 1944.

83. *Pravda*, July 17, 1943.

84. *Pravda*, Nov. 1, 1943.

85. Volkogonov, *Triumf*, pp. 174–75; John Barber and Mark Harrison, *The Soviet Home Front* (Cambridge, 1991), p. 208.

# 3

# Dateline Stalingrad

## Newspaper Correspondents at the Front

### Louise McReynolds

> Together we lived and served the Motherland,
> The sharp pen and the machine gun,
> We struck up a "front friendship,"
> The journalist, the writer, and the soldier.
>
> —A. Zharov[1]

THE NAZI INVASION in the predawn hours of 22 June 1941 presented Stalin's government with a distinctive communications problem. The enormity of the story precluded the possibility that it could be controlled by censors, however much the government wanted to manage the flow of information. The party line since the Molotov-Ribbentrop Non-Aggression Pact of 1939 had been to try to soothe readers' anxieties about war by preaching the invincibility of the Red Army and the superiority of the Soviet system. Hitler's *Blitzkrieg* laid bare these grandiose claims and the Stalinist state, faced with the need to mobilize public energy and maintain the morale essential to national defense, was forced to make adjustments in its propaganda machine. This gave birth to a new type of *voenkor*, or war correspondent, who could navigate the treacherous waters of communications between the state and a largely mistrustful readership. As Vasilii Grossman, one of the most popular of the new war correspondents, later pointed out, "the war was the arbiter of all fates, even that of the Party."[2]

Because it touches upon a society at every level, war greatly affects the rules of reportage. The war correspondent has traditionally held a glamorous position in the world of journalism, and neither Tsarist nor Soviet Russia made an exception to this rule. In addition to reportorial talents, a good war correspondent must show the courage of a private as well as command the respect of an officer because he (rarely "she") needs access to all soldiers. Vasilii Ivanovich Nemirovich-Danchenko became a newspaper star during the Russo-Turkish War of 1877, and his subsequent coverage of the Russo-Japanese and First World Wars gave him much greater fame among average Russians than his younger brother, the theater director, enjoyed.[3] The Soviet press, however, unlike its commercial predecessor, did not promote the journalistic canons of objectivity that dissociated reporters from the state, a separation that had given pre-revolutionary reporters such as Nemirovich-Danchenko an independent base of authority. On the contrary, the Soviet reporter was supposed to represent the government, and many were intentionally recruited from those social elements that gave the new regime its legitimacy: the worker correspondents, or *rabkory*; the peasant correspondents, or *sel'kory*; and the *voenkory* enlisted from the military.[4]

Originally, the *voenkory* were not war correspondents in the style of Nemirovich-Danchenko, who wrote about travel and other topics in peacetime. Rather, they covered the armed forces primarily in the newspapers produced by the military, the most important of which was the army's *Krasnaia zvezda* (The Red Star). As one future correspondent put it: "Like many from our generation, the war correspondent before 1941 was more interested in technology, art and literature, than artillery zones or grids of navigation."[5] They had their own newspaper, *Voenkor* (The War Correspondent), 1931–35, a quasi-political manual. A reading of bylines in *Krasnaia zvezda* between the purges of the High Command in the late 1930s and June 1940 indicates that the war correspondent came primarily from the officer corps and had license to criticize other officers in the interests of improving overall performance and discipline. The plethora of photographs in *Krasnaia zvezda* of officers assiduously studying their Marxism-Leninism, and stories about party activities in the army, shows that war correspondents were members of the military's ubiquitous political administration, the Glavnoe Politicheskoe Upravlenie, or GPU. This cadre did not, however, prove capable of providing the kind of coverage crucial to the battle and home fronts. If political reliability was a must, so too was the ability to inspire civilians as well as soldiers through prose.

The GPU, which had the responsibility of overseeing correspondents attached to the front, moved quickly. By 24 June, it was soliciting and assigning volunteers and organizing a more systematic instruction for war correspondents.[6] In addition to the major newspapers that circulated nationally, a number of special newspapers were established for publication by the various military units, especially those at the front. In the second half of 1941, for example, the military published 465 such newspapers, a number that rose to 757 by war's end.[7] Not only reporters, but editors, stenographers, printers, and photographers were needed. The Soviet government from its inception had considered journalism a branch of politics, and this held true in the military as well; for example, one could only take official courses on war correspondence at the military's Lenin Institute in Ivanovo or the Frunze Institute in Moscow, both of which specialized in political training for officers.[8] Several weeks before the outbreak of the war, the army began a lecture series for writers' groups on war correspondence; this suggests that it was anticipating the approaching hostilities and therefore was much less surprised than Stalin at Hitler's "infamy." The military could not, however, prepare so quickly the number of journalists suddenly in demand.[9]

The other official agency with a responsibility for war correspondents was the Communist Party's Administration of Propaganda and Agitation (Upravlenie propagandy i agitatsii, or UPA); a department of the Central Committee, UPA was empowered to formulate policy for the press. Wartime and postwar treatment of the relationship between the two agencies shows them working together smoothly on matters pertaining to war correspondence, although new glasnost revelations about the Second World War may well reveal undercurrents of tension and competition. The party affiliation of both organizations, GPU and UPA, makes it unlikely that conflicts between the two affected war coverage. When correspondents discuss in their memoirs the *politrabotniki* (political workers) with whom they worked, the latter appear as congenial members of the operation.[10] As the Ministry of Defense acknowledged: "Without newspapers, we are unarmed."[11]

In the week following the invasion, the GPU formally issued instructions that provided the foundation of war correspondence. The responsibility of the press was as follows: "To publicize the declaration of the Central Committee and Council of People's Commissars of 29 June 1941, in which the evil intentions of the Hitlerite gangs were disclosed and the program of the mobilization of the strength of the entire Soviet people was outlined; to mobilize troops for the selfless fulfillment of all military orders and to impart to them an unshakeable conviction in victory over the enemy; to train the troops in heroism, in the perfection of fighting skills; and to propagandize tirelessly the demands of the military oath, and the campaign to enhance discipline."[12]

This emphasis on inspiring the troops and maintaining discipline did not read especially well in a country whose primary centers of industry and agriculture had been invaded, and whose major cities were either falling or soon to come under siege. As *Krasnaia zvezda*, reporting on the "Second Day of Mobilization in Moscow" put it: "There is strict discipline at all points of mobilization. The reserves, just called up for duty, are filled with determination to fulfill their obligations to the Motherland." The same story reported how the deputy director of a factory (who in the previous year had been an ordinary worker) and his wife had put up a "wall newspaper" pledging their commitment to defend the Soviet system "with the last drop of blood." Mobilization "in Lenin's city" also displayed "immaculate order"; moreover, some of the reserves were treated to a showing of Sergei Eisenstein's *Alexander Nevskii* 1938 (see Kenez, this volume), a classic among propaganda films, which had been shelved following the Non-Aggression Treaty because of its anti-German tone.[13]

The official directives and the type of story they initially prompted stood little chance of inspiring optimism, and even less of sustaining it, as the German panzer divisions rolled eastward. A few war correspondents stand out as party hacks. Vladimir Stavskii, a member of the Writers' Union and the editorial board of the influential "thick" journal *Novyi mir* (The New World) before serving at the front for *Pravda* (The Truth) took his politics with him, as when he praised "the Great Stalin's" defense measures. Stavskii also found a metal worker from Moscow who, under fire in his dugout, asked his sergeant for paper because he wanted to apply for membership "in the Bolshevik Party of Lenin and Stalin." Party membership would help him to be "steadfast and brave to the end, to the utter defeat and destruction of the Hitlerite bands." Such sycophancy peppered Stavskii's correspondence, but he was among the minority who reported that "Stalin's strength is with us, his word is among us."[14]

In his famed radio broadcast of July 1941, Stalin called on the Soviet people to defend the Motherland, which was interpreted by many as a signal that he was subordinating the party to the nation. The names of many of the newly publishing military newspapers in part reflected this, e.g., *Za chest' Rodiny* (For the Honor of the Motherland) and *Vperëd, za Rodinu* (Forward, for the Motherland). The primacy of the party seldom dominated in war correspondence. Within a year, the UPA had drawn up a more specific blueprint for propaganda, which it coordinated with the GPU; the new orders reflected the official concern about who was receiving credit for maintaining an active defense, even in the occupied territories. Reporters were now to publicize "the battle experience of divisions, soldiers, and commanders of the Red Army and Navy in the Patriotic War of the Soviet Union against the German fascist aggressors, and also the experience of the party-political sections of the Red Army; the cooperation between the populations at the front with the fighting divisions of the Red Army; the vicious atrocities perpetrated by the German fascist aggressors—theft and violence against the peaceful populations of the occupied territories and the torture by Germans of Soviet prisoners of war."[15]

Two issues stand out in the new directives. First, correspondents had to advertise leadership, especially that of the party. Soviet readers were already well inured to this. The second point, however, which gave reporters the license to discuss violence openly and to sing the praises of individual heroes and heroines, opened a creative door for correspondents, although it did not suspend all official rules in Soviet journalism. Journalists and writers of fiction entered separate unions, but political demands on all who created Soviet literary culture were roughly comparable, which meant that they had to comply with the tenets of socialist realism. Officially adopted by the Writers' Union in 1934, socialist realism established the boundaries of what would be politically permissable in literature. With *partiinost'*, or propagation of party ideology, its foremost maxim, socialist realism delegated to writers the "task of ideologically remolding and educating . . . in the spirit of socialism."[16] The 1942 directive from the GPU and the UPA emphasized this as a reportorial function, especially with regard to publicizing the role of the party in winning the war. However, the license to publicize heroics and violence meant that writers could now discuss individuals and death, topics which pushed hard against the official limits.[17]

The changing profile of the correspondents influenced what and how they reported. Their great number and variety, including would-be poets contributing to small unit papers as well as the combination of military men and literati at the national press, lowered the possibility that GPU directives could create a politically correct stereotype. The nexus created at the point where the objectives of party, military, and journalism overlapped attracted the talented as well as the ambitious. The biographies of two Evgenii Petrovs exemplify this. The first, who survived and went on to become executive editor of *Sovetskaia Rossiia* (Soviet Russia), typified how support for the Soviet system could lead into a distinguished career in journalism. Born in 1917, he began working on the railroad in his native Archangel Oblast but had moved to the more interesting calling of journalism by 1935. A self-described "agitator," he recalled knocking on apartment doors to explain the Stalin Constitution of 1936. A year later he found his name in a front-page article with fellow students celebrating the twentieth anniversary of the Bolshevik Revolution. Drafted in 1940, he went immediately into the political branch. When war broke out, he was assigned to the Eleventh Army's paper, *Zemlia Sovetov* (The Land of Soviets). The end of the war found him in occupied Germany, editor of one of the divisional organs of the Sixty-fifth Army.[18]

The second Evgenii Petrov (real name, Evgenii Petrovich Kataev) embodied a more remarkable combination of party man and writer. Famous as Petrov of Il'f and Petrov, who had created *Twelve Chairs* and other popular parodies of the new Soviet society in the 1920s, he had survived the Great Purge and had condemned, with apparent sincerity, the Old Bolsheviks in the overtly political newspaper *Literaturnaia gazeta* (The Literary Gazette). After Il'f's death in 1937, Petrov went on to receive the Lenin Prize, join the party, and become editor of *Ogonëk* (The Little Flame).[19] Dispatched to Sevastopol to cover the siege for *Krasnaia zvezda*, he died after only two weeks in a plane crash when returning to Moscow.[20] He and his older brother Valentin Kataev, a leading socialist realist, while not the only siblings serving as correspondents, were undoubtedly the most famous.

Others came from more conventionally journalistic backgrounds, which also included connections with the party and a certain allegiance to the Soviet state. Sergei Dikovskii, who died covering the Winter War with Finland in 1940, stood out for the kind of heroics that made great soldiering as well as great reporting. Born in Moscow in 1907, the son of an artist, he grew up in Ukraine. Before covering the Finnish front for *Pravda* and *Komsomolskaia pravda* (The Komsomol Truth), he wandered the country in a variety of professions, from handling baggage at the railroad to singing in an opera chorus. His first taste of war correspondence had come in 1929 in Manchuria, reporting on border skirmishes for the local army's newspaper, *Trevoga* (The Alarm). A member of the Komsomol, he wrote stories of military heroes, some published collectively in book form as *Patriots*, and he eagerly returned to the front in the next war. In fact, he reportedly approached a number of commanders about his services, but refused assignment to any division until he found one that would send him directly into battle. His younger brother, Taras, a radio correspondent in Estonia, died in the German attack on Tallin in the following year.[21]

In the occupied zones, the correspondent sometimes created resistance newspapers. Vladimir Omel'ianiuk, who began as a reporter for his local paper in the Dzerzhinskii region of Belorussia, enrolled in the Belorussian Communist Institute of Journalism shortly before the war. Evacuated with other refugees one step ahead of the invading army, Omel'ianiuk decided to return to occupied Minsk and work in the resistance. A member of the underground party committee, he clandestinely listened to radio broadcasts and published sheets of news, which he transformed into a newspaper, *Zviazda* (The Star) by May 1942. Exposed by the Gestapo a month later, he was fatally shot, but the newspaper he founded continued until the end of the war.[22]

In other cases, journalists who were conscripted requested to be assigned to reporting duty. Musa Dzhalil, a Tatar poet who had written for *Krasnaia zvezda* and the Tatar-language edition of *Kommunist* (The Communist), found himself drafted into an artillery unit of the Second Army on the Volkhov front. Also a recent graduate of a short-term course on political education, Dzhalil asked to write for *Otvaga* (Courage), the regimental newspaper. Captured and shot after a daring stint with partisans, Dzhalil left notebooks of inspirational patriotic poetry that were published in Soviet papers throughout the war.[23] Boris Polevoi (see fig. 3), who became an important editor at *Pravda*, as well as a famous writer, had to wait until October 1941 before being reassigned from the trenches beyond his native city of Kalinin to the Moscow editorial offices of *Pravda*. From this central point, he traveled to cover other areas under attack, including Stalingrad during the siege of 1942. Referring to *Pravda* as "the town crier of Lenin's Party," Polevoi credited the paper with the ability to forge stamina at the front.[24]

The photographs and memoirs commemorating war correspondence show it, not surprisingly, to have been an overwhelmingly male enterprise. Ol'ga Lander, however, emerged as one of the premier photojournalists of frontline action. Leaving her young daughter with her mother for the duration, Lander also appears among the few who did not find postwar careers in journalism, despite her reputation. Describing her work forty years later, in the waning years of the veterans' generation, one of her male colleagues recounted that she considered her primary task to have been "to illuminate the cultural-educational work of the party and the Komsomol."[25] Whether or not that had been her objective, it is significant that her story was told by someone else.[26]

Party credentials of war correspondents certainly guaranteed that they would not openly criticize the system; but the comparatively broad scope given to them in reporting the human-interest side of war did not always stress party contributions to the war effort. The Union of Soviet Writers, with its problematic relationship to the party, supplied a number of the most popular war correspondents; also, of the more than one thousand union writers who volunteered, many fought and died as regular soldiers.[27]

Future Nobel laureate Mikhail Sholokhov is customarily listed among other authors who turned their talents to journalism, as is popular prerevolutionary novelist Aleksei Tolstoi. Combining the skills of professional journalists and literati, the correspondents produced a fundamentally original style of reportage, classified somewhere between the straight news story and the *ocherk*, or "sketch," from Russia's literary tradition, that combined fact with editorial commentary and descriptive embellishment.[28] The three most popular war correspondents, Ilya Ehrenburg, Konstantin Simonov, and Vasilii Grossman, also became politically important postwar writers. But the ties that connected them to the regime were not those manipulated by a puppeteer. The biographies of these three, like their reportorial styles, tell much about the opportunities for and the limitations on free expression made possible by war correspondence.

Ehrenburg earned his rank as the dean of war correspondents because his literary background included a brief stint reporting on the French front in World War I for the independent *Birzhevye vedomosti* (Stock Market Gazette), as well as his more famous coverage of the Spanish Civil War for the Soviet press. Born in Kiev in 1891, Ehrenburg combined the urbanity of a prerevolutionary intellectual with leftist politics, spending much time in Western Europe during the first two turbulent decades of Soviet rule. He eluded the purges that destroyed so many intellectuals of his background, quite possibly because his journalistic tirades against fascism voiced Stalin's foreign policy of collective security up to 1939. Like the former People's Commissar of Foreign Affairs, Maxim Litvinov, he was Jewish; both survived the changes signaled by the Molotov-Ribbentrop Pact. When war broke out, Ehrenburg could bank on his international contacts as well as his established Soviet audience; *Krasnaia zvezda* and *Pravda* (which shared an editorial office in Moscow during the war), enlisted his talents immediately, and Ehrenburg was the primary Soviet correspondent to have works translated at length into English.[29] Of his hundreds of articles that appeared in the national newspapers, many were collected into booklets that sold throughout the war, with circulations as high as 25,000.[30]

Ehrenburg visited numerous fronts. So great did the government consider his contribution to the war effort that once, when his automobile did not arrive on time at its destination, war planes were dispatched to find it. His particular reportorial gift did not, however, lie in the description of battles. Ehrenburg provided the political slant on events that helped readers put the war into a comprehensible context. He observed in *Krasnaia zvezda* on October 1941: "all distinctions between Bolsheviks and non-party people, between believers and Marxists, have been obliterated. . . . They pray for the Red Army in old churches, the domes of which have been darkened so they would not attract German pilots. Muftis and rabbis pray for the Red Army."[31] This sounded more authentic than the dispatches reporting perfect order amidst the chaos.

Ehrenburg's forte lay in his ability to move the war beyond the front, into the bigger questions posed by the battle against fascism, but without losing sight of the individuals victimized by Nazi ideology. In addition to his coverage of the war in Spain, he had visited Berlin as a foreign correspondent and also witnessed the fall of Paris. Ehrenburg's work possessed an international authority that others could not match: "I saw the German fascists in Spain, I saw them on the streets of Paris, I saw them in Berlin."[32] His stories describing and attacking German anti-Semitism appeared regularly in translation; but his claim that "once they [had] won their freedom, the Russian people forgot the persecution of Jews as a bad dream" was a clear distortion.[33] He later wrote that the authorities had objected to his reportage of heroic Jewish soldiers, and that they wanted him to try to appeal to American Jewry in hopes of gaining support for the long-awaited Second Front.[34] A major theme of Ehrenburg was the degradation of German culture, and articles on the corrupt *Kulturträger* implicitly argued for the superiority of Russian culture. Interviewing peasants in recently liberated villages in 1943, Ehrenburg wrote: "There is something terrible about the German himself. . . . 'They have befouled us'; that is the best way of putting it. . . . Now everybody has seen what their 'culture' is like—obscene postcards and drinking bouts. They were supposed to be a clean people. Now everybody has seen the lousy scratching wretches who turned a clean cottage into a public lavatory."[35] He remarked on the infamous irony that Hitler, "the cannibal who has killed more than five million people," was a vegetarian.[36]

Ehrenburg's graphic detailing of Nazi atrocities was among the most poignant examples of war correspondence. Describing the occupation of Berdichev, a city with a very large Jewish population, he wrote: "They undressed the three little Heifetz girls before their mother's eyes. The youngest was six. They ravished them, mutilated them, then killed them." Returning to Moscow, he met with another victim, "twenty-two-year-old Marina Boyko. She looks like an old woman; in Belostok the Germans maimed her and cut off her ears. Her mother they killed in a beastly fashion, and her seventeen-year-old sister, Nellia, they ravished and then killed. When I recall the face of Marina Boyko, I begin to fear for man."[37]

But many of the outrages perpetrated by the invaders were repeated by the Red Army as the soldiers marched toward victory in Berlin. Histories of the political rape of Eastern Europe by the Soviet government begin with stories of the physical violation of the women of the defeated nations. Vengeance, very much a part of Red Army behavior, was also a major theme of war correspondence. The 1942 directive to correspondents to report atrocities encouraged violent retaliation; Ehrenburg, in a piece on the November 7 anniversary of the Bolshevik Revolution, in 1941 foreboded the future as he also exonerated Soviet conduct: "The Russian people have a big heart. They know well how to love. They also know how to hate. . . . We shall repay the Germans for all the abuses, for all the grief. . . . We shall make [German] females cry their eyes out. . . . Russian widows will sit in judgement over Hitler. . . . For one hundred years Italians will be afraid to glance eastward."[38]

Simonov, who also published prodigiously in *Krasnaia zvezda*, provided a fitting counterpoint to the editorializing of Ehrenburg. Born during the First World War, he graduated from the Gorkii Institute for Literature in 1938. A writer who embraced the visionary new Soviet man, Simonov was stylistically well prepared to describe the courage of the individual soldier in battle. Earlier, in 1939, a literary critic in *Pravda* had found it "impossible not to criticize [him] for the deficiencies in his poetic language. I refer not only to his meager vocabulary. . . . He refuses to use metaphors, insisting instead on the prosaic details."[39] Two of Simonov's straightforward, unmetaphorical poems, "Wait for Me" and "Kill Him!" became classics of Soviet popular culture during the war years. Compilations of his articles and poetry from the front, published by *Pravda* in a series called "Life at the Front," had circulations of 150,000.[40] During the war the government also produced textbooks for secondary schools from the war correspondence of Simonov and others in a special "War Library for Schoolchildren" series.[41]

Where Ehrenburg analyzed and observed, Simonov situated himself in his stories self-consciously as the eyes of the nation, writing primarily in the first person because he often found himself in the thick of battle. In trenches and at airfields, Simonov scouted out the best and bravest of Russian soldiery, publicizing the individuals who constituted the Red Army. Pilot Alësha Khlobystov, for example, after having been shot down four times, was approached in his hospital bed and asked if he wanted a new plane. "He closed his eyes tightly in silence because he was afraid to respond aloud, afraid that he would cough so badly . . . that they would order him to stay in bed. Then he recovered his breath and [said] 'I do.' " Finding him again later, once more hospitalized for a bad parachute drop, Simonov wrote, "I remembered Khlobystov's face in the cockpit. . . . And I understood that this is one of those people who sometimes make mistakes, sometimes take unnecessary risks, but who have the kind of heart that you won't find anywhere, except Russia—a cheerful, indomitable Russian heart."[42]

One of the most widely traveled in the Soviet Union of the war correspondents, Simonov wielded a special authority. He served at the bloodiest front—Stalingrad—and much of what he observed there appeared in *Days and Nights*, the first volume of his trilogy of the Great Patriotic War. Another book covered his assignments *From the Black to the Barents Sea*, and he was the first to report from a submarine. Ehrenburg wrote that Simonov was the favorite of the executive editor of *Krasnaia zvezda*, Major General D. I. Ortenburg (who used the name "Vadimov" in the paper during the war, possibly to conceal his Jewishness), which helps to account for his key assignments.[43] Simonov covered Soviet partisan detachments; and was the first Soviet correspondent to introduce Marshal Tito to readers in his *Yugoslav Notebook*. In typical unadorned prose, he wrote, "I won't pretend that I can give you a portrait of this remarkable man in a short correspondence. I want only to outline a few fleeting sketches for you." Following a detailed description of his dress and comportment, Simonov told readers that "the marshal's face is lively, often smiling when he speaks, and striking because at the same time it radiates a special sense of calm."[44] The Croatian peasant made a comforting ally in 1945.

Simonov also catalogued the brutality and tragedy of the occupation. In the occupied Kuban, he described the "Gul'kevichi-Berlin" train transporting Russian workers to German factories. When volunteers did not respond to the propaganda of the good life in Berlin, "they took children to the commandant's headquarters and beat them; when that did not work, they threatened to shoot the parents."[45] With the Russian partisans in Kerch, he reported the summary trial and execution of a would-be informer: "He wanted to prove that he was not an enemy, that he was nothing more than a coward. But a coward was an enemy now."[46]

The third of the exceptional trio of correspondents, Grossman, combined elements of the other two. A Jewish intellectual born in Berdichev in 1905, trained as an engineer, Grossman began his writing career in the mid-1930s, specializing in stories of the struggle against the tsarist regime and of the Civil War. His most popular prewar work was the serial novel *Stepan Kol'chugin*, about the Bolshevization of a young worker. *Krasnaia zvezda*'s principal correspondent in Stalingrad during the siege, Grossman played an important role in the most strategically decisive battle of the Second World War. Collections of his pieces from Stalingrad were also published in *Pravda*'s "Life at the Front" series, as well as in a textbook for secondary schools.[47]

Supplying information from a front that hung in the balance for more than half a year proved no mean accomplishment, given the potential for national demoralization that defeat would have brought. Bad news had to be good, but at the same time, believable. Like Simonov, Grossman furnished the detailed particulars, although he was also less likely to place himself directly in the story. He described how the division commanded by Colonel Gurt'ev took its position: "The division moved forward and stopped in front of this factory. At its back was the cold, dark Volga. Two regiments defended the factory. A third moved into the deep ravine that connected the workers' settlement to the Volga. . . . Yes, at its back was the icy, dark Volga, at its back was the fate of Russia. The division prepared to stand to the death."[48] His detailing of this fight, and his portraits of the fighters, presented the ferocity of the German attack in images that underscored the courage of the defenders, but without trivializing the latter through hyperbole: "On the third day the German airplanes hovered over the division twelve, not eight, hours. They stayed in the sky after sunset, and from the high dark of the night sky the piercing cries of the 'Junkers' ' sirens started up, and like the heavy and constant blow of a hammer the demolition bombs rained down on the ground, blazing with smoky red flares."[49] His battle descriptions remain among the best of that genre from the Second World War.

Grossman also sought out the common soldier, "the guys," as the preeminent American war correspondent, Ernie Pyle, often commented, "that wars can't be won without."[50] Grossman shared Pyle's keen appreciation for details of the soldiers' private lives, and many of his articles read like Pyle's correspondence for the Scripps-Howard service. Both reminded readers that the experience of war would affect the personalities of those who fought it. Grossman, for example, began his sketch of twenty-year-old artilleryman Anatolii Chekhov, watching for German aircraft in the rubble around Stalingrad, with biographical details: "He has lived an unhappy life. The son of a worker in a chemical plant, this youth had a bright mind, a good heart, and remarkable abilities. . . . His father drank, and treated his wife, son, and daughter cruelly and unfairly." It was not the father's brutality, though, but "the iron and holy logic of the Patriotic War that turned him into a frightening person, an avenger." A man of substance rather than propaganda, Chekhov was recognizable to readers.[51]

Others who displayed better writing than political skills include Fëdor Panfërov, another member of the Writers' Union. Emphasizing the human interest in a politicized topic, he reported the Nazi murder of a peasant woman elected chairperson of her collective farm when the men—including her three sons—went to war. Panfërov drew a vivid picture of the old woman, as the Germans drew near, commanding grimly: "Burn the grain, don't harvest it."[52] Iurii Zhukov, corresponding for *Komsomolskaia Pravda*, ran excerpts from the diary of a fallen member of the Communist Youth League; rather than for the Party, the young soldier recorded, "we know what we're dying for—for the right to breathe. We know what we stand for—for Russia, for the Motherland."[53] And correspondents looked for another heroine similar to Zoia Kosmodem'ianskaia, the young victim of Nazi brutality who acquired a martyr's status when she became an early symbol of patriotic valor (see Sartorti, this volume).[54] Like all journalists, they wanted the big scoop.

The German army could not reap the spoils of its early successes. In the pivotal year 1943, the Red Army followed up on its winter victory at Stalingrad with a summer one at Kursk, which turned the tide of the war and allowed the Soviets to begin their counteroffensive. Feeling less defensive on all fronts, the Party began its own counteroffensive against the press. In May of that year the Central Committee directed the GPU to reorganize "the structure of its political and Komsomol organizations," and this must include "strengthening the military press and transforming newspapers into the primary center of political work; this must lead to a vitalization of party work, to an increase in party activities and Komsomol organizations within the Red Army."[55] Upon another order, the GPU called a congress of editors of military newspapers that July to explain the new policy. Typical of the new line was the censuring of *Za chest' Rodiny*, the newspaper of the Voronezh front for having "informed poorly on the role of party-political work."[56] A. A. Fadeev, a novelist who had first seen action in the Civil War and whose most important war correspondence for *Pravda* had come from blockaded Leningrad, gave the keynote address. Fadeev repeatedly directed attention to "skilled" (*kvalifitsirovannye*) writers, an Aesopian reference to status in the Union, but he also spoke repeatedly of the need to continue publicizing the heroics of individuals.[57]

The effects of the congress are difficult to gauge. Grossman attended it, but the admonitions given there did not seem to affect his style. However, he, Fadeev, Simonov and many others faced criticism after the Second World War, in the early years of the Cold War, for their insufficient acknowledgment of the Party's performance in winning the war. Selective evidence indicates that the military's *politrabotniki* began to take greater part in the newspapers, producing such stories as "Beneath Lenin's Banner— Onward to Victory" and "How to Increase Political Work among the Young Soldiers." Common sense, as well as tens of thousands of personal letters, indicates that soldier-readers preferred the more literary correspondence. The less secure party continued to sponsor seminars for the proper political training of *voenkory*.[58]

The dominant role of the Communist Party in all aspects of communications, coupled with the fact that even the Ehrenburgs downplayed Soviet casualties in favor of Soviet successes, raises the issue of propaganda. Writers not bound in party strait-jackets nonetheless presented a distorted image, and did so because they wanted to direct public opinion in a specific direction. The ill-fated Evgenii Petrov, before departing for Sevastopol, gave *Krasnaia zvezda* editor Ortenburg one condition upon accepting the assignment: "To write only the truth."[59] If reporters minimized the grimness of death and devastation by focusing attention instead on heroics, they were still reporting one version of the truth. As Simonov wrote, "Our job as war correspondents, as patriots, and as writers was to find, in the mass of wartime actions, not that which spoke about the difficulties of today, but that which spoke about the promises of a better future, about the triumphant end."[60]

Even more than in the First World War, propaganda functioned for all the belligerents as a powerful weapon in the Second. By the late 1930s, as one historian argued, propaganda "had the characteristics of a science, in the sense that a body of laws for it began to be formulated by scholars, a corpus of learning for the guidance of its practitioners." Hitler's Minister of Information Joseph Goebbels considered that "news policy is a weapon of war. . . . Its purpose is to wage war and not to give out information." He organized the famed propaganda companies (*Propaganda-Kompagnien*), which differed from the Soviet GPU and UPA in that they trained soldiers in journalism and then dispatched them to replace correspondents in the field; significantly, Germany's literary authors did not join the corps of war correspondents.[61]

The Soviet and Nazi states intentionally produced propaganda. It must be emphasized, though, that war changed the rules of communications. The so-called "totalitarian" regimes were hardly the only parties who manipulated information; Frank Capra's Oscar-winning "Why We Fight" film series anticipated television's docudramas with its imaginative use of facts. Nor was Soviet public opinion the only one Stalin needed to court. As Phillip Knightley has pointed out, the Soviet-German battlefront, despite its enormous importance, "remained throughout the most poorly reported part of the Second World War."[62] But the wartime alliance with the West, always precarious, also depended upon opening heretofore closed channels of communication and encouraging a modicum of trust. The Soviet government responded to its allies with a limited frankness that suited both the alliance and its own purposes. A comparative study demonstrated that Soviet war correspondence was sufficiently, if not extraordinarily, reliable.[63] Alexander Werth, the British correspondent who provided some of the best information from inside the USSR, concluded that "in the main, it was possible to get a fairly good general idea of what was happening," although he also noted that "foreign correspondents had to use great ingenuity and, in the case of some, a powerful imagination to piece together anything that looked like a coherent picture."[64]

Standard interpretations of the impact of World War II on the Soviet Union emphasize the fact that Stalin made concessions to non-party interests but also saw the viability of his system confirmed because it held together under the greatest imaginable stress.[65] This study of war correspondents supports both points. They did not assault either state or party, but they did describe violence and courage in language and images that expanded the official boundaries of literary culture. The Stalinist regime recognized this, and felt sufficiently threatened to put the journalists back in harness to the party once the Soviet army had begun its counteroffensive.

Official paranoia increased after the victory in Europe ended in Cold War, and it would be instructive to learn how many correspondents were accused of "rootless cosmopolitanism," the phrase employed by A. A. Zhdanov, Stalin's enforcer on cultural matters, to identify potential traitors to the system. The party undertook a political study of journalism in the immediate postwar period in order to debate the "contradictions" that apparently arose when some journalists wanted to continue the style of war correspondence.[66] Unfortunately, most of these journalists did not begin to produce their memoirs until the 1960s, in coincidence with the twentieth anniversary of the war, during the partial re-Stalinization associated with Brezhnev. Moreover, many of those who published had continued with party work and probably did not feel inclined to criticize their patron too harshly. The postwar careers of the Big Three, Ehrenburg, Simonov, and Grossman, however, can provide clues to the kinds of tension other journalists felt.

Ehrenburg, the most cosmopolitan, could use his reputation to defend himself against Zhdanov. Despite one novel of the invasion, *The Storm* (1947), he did not make a second career out of his war stories. Continuing his role as a political barometer in literature, Ehrenburg became best known for *The Thaw*, his 1954 novel that coined the synonym for Khrushchëv's early years; his memoirs, *People, Years, Life*, serialized in *Novyi mir* during Khrushchëv's final years, reclaimed numerous writers lost to Stalin's purges. Simonov, the most "politically correct" by Soviet standards, enjoyed a postwar literary-political career that included editorship of *Novyi mir* and status as Deputy Secretary to the Writers' Union. In addition, he rose to candidate member of the Central Committee in the early 1950s and was later elected to the Supreme Soviet. Still, official critics found fault with his realism because at times it "undercut socialist construction."[67] Simonov's war trilogy, begun with *Days and Nights*, continued with *The Living and the Dead* and finished with *Soldiers Are Not Born* in 1964. Like the war correspondence from which these semifictional novels derived, Simonov's clear and detailed descriptions did not surrender to party demands for hagiography. Despite nearly impeccable connections, like the others, Simonov fought more censors after the war than during it.[68] Grossman's postwar literary career was the most problematic because of the degree to which he became conscious of his Jewishness as Nazi barbarism came to light. His projected chronicle of World War II, originally entitled *Stalingrad* and intended for *Novyi mir,* left him open to charges of "cosmopolitanism" because of its Jewish hero. It appeared in abridged form as *In a Just Cause.* The expunged passages were reworked in the quasi-autobiographical *Life and Fate,* first published abroad in 1985. Making the main character a physicist rather than a journalist, Grossman did not address problems of war correspondence in this work, perhaps because he had enjoyed relative political and artistic freedom at the front.

How much credit can be attributed to Soviet correspondents for propagandizing the war effort effectively and mobilizing the public to expel the invaders? To what extent did the journalistic calls for repayment in kind, such as Simonov's "Kill Him!", encourage the savagery of the avenging Red Army? This became a sensitive postwar issue, but even well into glasnost Soviet writers defended the call for violence against the Nazis, noting the difficulty of separating them from the German people.[69] The direct effects of mass communications on public opinion cannot be quantified, but the thousands of letters from readers the correspondents reported in their memoirs reveal the solid ties between public opinion and journalists. It is not enough to say simply that state and society shared a common objective, and hence could unite in victory. The special significance of the Soviet war correspondents lay in their role as the principal transmitters of the culture of the shared experience of war, a culture that gave a cohesiveness to society, that kept the populace together in a way that the offical culture of state and party could not. If they left spots blank on the pages they wrote in Soviet history, they nonetheless wrote one of its most important chapters.

## Notes

I would like to thank Pat Polansky and Lori Emadi of the University of Hawaii's Hamilton Library for collecting the sources necessary to write this essay. Carol Stimson made helpful comments on an earlier draft.

1. Reprinted in *Zhurnalisty na voine,* 3 vols. (Moscow: Voennoe izdatel'stvo Ministerstva oborony SSSR, 1966), vol. 1, i.

2. Vasily Grossman, *Life and Fate,* trans. Robert Chandler (New York: Harper and Row, 1985), 109.

3. Louise McReynolds, *The News under Russia's Old Regime: The Development of a Mass-Circulation Press* (Princeton: Princeton University Press, 1991), 87–92, and passim.

4. V. N. Alferov, *Vozniknovenie i razvitie rabsel'korovskogo dvizheniia v SSSR* (Moscow: Mysl', 1970), 180–97.

5. Iurii Zhukov, "Voennyi korrespondent," *V redaktsiiu ne vernulsia*, 2nd ed., 2 vols. (Moscow: Politicheskoi literatury, 1972), vol. 1, 250.

6. S. I. Zhukov, *Frontovaia pechat' v gody Velikoi Otechestevennoi voiny* (Moscow: MGU, 1968), 14–15. See also, A. G. Kogan and M. A. Tseitlin, "Sovetskie pisateli vo frontovoi pechati (1941–1945)," in *Istoriia russkoi-sovetskoi literatury, 1917–1965 gg.*, 2nd ed., 4 vols. (Moscow: Nauka, 1968), vol. 3, 475.

7. Kogan and Tseitlin, "Sovetskie pisateli," 476–77; and S. Zhukov, *Frontovaia pechat'*, 6.

8. S. Zhukov, *Frontovaia pechat'*, 6; and *Velikaia Otechest. voina. Entsiklopediia* (Moscow: Sovetskaia entsiklopediia, 1985), 161.

9. I. Zhukov, "Voennyi korrespondent," vol. 1, 251.

10. M. V. Gur'ev, *Do sten Reikhstaga* (Moscow: VIMOSSSR, 1973), 25–29, and passim.

11. S. Zhukov, *Frontovaia pechat'*, 12.

12. Ibid.

13. *Krasnaia zvezda* (hereafter, *Kv*), 25 June 1941, no. 147.

14. Vl. Stavskii, *Frontovye zapisi* (Moscow: OGIZ, 1942), 152, 192, 236–37.

15. S. Zhukov, *Frontovaia pechat'*, 15–16.

16. Quoted from Victor Terras, ed., *Handbook of Russian Literature* (New Haven: Yale University Press, 1985), 430.

17. On one "dark day" alone, for example, *Krasnaia armiia* lost seventeen correspondents. *Sovetskie pisateli na frontakh Velikoi Otechestvennoi voiny*, vol. 78 of *Literaturnoe nasledstvo* (hereafter, *Lit nasled*). (Moscow: Nauka, 1966), vol. 1, 12.

18. Evgenii Petrov, "Sluzhba slova," *Biblioteka "Ogonëk"* 29 (Moscow: Pravda, 1970), 2, 18–19, 44–47.

19. A. A. Kurdiumov, *V kraiu nepuganykh idiotov* (Paris: La Presse Libre, 1983), 242–46.

20. *Lit. nasled.*, vol. 78, 1, 293.

21. Iurii Zhukov, "Pust' ne budet skidok nikomu i nikogda," *V redaktsiiu*, vol. 1, 7–18.

22. *Zhurnalisty na voine*, vol. 1, 83–84.

23. Ibid., 34–35.

24. Ibid., 36–37, 43.

25. N. Filippov, "Ol'giny mgnoveniia," in *Zhurnalisty na voine*, vol. 3, 223.

26. As *Pravda* reported on female aviators trying to join the Air Force during the war-scare summer of 1939, "Women can do every job that men can, but they work best at the rear." *Pravda*, 18 August 1939, no. 228. In action, though, the contribution of female pilots, however few, was remarkable. A. Griesse and R. Stites, "Russia: War and Revolution," in N. Goldman, ed., *Female Soldiers* (Westport: Greenwood Press, 1982), 61–84.

27. *Lit. nasled.*, vol. 78, 1, 12.

28. L. I. Lazarev, *Konstantin Simonov. Ocherk zhizni i tvorchestva* (Moscow: Khudozhestvennaia literatura, 1985), 88–92.

29. A. Rubashkin, *Publitsistika Il'i Erenburga protiv voinu i fashizma* (Moscow-Leningrad: Sovetskii pisatel', 1965).

30. For example, *Beshenye volki* (Moscow: Voenkorizdat, 1941) and *Rasskazy etikh let* (Moscow: Sovetskii pisatel', 1944).

31. Ilya Ehrenburg and Konstantin Simonov, *In One Newspaper: A Chronicle of Unforgettable Years*. Trans. Anatol Kagan (New York: Sphinx Press, 1987), 70.

32. Ehrenburg, "Gitlerovskaia orda," in *Beshenye volki*, 34.

33. Ilya Ehrenburg, *The Tempering of Russia*, trans. Alexander Kaun (New York: Knopf, 1944), 24.

34. Ilya Ehrenburg, *The War: 1941–1945*, trans. Tatiana Shebunina, with Yvonne Kapp (New York: The New American Library, 1964), 121.

35. Ilya Ehrenburg, *Russia at War* (London: Hamish Hamilton, 1943), 240–41.

36. Ehrenburg, *Beshenye volki*, 26.

37. Ehrenburg, *The Tempering*, 21.

38. Ehrenburg, *The Tempering*, 82–83.

39. *Pravda*, 18 July 1939, no. 197.

40. *Russkoe serdtse* and *Frontovye stikhi* appeared in 1944.

41. Simonov's *Pekhotinitsy* appeared in this series in 1944.

42. Simonov, *Russkoe serdtse*, 3, 8.

43. "Krasnaia zvezda," *Lit. nasled.*, vol. 1, 271.

44. Konstantin Simonov, "V iuzhnoi Serbii," *Iugoslavskaia tetrad'* (Moscow: *Pravda*, 1945), 14.

45. Konstantin Simonov, "Gul'kevichi-Berlin," in *Ot Chernogo do Barentsova moria* (Moscow: Sovetskii pisatel', 1944), 37.

46. Simonov, "In the Quarries of Kerch," in *In One Newspaper*, 124.

47. Grossman's "Pis'ma iz Stalingrada" appeared in the pamphlet *Napravlenie glavnogo udara* in 1944, the same year that his *Oborona Stalingrada* was published for schoolchildren.

48. Grossman, "Pis'ma iz Stalingrada," 3.

49. Ibid., 9, 11.

50. *Ernie's War: The Best of Ernie Pyle's World War II Dispatches*, ed. David Nichols (New York: Random House, 1986).

51. Vasilii Grossman, "Glazami Chekhova," in *Oborona Stalingrada* (Moscow-Leningrad: DETGIZ, 1944), 47, 55.

52. F. Panfërov, "Ubiistvo Ekateriny Pshchentsovoi," *Kv*, 7 December 1941, no. 288.

53. I. Zhukov, "Voennyi korrespondent," 252.

54. Vil' Dorofeev, "Atakuiushchie pravdisty," in *V redaktsiiu ne vernulis'*, I, 337–67.

55. S. Zhukov, *Frontovaia pechat'*, 18–19.

56. Ibid., 19.

57. See A. A. Fadeev, "Doklad na soveshchanii redaktorov frontovykh i armeiskikh gazet v Iiule 1943 g.," in *Lit. nasled.* vol. 78, 1, 305–18.

58. S. Zhukov, *Frontovaia pechat'*, 20, 22–23.

59. Kogan and Tseitlin, "Sovetskie pisateli," 482.

60. Lazarev, *Konstantin Simonov*, 82.

61. Quotations from Joseph Mathews, *Reporting the Wars* (Minneapolis: University of Minnesota Press, 1957), 86, 186–87.

62. Phillip Knightley, *The First Casualty: From the Crimea to Vietnam—the War Correspondent as Hero, Propagandist, and Myth Maker* (New York: Harcourt Brace Jovanovich, 1975), 244.

63. Mathews, *Reporting the Wars*, 186.

64. Alexander Werth, *The Year of Stalingrad* (New York: Knopf, 1947), 132.

65. Susan Linz, ed., *The Impact of World War II on the Soviet Union* (Totowa, NJ: Rowman and Allanheld, 1985).

66. On the early postwar official criticism of war correspondence, see N. I. Dushkina, "Zhurnalistika i kritika," in *Istoriia russkoi-sovetskoi literatury, 1917–65 gg.*, 2nd ed., 4 v. (Moscow: Nauka, 1968), vol. 3, 455–56, 466–67.

67. Deming Brown, "World War II in Soviet Literature," in Linz, ed., *The Impact of World War II*, 244.

68. K. M. Simonov, *Pis'ma o voine, 1943–79*, ed. L. I. Lazarev (Moscow: Sovetskii pisatel', 1990), 374.

69. Aleksandr Rubashkin, *Il'ia Erenburg* (Leningrad: Sovetskii pisatel', 1990), discusses Ehrenburg's famous article "The Justification of Hate," 334–337.

# 4

# Radio Moscow

## The Voice from the Center

### James von Geldern

B ROADCAST RADIO WAS the most far-reaching outlet available to Soviet authorities during the Great Patriotic War, when the medium's unique potential became fully and finally apparent. Radio had an impact that went far beyond its programming. At a time when the familiar world was being shaken by modern science and culture, radio helped hold it together. Military technology engulfed vast spaces in death and destruction; radio technology humanized and domesticated the new world. Broadcasting made listeners aware of the knowable world, which had expanded beyond the human consciousness, and it kept millions of people in touch with each other. Amid overwhelming turmoil, radio reminded citizens cut off from country and kin that the community survived. It supported faith during the bleakest days of the war; when it fell silent, as Radio Leningrad did for three frigid days in January 1942, people despaired. The need to hear a human voice was so overpowering that many in the starving city risked their lives in a crosstown trek to Radio Center. The voice of radio was affirmation that the city survived.

Wartime radio programming reflected policies followed by other media, but it also bore traces of a unique pedigree. Radio was still young at the onset of war and carried the stamp of recent cultural politics. Programming was deeply politicized and constricted by intrusive censorship. Choked by layers of supervision, radio could not at first respond to modern war's rapid pace, and, in the catastrophic autumn of 1941, it failed its listeners. The absence of trustworthy communication could have been fatal, and the State Radio Committee was forced to enact reforms. Within months, broadcast programming had traded stale formulas for spontaneous interviews, and political slogans for heartfelt emotions, thus providing a more immediate and flexible form of communication. Even before the Red Army had gone on the offensive, Radio Moscow reconquered the audience at home, and soon won new listeners abroad. By 1943, radio was a presence in most Soviet homes and trenches, and it was heard—whether or not legally—throughout Europe.


Born in the 1920s, Soviet radio evolved alongside the socialist state, whose leaders appreciated its reach and feared its potential. Their ambivalence shaped the growth of the medium. In the late 1920s and early 1930s local radio flourished, but later measures were taken to consolidate broadcasting throughout the country. Central control hamstrung radio workers and alienated part of the audience; it also reinforced nationwide integration by ensuring common broadcasts, essential for a vast country where radio was the prime source of information.

The effectiveness of Radio Moscow was determined from the outset by the use of wire-fed instead of ether transmission. The decision, made in the late 1920s, had a variety of motives. Authorities claimed technical advantages: the wire system allowed for more local broadcasting; it improved reception; and more people could afford the simplified receiver. Yet Soviet wired reception was notoriously bad, and local broadcasting depended on administrative support, not consumer technology.[1] Wire broadcasting was in fact an impediment in the countryside. Political considerations were probably more decisive. Radio, which matured as a mass medium at the same time as the German and Soviet propaganda states, could penetrate borders and render any population accessible to outside messages.[2] Counterpropaganda was as urgent a task as propaganda, and with wire transmission only a small group of ham operators could listen to foreign broadcasts. The system yielded additional advantages during the war, when important broadcasts could be conducted without tipping off the Germans, who could not track the signal. That is how Radio Leningrad sustained its population during the blockade.[3]

Soviet radio development before the war compared reasonably well with the West. Though per capita radio ownership was relatively low, total receiver production was among the highest in the world.[4] By early 1941, an intensive radiofication program had placed most of the country under the broadcast net of Radio Moscow; many areas were served also by republic, oblast and local radio services. Programs were broadcast via medium- and long-wave to local relay points, where they were received and piped into homes and factories. There were over 100 broadcast stations in the country, a million private radios and six million public amplifier-receivers, with an estimated thirty million regular listeners. Service was still inadequate in the non-Slavic republics and in the countryside; there were sixty-seven receivers per thousand population in cities, eight in the countryside, and three in the non-Slavic republics. Yet even then, radio was the leading source of first-hand news.[5]

The prewar politics of radio programming were more problematic, and would inflict great damage on early wartime broadcasting. The radio boom in Russia had co-incided with the First Five-Year Plan and Cultural Revolution, 1928–1932. Local activity was vital, boasting thriving municipal and republic studios—particularly in Ukraine and Belorussia—and a network of amateur radio operators. Central control was weak and contested, and the relatively meager programming of Radio Moscow was supplemented by local broadcasts, which were not yet subject to strict ideological control. Live, spontaneous genres—local reporting, radio sketches (*ocherki*), city-to-city talk shows (*pereklichki*)—were most popular. But the centralizing impulse that realigned the media in the 1930s reached radio, too. From 1934 on, the Radio Committee put intense pressure on local radio workers to toe the line. Particularly important was a summer 1934 conference in Leningrad, where local dominance of programming was contested and defeated. Local productions, chiefly from factory clubs, were soon banned. Central programming, which local stations were now obliged to transmit, formed the bulk of the schedule, while supplementary local work was limited to two and a half hours daily.[6] Unpredictable genres like the live report gave way to prepared political statements, music and literary readings. Intimacy and immediacy were further weakened by the introduction of recording technology. The fear of spontaneity grew so strong that in 1937 the final live genre, the talk show, was banned outright.[7]

The changes did not necessarily diminish quality. Though broadcasts were subordinated to political campaigns concerning the Five-Year Plan, Stakhanovite labor, party loyalty, etc., they were also somewhat professionalized. Renowned writers such as Aleksei Tolstoi, Sergei Tretiakov, Semën Kirsanov and Aleksei Surkov came on the air to provide commentary and read their works. The generation of news readers that would gain fame during the war—Iurii Levitan, Nataliia Tolstova, Ol'ga Vysotskaia, Osip Abdulov—first rose in the profession at that time.[8] Exciting programming did not vanish entirely: reports on the Cheliuskin rescue, the polar expeditions, and record-breaking aviators won radio a huge audience. Musical programming received a particular boost from the reforms. A series of musical educational programs ("Musical-Cultural Minimum") was introduced along with lectures on music appreciation and talks by Soviet composers.[9]

The great shortcoming of the reforms became apparent in 1941, when Soviet radio proved incapable of responding to the war. Response to rapidly developing events was impaired by prebroadcast censorship, which required a lag time from ninety minutes for news items to two hours for other programming. All materials had to pass the censor, after which no digression from the written text was permitted.[10] Central control also weakened the republic (chiefly Ukrainian and Belorussian) and local broadcasting, which in wartime could have relayed information about German attacks to the center, and later could have operated in occupied lands. These units had been targeted by a 1937 *Pravda* editorial, "Putting Radio Broadcasting Back in Shape," and were soon subordinated to Moscow.[11] The most damaging result of pre-1941 policy was that radio, along with the other news media, was discredited by its reporting of the Finnish and Polish campaigns. Though Radio Moscow dispatched its most famous correspondents—Viacheslav Sysoev and Grigorii Nilov to Bialystok and Lwów, and Nilov and Vasilii Ardamatskii to Karelia—their impassioned reports, particularly from the Finnish woods, proved unreliable.[12] Skeptical Soviet listeners could no longer accept news reports unconditionally.

Radio Moscow's conduct at the outset of the German war exhibited all the familiar vices. Since the possibility of an invasion was taboo, there were no contingency plans. Staff members only warning was a question, asked by their director in early June: if we suddenly need to play war songs, are you ready? They were not. There were no correspondents on the Ukrainian and Belorussian fronts, and Ian Boretskii, who reported from Kiev on the 22nd, was there only incidentally, to broadcast an important soccer match. Bombs began falling early on the 22nd, and Boretskii and the Minsk correspondent quickly phoned in reports. But confronted by a fast-breaking story with complex political implications, and lacking instructions from the authorities, radio met the invasion with silence. Scheduled programming was run, which included a talk on "Darwinism in Soviet Science," gypsy songs, and classical music.[13] Radio, which in principle was the first source of information for citizens—newspapers only came out in the evening, and did not reach many localities for another week—offered no announcements in spite of rumors filling Moscow and citizens constantly calling in for confirmation. The news led with items on a Leningrad regatta and a carnival in Tashkent.[14] Alarmed radio workers streamed into the Gorky Street headquarters, but aside from pulling all German news from the air, no changes were made. Standard weekend musical fare—marches and classical music—played on, and a professor rhapsodized on the beauties of Russian nature. Regular news reports were aired without any mention of war, though the military, patriotic theme was played up and a war broadcast was prepared for the moment that permission came from the Kremlin.[15]

The first announcement of war came at twelve noon, when at Stalin's request Molotov spoke to the country on the radio. His speech struck chords that would ring true throughout the war, but the delivery and rhetoric lacked conviction.[16] Moreover, Molotov repeated old mistakes, above all the vow that Soviet arms would soon crush the fascist aggressor. That message would seem hollow for many months. Once the announcement was made, radio went over to war footing: bulletins were on the air within forty-five minutes; Aleksei Surkov, Vasilii Lebedev-Kumach and Ilya Ehrenburg made brief morale-boosting statements; correspondent reports, praising exaggerated Soviet heroism and resistance, were filed; and appropriate music plugged the gaps. A scheduled broadcast of Prokofiev's ballet *Romeo and Juliet* from the Bolshoi Theater was attempted, but it was interrupted by bulletins from the front.

In the early days of the war, radio transmission to occupied territory and near the front was almost impossible. The Germans captured many relay points, completely halting wire transmission. Since Radio Moscow was broadcast mostly on long- or middle-wave bands, the western territories—including recently incorporated territories in Ukraine, Belorussia, and the Baltic states, where Soviet sentiment was weak—were often beyond reach.[17] The situation was further complicated by a 1940 decree of the People's Commissariat of Communications, which had confiscated private radio receivers. The absence or breakdown of communications in the summer and autumn of 1941 caused untold suffering; residents of the border republics were caught unawares by the invasion; and the army itself was so poorly equipped that even a general needed a captured receiver to get essential information.[18]

Early in the war, the State Radio Committee decided to merge central broadcasting's two channels into one, and to convert from long- and medium-wave transmission to medium- and short-wave, by which it was easier to reach all parts of the country, including occupied territory. Radio Moscow soon established broadcasts to the occupied zones of Ukraine, Belorussia, Karelia, Moldavia, Lithuania, Latvia and Estonia in their native languages. The most important broadcast towers were evacuated east. Blockaded Leningrad not only succeeded in saving all equipment, it even constructed a new station, claimed to be the world's most powerful.[19] Other new and powerful transmitters were erected in the Ural Mountains, and by 1943, broadcasting had reached prewar levels. Since radio construction was given top-level priority, service was immediately restored when the western republics were recaptured from the Germans.

At its wartime height, Radio Moscow provided eighteen and a half hours programming daily, with an equal division between news and cultural programs. The daily schedule offered fourteen editions of "The Latest News," five children's programs, four programs of letters to and from the front, three literary and eighteen musical programs. There were also frequent special programs for peasants, youth, the army, navy, and other groups. Music was dominant, occupying over ten hours a day; though literary readings were quantitatively few, they were popular and commanded prime broadcast scheduling—perhaps due in part to the wholesale German destruction and burning of books, and the difficulty of producing replacement books.

News programming was instrumental in restoring public confidence in Radio Moscow, but it took time and struggle. Early war programming fell back on slogans that had been exhausted in the 1930s, including broadcasts like "Ceaselessly Preparing New Reserves for the Red Army," or "The Stakhanovites of War."[20] Other old reflexes survived through 1941. Even after the embarrassing broadcast lag of June 22, directors hesitated to share bleak news from the front without high-level authorization. In August, Radio Committee Chairman Polikarpov demanded that no news be broadcast without his personal approval. The strong arm of censorship was evident in early months, when old formulas concealed the obvious truth of the retreat. There were in fact unwritten instructions that the retreat should not be mentioned on the air.[21] Newscasts either made little reference to the war or else claimed that the fascist enemy was reeling from Soviet attacks; Stalin in his November 7, 1941, broadcast claimed that 4.5 million German soldiers had been taken out of action, and that the Wehrmacht was terrified of Soviet bayonets and cavalry.[22] These were clichés of the pre-Blitzkrieg era.

The audience, aware of the military debacle despite official silence, suffered a serious drop in morale. There existed few credible sources of information, and none that could report events as quickly as radio. Authorities responded to the situation by creating broadcast formats that avoided crude propaganda and added the flavor of spontaneity, yet preserved central control. First and most important was the creation of Informbiuro two days after the start of the war. Informbiuro centralized responsibility for news even more than before—it was in charge of both reporting and interpreting events—but it also streamlined the process by removing competing organs of censorship. This allowed for the rapid relay of fast-breaking news, and eliminating organizational ambiguities that made censorship a reflex of self-protection. More authority created more latitude for a variety of news, good and bad, and Radio Committee directors found in the end that they could trust citizens with bad news. Horrible stories of the German occupation, which proved a particularly effective propaganda measure, began early in 1942 and continued throughout the war.[23]

News reporting was greatly improved by the assignment of war correspondents to the front. The politics of false peace had prevented reporters from observing the initial stages of the invasion. Radio Moscow dispatched correspondents in the days immediately after June 22, but they rarely got far. Aleksei Surkov filed one of the earliest reports from Moscow's Belorussia Station, where he described troop trains departing for the front. Battle correspondents had no military authorization, and they often found themselves unwanted and ordered back home.[24] By autumn, an agreement had been signed by Polikarpov and General Zhukov, under which correspondents were accredited by the military—they were sometimes given military rank—and able to travel about the front with army cooperation. By 1942 the corps was thoroughly professional, aided by a joint Agitprop-Army regulation that put knowledge above political reliability in the selection of correspondents.[25] The series "Dateline Western Front!" was one result of the collaboration; it broadcast reports recorded on the front, where background noise lent a new authenticity.

Mobile units were formed by November 1941, and when the front approached Moscow, correspondents were able to visit the troops during the day and broadcast that same evening.[26] Their work was facilitated by the Shorinophone recorder, named after its inventor, Aleksandr Shorin, which was an adaptation of film technology. The machine, a somewhat belated discovery used only in the Soviet Union, was unreliable, bulky (it weighed about a hundred and eighty pounds), and required an electrical source.[27] Yet it proved useful: in the first year of the war, it recorded the voices of units—such as the battleship *Kirov*—that the Germans had claimed destroyed, and later it thrilled listeners with battle sounds taken from a bomber and an attacking tank. Once the partisan war had grown, favorite broadcasts for front and rear were stories of partisan attacks, recorded behind enemy lines by the partisans themselves and flown back to Moscow. Intrepid reporters and technicians recorded stories under fire from Malakhov Kurgan in encircled Sevastopol, from the Dnieper crossing, and later from Stalingrad.[28]

After its meek initial reaction, Soviet radio recovered some of the boldness needed to restore civilian morale. On July 3, 1941, after a two-week silence, Stalin spoke to the nation from an improvised Kremlin studio. The speech, which lasted a mere twelve minutes, was a sure-footed performance summoning emotions that would hold citizens together throughout the war. Most memorable was the appeal to "brothers and sisters," evoking blood-based, non-political ties that were previously condemned. At a time of rampant fear, which had only been fanned by radio's silence and false bravado, Stalin spoke confidently of the fate of Napoleon and Kaiser Wilhelm, who had also penetrated deep into Russia. The speech as a whole was strong, and it fixed several effective lines of propaganda for the remainder of the war. Even more important than the words was the fact that Stalin had responded, admitted terrible losses, and rallied his people to the cause.[29]

November 7, 1941, brought another important broadcast: the anniversary parade from Red Square. It was arranged in great secrecy, to prevent any raid by German bombers. The night before, in a broadcast from Maiakovskii Metro Station deep below the city, which caused sound technicians countless difficulties, Stalin had spoken to the nation. Then on the morning of the seventh, a team of commentators headed by Surkov and Vadim Siniavskii (the soccer commentator who had reported prewar holiday demonstrations) was brought to the square for a live—and for the first time in years, extemporaneous—broadcast. Marshal Budënnyi, still a popular hero, led the parade, which was reviewed by Stalin and the Politburo.[30] Though the display of saber-bearing cavalry might have seemed hopelessly outdated, Stalin's decision to stay in the city was a source of pride for Soviet people to the end of the war. His role in lifting morale cannot be overestimated.

By late 1941, programming for frontline troops was receiving special attention. At first "Dateline Western Front" was the only offering, but other programs soon joined it on the air. Every Monday an important political figure would deliver a morale-boosting speech, and for a half hour on Tuesdays and Thursdays, conversations about military themes were aired. More popular were the "Red Army Hours" broadcast on Wednesdays and Saturdays, which featured entertainment, as did the "Listen Up, Front Lines" program. Concerts featuring popular singers were given, with Ivan Kozlovskii being a favored guest. Authorities went to great lengths to safeguard these broadcasts; in Leningrad trenches were hooked into the wire network, and there were nighttime broadcasts for garrisons behind enemy lines. Outside Moscow, there was even a transmission from an aircraft flying over the trenches.[31]

Programmers devoted particular attention to relations between the military and civilians, and their success was recognized at home and abroad. On "Listen Up, Front Lines" soldiers heard about the hard work being performed in factories and kolkhozes, much of it by women.[32] The broadcast's credibility was probably helped by the fact that soldiers were hearing similar news in letters from home. There were other broadcasts devoted to the theme of front-rear relations: "From the Urals to the Front," "Workers of the Rear Are with You, Comrade Warriors," and "Communists and Young Communists in Battle."[33] Also effective were supplementary communiqués concerning the feats of individual soldiers. This was a practice common to all the Soviet media, one that so bolstered morale that Goebbels praised it and tried unsuccessfully to copy it. His failure was due to the military high command, which resented attention paid to the lower ranks, and to Nazi Party members who begrudged any praise directed at the military.[34]

Strong ties between front and rear were maintained by the daily series "Letters from the Front" and "Letters from the Rear," the most avidly followed of all Radio Moscow programs. Millions of families were torn apart by the war, personal letters often did not reach their destination, and families had no information on the whereabouts of missing soldiers. Their last remaining hope was that a message would come over the airwaves. There were ten daily broadcasts totaling two and a half hours, which produced many a happy tale of families reunited. The program in fact continued for years after the war, and twenty years later it was still reuniting families. Both programs were up and running by August 1941: they received about 50,000 letters a month, each of which was carefully catalogued and stored, and ten percent of which were read over the air.[35] At first, letters underwent "literary reworking" before being read; and they were delivered by famous actors, such as Vera Pashennaia of the Malyi Theater. But within a year, there were enough complaints about stiff language that the directors put letters on the air without "correction." Mobile correspondents were assigned to record soldiers reading their own letters, and civilians were invited to the studios to read theirs.[36]

For the first time in history, near-universal participation was possible during the Great Patriotic War; almost every family had someone on the front, and its course was followed daily throughout the country. The whole record of wartime radio suggests that a new relationship was forged between radio and listener that allowed for more openness and intimacy; programming addressed the concerns of average people more than it had before. By 1942 Radio Moscow had recovered its authority, and soon became a trusted news source for much of the population. Its ability to convince citizens was fully recognized by the Germans: Radio Center on Moscow's Gorky Street became a target of bombers—a huge dud landed in its courtyard—and Levitan, the most respected reader, had a price set on his head by Goebbels.

Many of the adjustments made in wartime revived practices developed during the infancy of radio, including many associated with the Cultural Revolution. This ran counter to a trend seen elsewhere during the war, when radical cultural forms were forsaken for more traditional ones. As in the years 1928–32, reporters were dispatched to interview simple people and capture their voices and thoughts; ad libs were allowed, sometimes even encouraged; work on location, where background noise roughened the recorded texture, was common; and creative genres like the radio sketch and radio play were revived. On-site documentaries from the factory floor or front line returned, as did intercity *pereklichki* and rallies.[37]

In isolated Leningrad, spirited broadcasting was essential to public confidence. The once-banned *pereklichka*, a distinctly Leningrad form originated in the 1930s, found new applications. Any contact with the outside world was a great morale booster during the war, since no other form of public rally was possible, and programs such as an October 1941 *pereklichka* with Moscow were very popular.[38] Wartime also created new topics for the aggressive satire common in the early 1930s. Mikhail Zoshchenko and Evgenii Shvarts put their sharp pens to work for the "Leningrad Radio Chronicle," where they mocked—in a style reminiscent of earlier years—panickers, chatterboxes and loafers, old terms that had taken on new meanings in war conditions. The "Radio Chronicle" was a direct continuation (many of the writers were the same) of the popular 1930s series "*Veselye ochki*" and "*Davaite ne budem*," which had run at 10 AM Sunday mornings and tempted huge audiences away from church.[39]

It was not only news broadcasting, but also cultural broadcasting that attracted listeners to Radio Moscow during the war. Credit should be given not only to programming but to its new context. Old formulas suddenly rang true; and programs that had been irrelevant were now a matter of vital concern. Since the audience already shared officially supported sentiments, the annoying apparatus of listener edification—including gung-ho marches and political jingles—could be abandoned. Music had only to be "patriotic," which meant Russian folk or classical music, nineteenth-century masters, and twentieth-century music untainted by the avant-garde. Perhaps surprisingly, the German classics—Beethoven and Bach—were also popular, because they were played with the tacit understanding that their tradition had been repudiated by the Nazis. Unburdened by Nazi-style racial theories of culture, Radio Moscow could make any music patriotic, by claiming that all great culture was antagonistic to the black hordes of Hitler. The emotional power of classical culture received its most stirring embodiment in Dmitrii Shostakovich's Seventh Symphony, which premiered over Radio Leningrad in the hard winter of 1942 (see Robinson, this volume).

Classical culture was elevated to cult status during the war, reinforced by strong doses of cultural programming on Radio Moscow. Its "eternal values" were given a distinctly contemporary spin. Ilya Ehrenburg excoriated the Nazi savages for defiling French and European culture; Lev Magrachev, the popular Leningrad commentator, bemoaned the descent of the German race into barbarism.[40] Culture—in the abstract as well as the concrete—became a rallying point for Russians. An anti-fascist radio rally of November 1942 united the writer Aleksei Tolstoi, the actor Nikolai Cherkasov, and Shostakovich, who together called on the people to defend Russian culture against the Huns.[41] Broadcasts from the Bolshoi Theater in Moscow, high temple of the cult of culture, were common, as were symphonic performances—even in Leningrad, where the radio orchestra eventually dwindled to seven people. Dramas were broadcast live from the capital in the series "Theater at the Microphone," featuring Russian classics and wartime Soviet works, with a new production almost every other day. Topical plays, particularly Aleksandr Korneichuk's *Front*, won a large listenership. For some sumptuous operatic recitals, commentators attempted to describe the production during the action—this of course only interfered. But the broadcasts were still popular because, as one listener wrote, "Listening and not seeing is better than not listening and not seeing."[42]

The most popular of Radio Moscow's cultural programs were literary readings, which were followed with a devotion that might surprise students of Western commercial radio. The works of Lev Tolstoy enjoyed an immense audience during the war. *War and Peace*, which had powerful contemporary resonance, was read by the actor Dmitrii Orlov over the course of thirty broadcasts, maintaining a constant audience throughout; and readings of his *Sevastopol Stories* were broadcast during the siege of that city, which enhanced the historical parallels. Radio programmers exploited the popularity of classics by scheduling frequent readings, conducted by such master readers as Orlov and Iakhontov.[43] By the end of 1944, a new literary reading was being prepared every day, attesting to the genre's popularity.

Soviet literature of the prewar variety was absent from the air. There were occasional readings taken from the 1920s: Il'f and Petrov were favorites.[44] The heavily politicized writings of the 1930s were shunned, even though writers of that period gained great popularity reading their wartime work over the air. Konstantin Simonov read his war lyrics, Konstantin Paustovskii spoke of the Sevastopol sailors, Nikolai Tikhonov read his blockade stories, and Aleksandr Fadeev read from an early version of *Young Guard*. Soviet writers were in fact so popular that Radio Moscow prepared a series of sketches on their lives. Surely the most popular reading of the war was Aleksandr Tvardovskii's *Vasilii Tërkin* in Orlov's rendition, which began in the hard winter of 1942, when the poem was only half done. Tvardovskii himself admitted that the poem owed its tremendous popularity to radio.[45]

Radio sketches, the interpretive journalism that had flourished in the early 1930s, returned with the slackening of censorship. In 1942 Radio Moscow began a regular series entitled *From the Notebooks of Soviet Writers*, which featured longer sketches from such writers as Leonid Sobolev, Pëtr Pavlenko, Lev Kassil', and Vladimir Beliaev. Back-against-the-wall determination was an outstanding feature of the most famous radio sketches, all of which were read by the authors themselves. Ilya Ehrenburg read his famous pieces, many of which also appeared in *Izvestiia*, and Boris Gorbatov read his stories, including the popular "Life and Death."[46] Again, writers' ability to stir hearts was most fully realized in Leningrad, where Vsevolod Vishnevskii's speeches and the sketches and the verse of Vera Inber and Ol'ga Berggol'ts (see fig. 4) helped Leningraders through the harsh winters and inspired the rest of the country in weekly all-Union broadcasts.

Soviet radio boasted over two hours of children's programming per day. Leadership was provided by Radio Leningrad, which had a strong prewar tradition of children's broadcasts. At the outset of war, the supervisory Children's Sector of the Radio Committee was closed, which removed a layer of political tutelage. There were still parallels to adult programming: readings of the Russian classics were common, as were reports on the lives of heroic soldiers. Programs about children—usually brave Pioneers—bore the marks of adult supervision. The roles given to children in such programs were often reflections of adult roles: brave fighters, suffering martyrs, etc. Yet there were also readings by the wonderful writers Samuil Marshak, Agniia Barto, Lev Kassil', and special children's plays that were truly for children. An adventure series, "The Amulet," won particular popularity in the winter of 1942–43; it featured three kids and an absent-minded professor, whose search for an amulet took them to various eras in the past. And in 1944–45 "Try and Guess," a game show, successfully combined military education and fun.[47]

Ultimately, radio's greatest asset was the power to create intimate ties over a span of thousands of miles. Stalin's speeches were instrumental in reclaiming that potential: his decision to address citizens as "brothers and sisters" animated a sense of family that thrived throughout the war. Wooden, with a flat accent exaggerated in anecdotes, the voice of a cruel dictator was an odd vehicle for intimacy; surely the credit belonged equally to the medium which yielded similar advantages elsewhere. In America, President Roosevelt's "Fireside Chats" had enraptured listeners; in Britain, Winston Churchill rallied citizens in the bleakest days of the war; the leader's voice lifted morale in a time of crisis, where paradoxically the voices felt most intimately were those that were most distant and imposing.

The emotional tug was most evident in the voice of Iurii Levitan. Levitan, whose booming, authoritative delivery was unmistakable, was the only Radio Moscow announcer allowed to read orders of the High Command (totaling twenty-seven during the war) and the texts of Stalin's speeches. For many military men, Levitan was the voice of Headquarters.[48] It was a responsibility that kept him in Moscow and on constant alert throughout the war. He had earned that signal honor by 1934, still a young man, when he read for radio listeners Stalin's speech to the 17th Party Congress—all five hours of it—without a quiver in his voice.[49] By the late 1930s, Levitan was assumed to be the voice of Stalin. His eminence was codified in 1938, when the State Radio Committee formed a commission to evaluate readers, who henceforth were categorized by the materials they were authorized to read. Only a small group could read the leading news and high state proclamations. Ol'ga Vysotskaia, who also received the highest classification, recalled that when reading such announcements, she and her colleagues assumed a severe, restrained, measured voice.[50] Levitan's reading was exalted—he was speaking for Stalin personally—yet he is remembered with an intimate, personal gratitude, and his voice was an inseparable part of the wartime experience. The voice was unshaken in the dark days of retreat, and later rang loud with news of great victories. It proclaimed the victory salutes of 1943–45, which were broadcast to the entire country (even the fireworks displays), and in 1945 it brought the final news of German surrender.

Levitan also represented, for many parts of the country, occupied and unoccupied, the voice of the "mainland" (*bol'shaia zemlia*), the core of the country that anchored and integrated the periphery. It was a role he had assumed in the 1930s, during the great era of polar exploration, when he conducted special late-night broadcasts for the Cheliuskin and Papanin expeditions. The first months of war brought chaos and dislocation, as if the world were crumbling; Radio Moscow readers acted like ambassadors for the center.[51] The actor Vladimir Iakhontov, whose wartime readings were beloved, said: "Living without listening to the radio was impossible. Radio informed, signaled and guided us, kept kin and loved ones linked together. The voice that said 'Dateline Moscow' grabbed listeners' attention, comforted them, instilled hope in them. People listened to it all over the country, thousands of miles away."[52] It represented the center, with all the political and cultural punch that notion carried.

Radio fully realized its ability to integrate center and periphery during the war, when it broadcast over enemy lines to occupied territory. It added a new dimension to warfare, and redefined the relationship between front and rear. Geographic isolation and military obstacles were no longer unbreakable; there was a mutual awareness in wartime society that had been absent in previous wars. Radio communication bound classes and regions; and it maintained a dialogue—often polemical—with other countries. Broadcasts were essential to maintaining civilian support for the war effort, but their power went beyond simple communication. They assured the center and periphery of the other's existence, and also assured themselves of *their own* importance. The center knew it was important by the fact that the periphery needed to hear from it; the periphery knew it was valued because Moscow wanted to talk to it.

Maintaining contact with occupied territories was at the top of the agenda, but the task was complicated by ethnic politics. One of the first measures taken was to ensure transmission. The PB-1 Komintern station built in 1933 was already capable of reaching most of the cut-off zones. Other transmitters were evacuated to the Urals, and middle-wave stations were converted to short-wave. Broadcasts were initiated to the Slavic, Baltic, Caucasian, and Central Asian republics, and they were staffed by native news readers evacuated to Moscow.[53] Yet Soviet authorities had previously so incapacitated multinational broadcasting that its wartime utility was dubious. The Ukrainian and Belorussian stations had been crippled in 1937. In the Baltic territories and Bessarabia, Radio Moscow correspondents were associated with the occupying forces: immediate prewar broadcasts had included such pieces as "Triumph of the Lithuanian People" and "Bessarabians Return to Their Homeland."[54] Citizens of the occupied territories were likely inclined to listen to German broadcasts; such, at least, was the operative assumption of the Ukrainian Radio Shevchenko, whose assignment was counterpropaganda against Radio Weichsel (German for the Vistula River) broadcasts.[55] Only after the western territories had been recovered, and the exclusive wire network reestablished, was Soviet radio confident of its audience there.

An enduring myth about Radio Moscow is that it sustained the partisan movement through its darkest hours—the film *She Defends the Motherland* (see Kenez, this volume) created the image of peasant partisans huddled around a crystal set listening to the center. In his July 3, 1941, speech, Stalin called for the formation of partisan units, but his summons—despite the legend—often went unheard. The countryside, particularly the western territories, had been neglected in the prewar radiofication drive, and few radios were available; those few were hooked to the wire network, which the Germans had already captured; most partisan radios were rigged for Morse reception. Soviet authorities had recognized the problem by November; when Stalin addressed the partisans (who as yet hardly existed) in his anniversary speech, the speech was printed in leaflets dropped behind enemy lines in case nobody had heard.[56]

There was something very Bolshevik in the early partisan broadcasts, which served the same organizing function for the partisans as newspapers had served for the prerevolutionary underground. The rare partisan with a short-wave receiver would receive and then stenographically transcribe Radio Moscow. The records would be typed out, printed on secret presses, and then distributed by secret couriers. News-delivery groups later served as the nuclei of the partisan underground—as did the Krasnodon circle later glorified in Fadeev's *Young Guard*.[57] Despite the obstacles, broadcasting was instrumental in establishing contact with occupied territory and maintaining morale. In late 1941 German radio spliced Soviet broadcast segments into a counterfeit announcement of Moscow's surrender (also alluded to in *She Defends the Motherland*). Every broadcast from Moscow belied that claim, and was a source of hope. Though attentive to the partisans, the Radio Committee waited until May 1942, when the movement had gained strength, to initiate regular broadcasts.[58] The weekly program, whose call ran "Listen to us, brothers and sisters on the other side," contained practical advice for partisan units, including spots on "How to Destroy Transport," "The Simonov Antitank Gun," "Ambushes," "Abandoning a Firefight," "The Art of Camouflage," and "Shooting Fascist Planes Down with Infantry Weapons."[59] The audience, judging by the programs, consisted of real partisans, and broadcasts continued until October 1943, when the advance of the Red Army made them obsolete.

Counteracting Nazi radio was an important assignment despite the fact that most

Soviet citizens had no access to foreign broadcasts. There was good reason to: German broadcasts did reach occupied territory; they filtered over to Soviet territory by word-of-mouth; and Allied nations, whose support the Soviets needed, could also hear Nazi radio. At first the Germans proved more adept at radio warfare, and they easily parried Russian braggadocio: premature announcements of victory, and euphemisms such as "fighting in the direction of," which ignored the question of whether Russians were advancing or retreating. The Germans caused acute embarrassment by tallying Russian counts of Wehrmacht casualties for the 1941–42 campaign, which came to one-sixth of the entire German population.[60] Early Russian counter reports were feeble, perhaps worse than silence. Magrachev attacked a June 22, 1941, German broadcast that claimed advances along the entire Russian front. The report, Magrachev averred, was patently false, since there were *some* pockets of resistance along the front.[61] Nazi radio also gave listeners food for thought with reports of primitive living standards on captured Soviet territory and GPU crimes—the Katyn graves were a powerful blow. When *Pravda* published reports about German atrocities, Nazis countered with reports of cannibalism in Soviet cities.[62]

Radio Moscow recovered and soon gained credibility over its German rivals. There were several factors: relative reliability, the willingless to trust listeners to reach their own conclusions, and improved fortunes in the war. Ultimately, the Soviets profited most from clumsy Nazi broadcasting, which undermined its own credibility and insulted its audience. German radio suffered a credibility gap from the time of its first eastern broadcasts, when Goebbels's strategy was to mask the impending invasion with gossip. The strategy's short-term success was offset by long-term distrust. Later broadcasts featured strong doses of Nazi racial theory, against the will of Goebbels, but at the behest of Alfred Rosenberg, erstwhile party ideologist and Minister for the Eastern Territories. The occupied territories offered an audience open to anti-Soviet and anti-Semitic sentiment, particularly in relation to the "Bolshevik Jews." But the equal time devoted to the dogma of the Slavic *Untermensch* obviously found little resonance on Slavic territory. Goebbels's insistence on programs stressing the fight against Bolshevism, not the Russian nation, went unheeded; Radio Moscow often played back broadcasts in which Nazis discussed plans for destroying the Slavic races.[63]

German credibility was suffering at the same time because the tide of war was changing after Stalingrad; grandiose claims were no longer matched by battlefield success. Radio Moscow deftly countered their false claims, and the claims of their Italian allies, as when they announced the downing of forty-four Russian planes over Leningrad on a night when no planes had flown.[64] Radio Moscow learned that the best way to raise morale was not to exaggerate, a strategy that reaped benefits when cautious forecasts for Stalingrad were exceeded by reality. German radio had long ago trumpeted a Wehrmacht victory.

The greatest turnaround was performed by the foreign-broadcast arm of Radio Moscow, once a neglected mouthpiece. Before the war, the Nazis had had more for-eign-broadcasting experience than the Soviets, due to the ethnic politics of the time, when radio helped the weakened German state maintain contact with Germans in other lands: the Ruhr, Sudetenland, Upper Silesia, etc.[65] But by 1942 several factors had allowed Radio Moscow to establish effective service to Germany and occupied Europe. Although they had paid less attention to international radio than had the west-ern powers, the Soviets were ahead technologically: the PB-1 Komintern station was easily capable of broadcasting throughout the continent. Early on, in 1929, the Rus-sians had established a German service, Radio Marikhen, that within several years was staffed by highly capable expatriate Germans. The broadcasters were provided with an extensive library of German propaganda and ample financial resources.[66] When German aggression began in Europe, an organization was already in place, and the flood of refugees provided Radio Moscow with a corps of thirteen native broadcasters working in most of the European languages. This was a distinct advantage over the Germans, because Radio Moscow announcers were not compromised by association with the enemy.[67]

Radio Moscow clearly came out ahead in the chess game of counterpropaganda. Programmers had a clear grasp on their audience, which they divided into five sec-tions: Germany, its satellites, occupied countries, neutral countries, and the Allies. Some programs were targeted: for Slavic countries, there were special broadcasts on Slavic patriotism, with an emphasis on stoicism in the face of death.[68] For the German audience, there were programs on conditions in the German rear. Some of these clev-erly employed letters taken from captured and killed soldiers, which spoke of large-scale corruption and favoritism. The prevailing strategy was one that could be applied in all directions: break down Nazi arguments; show that Nazi power had been weak-ened; show Nazi barbarism.[69] The Germans' increasingly empty claims were punc-tured: when they boasted of rapidly constructing an Atlantic defense wall, Radio Mos-cow calmly pointed out that their figures would demand 150 percent higher concrete production than all prewar Germany could muster. Soviet work became so effective that the Italian announcers Appelius and Ansaldo devoted a special program, "Mos-cow's Lies on the Ether," to countering Radio Moscow. Their effort was foiled by the clever trick of a "ghost voice." During the broadcast, Moscow would tune in on the same frequency, and during pauses, a mysterious voice would counter any claims made. A curt rejoinder could undermine a half hour's tirade. Soon, Moscow created the "Voice of the People" to interrupt German broadcasts, whose victim became, among others, Joseph Goebbels.[70]

By war's end, Radio Moscow was transmitting to audiences throughout the So-viet Union and Europe with success. Battlefront progress helped expand Soviet radio's authority and audience, but credit is due as well to policy decisions taken at the beginning of the war. Technological resources were protected and enriched in the midst of a confused retreat; skilled radio workers were given latitude; and programming forsook narrow politicking to win a broader listenership. In 1945, when Radio Moscow triumphantly broadcast the raising of the red flag over the Reichstag and the many-gunned victory salutes on Red Square, it had an extensive and sympathetic audience. Still, the greatest accomplishments of wartime radio came in the dark early days of retreat, when it performed unique functions and helped stanch disaster. Broadcasting in World War II performed a role similar to that of the airplane in World War I: it rendered old lines of demarcation penetrable. Previous models of warfare involving fixed areas defined by battlelines became obsolete. Tanks had shattered the tactics of position and counterattack; new communications linked vast areas and made front lines porous. As German forces moved deep into Soviet Russia, radio maintained contact, and preserved the unity that eventually defeated the invaders.

## Notes

Support for research on this paper came from the Kennan Institute for Advanced Russian Studies. Special thanks are due to Doug Brown of Georgetown University for his timely advice and assistance.

1. A.D. Fortushenko, *50 let radio* (Moscow: Sviazizdat, 1945), 75–76; I. E. Goron, *Radioveshchanie* (Moscow: Sviazizdat, 1944), 10; V. Stepanov, "Moshchnoe sredstvo propagandy," *Izvestiia* (16 December 1944), 2.

2. K. R. M. Short, ed., *Film and Radio Propaganda in World War II* (Knoxville: University of Tennessee Press, 1983), 3.

3. Alex Inkeles, "Domestic Broadcasting in the USSR," *Communications Research 1948–1949*, ed. Paul F. Lazarsfeld and Frank N. Stanton (New York: Harper and Brothers, 1949), 245.

4. Inkeles, 248.

5. V. B. Dubrovin, *K istorii sovetskogo radioveshchaniia* (Leningrad: Izd-vo Leningradskogo universiteta, 1972), 66–67; N. F. Pogodin, "Mikrofon v derevne," *Radioslushatel'*, no. 45–46 (1929), 4–5; A. Fortushenko, "Tekhnika sovetskogo radioveshchaniia," *Izvestiia* (16 December 1944), 2; Inkeles, 235–39.

6. Dubrovin, 51–54; Inkeles, 276–77.

7. Prikaz N° 511 po VRK pri SNK SSSR, "O zapreshchenii radioperklichek," 29 October 1937, in *Istoriia sovetskoi radio-zhurnalistiki: dokumenty, teksty, vospominaniia, 1917–1945* (hereafter, *Istoriia*) (Moscow: Izd. Moskovskogo universiteta, 1991), 62.

8. Evgenii Riabchikov, "Golos vremeni," *Iurii Levitan: 50 let u mikrofona*, ed. V. M. Vozchikov (Moscow: Iskusstvo, 1987), 91.

9. N. A. Tolstova, *Vnimanie, vkliuchaiu mikrofon!* (Moscow: Iskusstvo, 1972), 134–40; Inkeles, 262.

10. Prikaz N° 45 po VRK pri SNK SSSR, "O poriadke sdachi mikrofonnykh materialov," 14 February 1939, in *Istoriia*, 62–64.

11. "Navesti bolshoi poriadok v radioveshchanii," *Pravda* (22 July 1937), 1.

12. V. A. Goncharov, "S mikrofonom po strane" (1940), *Istoriia*, 387–89.

13. O. Kudenko, *Podvig naroda* (Moscow: Iskusstvo, 1971), 14, lists the programming schedules for June 22, 1941.

14. M. Shalashnikov, "Stranitsy voiny," *Radioprogrammy* (18 June 1961), 2.

15. For the chaos and confusion of those days, see N. M. Potapov, "V pervyi den'," *Radio v dni voiny: ocherki i vospominaniia vidnykh voenachal'nikov, izvestnykh pisatelei, zhurnalistov, deiatelei iskusstva, diktorov radioveshaniia*, ed. M. S. Gleizer and N. M. Potapov (Moscow: Iskusstvo, 1982), 9–13; and Tolstova, 177–80.

16. *Istoriia*, 221–22; the delivery is described in Alexander Werth, *Russia at War, 1941–1945* (New York: Carroll and Graf, 1984), 159–69.

17. K. Sergeichuk, "Radio v Sovetskom soiuze," *Pravda* (7 May 1947), 3. The figures in *Razvitie sviazi v SSSR, 1917–1967* (hereafter, *Razvitie*) ed. N. D. Psurtsev (Moscow: Izd. Sviazi, 1967), 262, suggest that the entire western network was practically destroyed.

18. Sovet Narodnykh Komissarov SSSR, "O vozvrate naseleniiu, uchrezhdeniiam i prepriiatiiam radiopriemnikov, priniatykh v 1941 godu na khranenie organami Narkomata sviazi," 14 March 1945, in *Istoriia*, 35; I. Batov, "Levitana znali vse," *Iurii Levitan*, 41.

19. A. Puzin, "20 let radioveshchaniia v SSSR," *Pravda* (16 December 1944), 3; *Razvitie*, 261; Fortushenko, "Tekhnika," 2.

20. V. G. Kovtun, "Veshchanie Leningradskogo radio dlia molodëzhi v gody Velikoi Otechestvennoi Voiny," *Problemy zhurnalistiki*, vyp 4 (Leningrad: Izd-vo LGU, 1974), 64–65.

21. Prikaz N° 407 po VRK pri SNK SSSR, "O poriadke vizirovaniia radioperedach." 24 August 1941, in *Istoriia*, 72; Vasilii Ardamatskii, "Zametki o rabote na voine," *Radio v dni voiny*, 32–34.

22. *Istoriia*, 235–37, 248.

23. See for instance "Govorit zapadnyi front," 25 March 1942, in *Istoriia*, 248.

24. Surkov's transcript is in Kudenko, 40. On early frontline reporting, see M. Gleizer, *Radio i televidenie v SSSR, 1917–1963 (fakty i daty)* (Moscow: Izdi Sviaz', 1965), 90–93; Ardamatskii, 31–33.

25. Upravlenie propagandy i agitatsii TsK VKPb i Glavpolituprav Krasnoi Armii, "O rabote voennykh korrespondentov," 1942, in *Istoriia*, 32–34.

26. Georgii Evstigneev, "Pozyvnye muzhestva," *Radio v dni voiny*, 22–25; Kudenko, 16.

27. *S perom i avtomatom* (Leningrad: Lenizdat, 1964), 162–65, describes some of the practical difficulties involved.

28. Arkadii Fram, "S mikrofonom i bloknotom," *Radio v dni voiny*, 70–73; L. Magrachev, *Golosa zhizni* (Leningrad, 1962), 19; Kudenko, 42–52, gives texts for some outstanding recordings; Kassil', 2. See also A. M. Spasskii, "Po dorogam voiny. Zapiski frontovogo zvukooperatora," *Radio v dni voiny*, 165–73.

29. The text in *Istoriia*, 223–26, is from *Pravda* (3 July 1941). See Werth, 162–68, or Dina Iablonskaia and Mikhail Shul'man, *Odessa–Tel-Aviv i Radio—liubov'moia* (Tel-Aviv, 1985), 135 for the response.

30. I. T. Peresypkin "Vospominaniia narkoma," *Radio v dni voiny*, 141–43; for the text of broadcast, and announcers' recollections, see "Parad na Krasnoi ploshchadi 7 noiabria 1941 goda," in *Istoriia*, 229–37; and Vadim Siniavskii, "O samom pamiatnom," ibid., 395–402; and Aleksei Surkov, "V efire—Krasnaia ploshchad'," in ibid., 219–23. There are many testaments to the success of the broadcast: see in particular Vera Inber, *Leningrad Diary*, trans. Serge M. Wolff and Rachel Grieve (London: Hutchinson, 1971), 31, and Lev Kassil', "Vsesvetnoe slovo," *Literaturnaia gazeta* (16 December 1944), 2.

31. *S perom i avtomatom*, 157; Tolstova, 183–85, 197.

32. *Radio v dni voiny*, 263.

33. Kudenko, 18.

34. Robert Edwin Herzstein, *The War That Hitler Won* (New York: G. Putnam's Sons, 1978), 180; Matthew Gordon, *News is a Weapon* (New York: Knopf, 1942), 180.

35. Lev Kassil', "Deviat'minut, radiorasskaz," *Istoriia*, 244–47; G. Kazakov, "Pis'ma na front," *Radio*, no. 2 (1946), 12–13; Dubrovin, 69; Inkeles, 286. Vera Kabluchko and Mikhail Gleizer, "Dva milliona pisem," *Radio v dni voiny*, 207–18, record the memories of two Radio Committee workers in charge of registering letters.

36. Tolstova, 190; *Istoriia*, 74–75; Spasskii, 165–73.

37. Dubrovin, 31–40; *S perom i avtomatom*, 161.

38. Inber, 12; Kudenko, 20–22; Kovtun, 62.

39. O. Berggol'ts, "Govorit Leningrad," *Deviat'sot dnei* (Leningrad, 1962), 411; T. A. Marchenko, *Radioteatr* (Moscow: Iskusstvo, 1970), 62–64.

40. I. Erenburg, "Slushai, Parizh!", in *Istoriia*, 242–44; L. Magrachev, "Vot ona, ikh kultura," in Kudenko, 41.

41. Text in "Antifashistskii miting rabotnikov iskusstva i literatury," 29 November 1942, in *Istoriia*, 258–62.

42. V. Ardamatskii, "Literatura po radio," *Literaturnaia gazeta* (16 December 1944), 2.

43. Ardamatski, 2; N. Iu. Verkhovskii, *Kniga o chtetsakh* (Moscow: Iskusstvo, 1950), 218-41.

44. O. Abdulov, "Kniga v efire," *Literaturnaia gazeta* (16 December 1944), 2.

45. A. T. Tvardovskii, "*Vasilii Tërkin* Dmitriia Orlova," in *Istoriia*, 405–06.

46. S. Gurevich and V. N. Ruzhnikov, *Sovetskoe radioveshchanie* (Moscow: Iskusstvo, 1976), 200–03; Ardamatiskii, 2.

47. *Istoriia*, 70–71; Dubrovin, 44; Gurevich, 205–07; Marchenko, 86–87. Texts for children's broadcasts are in *Istoriia*, 256–58, 272–75, 290–95.

48. *Iurii Levitan*, 41.

49. Mikhail Platov, "Glavnyi diktor strany," *Iurii Levitan*, 111–12.

50. V. Kovanov, *I slovo—oruzhie* (Moskva: Sovetskaia rossiia, 1982), 80.

51. Tolstova, 131–37.

52. V. N. Iakhontov, "Teatr odnogo aktëra," *Istoriia*, 403.

53. B. Beliaev and A. Elkin, *Iaroslav Galan* (Moscow: Molodaia gvardiia, 1971), 141–42; and the recollections of readers in *Radio v dni voiny*, 79–126.

54. "Iz otchëta redaktsii *Poslednykh izvestii*," in *Istoriia*, 69–70.

55. Beliaev, 142.

56. Werth, 250.

57. Beliaev, 149; Stepanov, 2.

58. I Prikaza N° 129/a po VRK pri SNK SSSR, "Ob organizatsii redaktsii radioveshchaniia dlia partizan i naseleniia sovetskikh raionov, vremenno okkupirovannykh nemetskimi voiskami," 22 May 1942, in *Istoriia*, 74.

59. See Georgii Rzhanov, "Partizany slushali Moskvu," *Radio v dni voiny*, 79–82; "Spetsperedacha dlia partizan," 6 iiunia 1942 goda, in *Istoriia*, 253–55; Gurevich, 183.

60. Willi A. Boelcke, ed. *The Secret Conferences of Dr. Goebbels: The Nazi Propaganda War, 1939–1943* (New York: E. Dutton, 1970), 216, 305; Gordon, 172.

61. A transcript of the broadcast is in Kudenko, 39–40.

62. Boelcke, 178, 228.

63. Herzstein, 351–54; Kudenko, 40–41.

64. M. L. Frolov, *Reporter u mikrofona* (Leningrad: Lenizdat, 1966), 87.

65. Short, 25–31.

66. See V. Ostrogorskii, *Radiostantsiiu nazyvali Marikhen* (Moscow, 1972), for the station's work from 1929 to 1945; *Radio v dni voiny*, 145–50.

67. Gurevich, 189–91. See Kovanov, 89–91, for descriptions of the foreign broadcasters.

68. Mikhail Gus, "Spetsialnyi korrespondent radio," *Radio v dni voiny*, 233; Kudenko, 18.

69. Harold Ettlinger, *The Axis on The Air* (NY: Bobbs-Merrill, 1943), 275.

70. Ettlinger, 278–79; *Radio v dni voiny*, 162; Gurevich, 197; Kudenko, 18.

# 5

# Composing for Victory

## Classical Music

### Harlow Robinson

You could finally talk to people. It was still hard, but you could breathe. That's
why I consider the war years productive for the arts. This wasn't the situation
everywhere, and in other countries war probably interferes with the arts. But in
Russia—for tragic reasons—there was a flowering of the arts.
—Dmitrii Shostakovich[1]

FOR SOVIET COMPOSERS, even more than for writers or visual artists, World War II proved
to be a period of remarkable productivity and relative creative freedom. Whether
genuinely inspired by the life-or-death struggle against Hitler's armies, or relieved by
the relaxation of the intimidation and terror Stalin had been directing against them
(and all other cultural workers) since the late 1930s, they responded to the national
crisis with a flood of new works. Despite its complexity, which demands many hours
of reflection and concentration, the genre of the symphony enjoyed special popularity:
no less than thirty were composed in the USSR between 1941 and 1945.[2]

Not surprisingly, the highly flexible and mobile form of the "mass song," which
had already become a leading genre in Soviet classical as well as popular music in the
1930s, also flourished (see Rothstein, this volume). Composer Aram Khachaturian later
recalled that during the first two days after the Nazi attack on Russia, more than forty
such songs were composed, production-line style, at a hastily established "song headquarters" at the Union of Composers in Moscow. According to Khachaturian, who
would join the Communist Party in 1943, he and his colleagues approached this task
with a combat mentality. "Soviet songs are weapons to be used in battle," he said. "It
is our duty to forge them with total passion and a deep sense of responsibility, pouring
into them all our talent, skill and knowledge."[3] Oratorios and cantatas set to topical
texts also flourished, two of the better-known examples being Iurii Shaporin's oratorio

*Saga of the Battle for the Russian Soil* (*Skazanie o bitve za russkuiu zemliu*, composed 1943–44) and Nikolai Miaskovskii's poem-cantata *Kirov Is with Us* (*Kirov s nami*, 1943, with text by Nikolai Tikhonov).

Not all the symphonies, songs, oratorios, cantatas, operas, ballets and chamber music created by Soviet composers between 1941 and 1945 proved to be masterpieces, of course. Not infrequently, outraged emotion, sentimentality and tendentiousness overwhelmed the required artistic distance and self-control. But the list does include several of the most celebrated products of Soviet culture, works that have also achieved a secure niche in the pantheon of twentieth-century world culture. Dmitrii Shostakovich's Symphony No. 7 ("Leningrad") and Symphony No. 8; Sergei Prokofiev's Symphony No. 5 and his opera *War and Peace*; and Khachaturian's ballet *Gayane*. *Gayane*, an exotic love story set in the Armenian mountains and promoting the idea of friendly coexistence between the many different ethnic groups of the USSR, received its premiere on December 9, 1942, in Perm, where the Kirov Ballet was in evacuation. Prokofiev also worked in Perm in 1943, completing his ballet *Cinderella*, which was staged for the first time by the Bolshoi Ballet on November 21, 1945.

Since concerts are by their nature social occasions for both performers and audiences, the premieres of these and other works also became important opportunities for building and sustaining public morale at a time when Soviet citizens frequently felt isolated and fearful. Indeed, the premieres of Shostakovich's Seventh Symphony in 1942 and of Prokofiev's Fifth in 1945 were two of the most important (arguably, even the most important) cultural events of the entire Soviet war effort, and provided vivid illustration of music's special power to galvanize, unite, and inspire.

Operating under circumstances that were at times extremely difficult (evacuation, crowding, rationing, illness, physical and emotional exhaustion), Soviet orchestras, musicians, and opera and ballet troupes rose to the composers' challenge, presenting countless performances of new and standard repertoire in halls that were often unheated and poorly lit. Groups of musicians and dancers frequently performed at the front, proving, as a historian of the Soviet ballet has written, that "the muses can go into combat along with the soldiers."[4] During the first months of the blockade of Leningrad, dancers of the Kirov Ballet even performed military service themselves by taking turns guarding the theater around the clock.[5] Some young musicians and dancers were so overwhelmed by patriotism that they simply joined the armed services. So did a few composers. Veniamin Fleishman, a promising student of Shostakovich, was only twenty-eight when he died as a volunteer fighter in 1941, leaving behind an unfinished satirical opera, *Rothschild's Violin*, later completed by his teacher.[6]

Throughout the war, performances of classical music were also prominently featured on Soviet radio. Beamed to all corners of the country, they played an important role in maintaining morale and creating the sense of a shared Russian/Soviet cultural heritage worth fighting for. Similarly, the international language of classical music became a valuable tool in cementing the anti-Hitler Western alliance. Immediately accessible to listeners in Great Britain and the United States without the intermediary step of translation (as in the case of literature) or dangerous transportation (as in the case of visual art), music—especially instrumental music—created a sonic bridge over Germany from the USSR to the West.

Thanks to radio (see Von Geldern, this volume) and the strengthening of Soviet-American military and cultural ties, during World War II Soviet music and composers became widely known in the United States for the first time. At the same time, Soviet composers and musicians, who had been operating in almost total isolation since the early 1930s, received greatly increased exposure to Western (especially American) music. Toward the end of the war, special concerts featuring works by contemporary British and American composers were held in Moscow, and several books and brochures on Western music were published. Individual composers were even encouraged to correspond with Western musicians and scholars. In the United States, the National Council of American-Soviet Friendship was set up under the chairmanship of Russian-born Serge Koussevitzky (Sergei Kusevitskii), the conductor of the Boston Symphony, in part to encourage Soviet-American musical exchange.[7]

Another intriguing and unexpected side effect of the war was a new interpenetration of the musical culture of Russia and the other Soviet republics. Evacuated for extended periods to the Caucasus and Central Asia, composers, musicians, choreographers and dancers from Moscow and Leningrad made their local counterparts more familiar with European traditions even as they gained knowledge of indigenous non-Western musical traditions. This cross-fertilization yielded very concrete results. Russian composers began to incorporate native musical ideas into their own compositions: one of the most successful examples is Prokofiev's use of Kabardinian themes in his String Quartet No. 2, composed in 1941 while he was living briefly in evacuation in Nalchik, capital of the Kabardo-Balkar Autonomous Republic in the northern Caucasus.[8] But the influence also operated in the opposite direction: in 1944, the first conservatory was opened in Alma-Ata, the capital of the republic of Kazakhstan, with help from evacuees from European Russia.[9]

Two figures towered over the Soviet musical establishment during the war years: Sergei Prokofiev (1891–1953) and Dmitrii Shostakovich (1906–75). In many ways their story is the story of Soviet wartime classical music. At home and abroad, their compositions came to symbolize the desperate Soviet war effort and the stubborn survival of the highest level of human civilization amidst death and destruction. Well-established on the international musical scene long before Hitler's attack on Russia in June 1941, both were at the height of their careers as the Great Patriotic War began. Because music is a universal language and because both composers were already known there, in America Prokofiev and Shostakovich became the leading Soviet cultural heroes of the war era. *Time* magazine devoted a cover story to each, portraying the meek and shy Shostakovich in an uncharacteristically martial pose: wearing his Civil Defense firemen's helmet, he stood ready to save Leningrad from flames raging in the background.[10]

Strange as it may sound, for Prokofiev and Shostakovich World War II actually came at a most opportune moment. On the eve of the Nazi attack on Russia, both composers found themselves in a highly vulnerable position. Shostakovich was still recovering from the vicious 1936 official attack on his opera *Lady Macbeth of Mtsensk*, which had been banned from the Soviet stage after being denounced by Stalin as obscene, dissonant, and degenerate.[11] Although his official reputation had apparently been restored with the premiere of his well-received Fifth Symphony in early 1938, Shostakovich still lived in constant fear of Stalin's unpredictable wrath, and watched in terror as close friends and associates disappeared all around him. Nonetheless, Shostakovich continued to behave and compose in a dangerously individualistic fashion, producing ambiguously understated symphonies like the Sixth (completed in October, 1939) and refusing to turn out the expected paean to Stalin on the solemn occasion of his sixtieth birthday on December 21, 1939.

Prokofiev's vulnerability stemmed more from his many years spent abroad. After leaving Russia in early 1918, not long after the Bolshevik Revolution, he had lived first in America and then in Europe for nearly twenty years, returning permanently with his family to Moscow only in early 1936. At a time when Stalin had come to view the world beyond the USSR with hatred and suspicion, Prokofiev's globe-trotting and many foreign connections were regarded as highly questionable and potentially traitorous. For that reason, he was eager to prove his Soviet patriotism and trustworthiness, to find a musical style that would satisfy the demands of the official cultural establishment while retaining his artistic integrity.

Fortunately for him, it was precisely at that moment that he encountered film director Sergei Eisenstein (1898–1948). Like Prokofiev, Eisenstein had worked briefly in America, and was also viewed with deep skepticism by Stalin's cultural commissars as an individualist with disturbingly avant-garde and cosmopolitan tendencies. Capitalizing on rising fears in the USSR over Hitler's increasingly aggressive behavior in Europe, these two great artists agreed to collaborate on a blatantly anti-German and heavily supervised epic film, *Alexander Nevskii* (see Kenez, this volume). Completed in November 1938, after a mere five months of work, this cartoonish, almost operatic biography of the legendary thirteenth-century Novgorod prince famous for defeating an army of invading Teutonic knights achieved an enormous ideological and popular success. Both Eisenstein and Nikolai Cherkasov, the actor who played Nevskii, received the prestigious Order of Lenin. *Nevskii* was, in fact, one of the first examples of wartime culture, with its stirring musical call to arms (especially the chorus "Arise,

O Russian People") and vilification of the (then only anticipated) enemy as child-burn-ing murderers.

When Stalin and Hitler signed their non-aggression pact in August 1939, how-ever, *Nevskii*'s blatantly anti-German message became an embarrassment, and it was shelved until after the German attack upon Russia.[12] Prokofiev's position was further weakened by the arrest of his longtime friend and collaborator, the anti-realist stage director Vsevolod Meyerhold. When seized by the KGB in June 1939, Meyerhold was working with Prokofiev on the first production of his new opera, *Semën Kotko*.[13] Im-prisoned and tortured, Meyerhold died six months later. It was, perhaps, anxiety over Meyerhold's fate that led Prokofiev to write the propagandistic cantata *Zdravitsa*, a fawning, monumental sixtieth-birthday tribute to Stalin that depicts the USSR flourish-ing in happy pastoral serenity under the benign leadership of its Communist *pater familias*. But Prokofiev was simultaneously producing music of an entirely different sort. On January 11, 1940, the ballet *Romeo and Juliet* received its world premiere at the Kirov Theater in Leningrad, its streets dark because of the proximity of the Soviet war with Finland.

Seventeen months later, the German attack on Russia found Prokofiev at work on another ballet, *Cinderella*.

> On June 22, a warm sunny morning, I was sitting at my desk. Suddenly the houseman's wife appeared and asked me, with an anxious expression, if it was true that "the Germans have attacked us and they are saying that they're bombing the cities." The news astonished us. We went over to see Sergei Ei-senstein, who lived not far from us. Yes, it turned out to be true. . . . Everyone immediately wanted to make a contribution to the struggle. The first response from composers was, naturally, heroic songs and marches—music that could resound directly at the front. I wrote two songs and a march. . . . [These even-tually went into the Seven Mass Songs, Op. 89. HR]
>
> It was during these days that my idea of writing an opera on Tolstoy's novel *War and Peace* assumed a definite outline. The pages that told of the strug-gle of the Russian people against Napoleon's hordes in 1812, and of the ex-pulsion of Napoleon's army from Russian soil, became somehow particularly relevant.[14]

The fanciful *Cinderella* was now put aside, and would be completed only three years later.[15] *War and Peace* became Prokofiev's major project for the remaining years of the war, although this ill-fated historical opera would have to wait for many years—until long after Hitler had been defeated—for its first complete performance.[16] During the war years, in addition to the first version of *War and Peace*, Prokofiev also created his Symphony No. 5, the String Quartet No. 2, two piano sonatas (Nos. 7 and 8), a flute sonata (also transcribed for violin), five film scores (including one for Eisenstein's *Ivan the Terrible*), several large orchestral works, and numerous songs and piano pieces. These four years were, in fact, one of the most productive periods in the composer's life. So intense was the pace that Prokofiev—like many Russians of his generation—was left weakened and spent. These were the last years in which he would command the full strength of his talent, energy, and health.

Like other Soviet cultural figures, Prokofiev spent most of the war moving around the vast spaces of the Russian and Central Asian interior. Soon after the German invasion, many composers were evacuated to various cities to the east. On August 8, 1941, Prokofiev and his new companion Mira Mendelson joined a group of Moscow Conservatory professors (including his old friend, the composer Nikolai Miaskovskii), actors from the Moscow Art Theater (including Anton Chekhov's elderly widow, the actress Ol'ga Knipper-Chekhova) and other "artistic workers" on a special train.[17] They pulled out of the capital, already seriously damaged by German bombs, on an overcast and solemn evening. "We all shared one thought," Ol'ga Lamm, the daughter of musicologist Pavel Lamm, later observed. "Will we ever again see those we are leaving behind—and when?"[18]

After a three-day train trip, Prokofiev and his colleagues arrived in Nalchik in the Northern Caucasus. There, living in cramped quarters in a tiny hotel room, he composed the first six scenes ("Peace") of *War and Peace* and several other major works. But the German army was fast approaching the northern Caucasus, and the cultural refugees from Moscow were again loaded onto railroad cars and transferred southward to Tbilisi in Georgia. During six months there, Prokofiev (with literary and dramatic help from Mendelson) managed to complete the remaining scenes of the opera, as well as the Sonata No. 7 (Op. 83) for piano. Often interpreted as a dramatic illustration of the driving intensity of his (and Russia's) fight for survival, especially in its compact and ferocious concluding movement (*precipitato*), the sonata was premiered with great success by Sviatoslav Richter in 1943. Richter himself claimed to see the work as symbolic of humankind's victory over the forces of evil and disorder.[19] The Soviet cultural bureaucrats also approved of the Seventh Sonata's insistent, even militant energy. In 1943 they awarded it a Stalin Prize (second class)—the first official Soviet prize Prokofiev had ever received. Over the next few years, mostly for the music he wrote during the war, Prokofiev would receive many more official honors and titles, finally solidifying his previously ambiguous position in the Soviet musical establishment.

From Tbilisi, Prokofiev moved on to Alma-Ata in Kazakhstan, where the major Soviet film studios had taken refuge. Eisenstein, who was working there, had invited the composer to Kazakhstan to collaborate on another historical epic film biography, this time about Tsar Ivan IV ("The Terrible"), one of Stalin's favorite Russian rulers, whose relevance as a strong military leader made him an especially appropriate subject at the moment.[20] To reach Alma-Ata, Prokofiev and Mendelson had to travel by boat across the Caspian Sea, then by train across desert wasteland, carrying drinking water from Tbilisi. They arrived in the capital of Kazakhstan after nearly a month in transit, in June 1942. But Prokofiev and Mendelson were fortunate. Evacuated from threatened Tbilisi, their Moscow colleagues (including composers Miaskovskii and Iurii Shaporin) were sent to Frunze (now Bishkek), the capital of Kirgizia (Kyrgystan), where they endured living conditions "a hundred times worse" than in Tbilisi or Alma-Ata.[21] Prokofiev remained in Alma-Ata for most of the next year, working on a variety of projects, including (besides the rest of *War and Peace* and the score for *Ivan the Terrible*) several highly propagandistic films intended to inspire soldiers and citizens in the struggle against Hitler.[22]


The early years of the war were no less eventful and dramatic for Dmitrii Shosta-kovich. Unlike Prokofiev, who had celebrated his fiftieth birthday just two months before the German attack on Russia, Shostakovich, at age thirty-four, was still young enough to consider enlisting. Shocked by the threat to the city in which he had spent his entire creative life, he attempted to volunteer, but (fortunately for posterity) his poor eyesight kept him from combat. Rejecting several offers of evacuation during the summer of 1941, as Hitler's armies raced towards Leningrad, Shostakovich (see fig. 7) joined the Civil Defense brigade (whose job was to project the city's countless architectural treasures from fire) and sent his family out of danger. At the same time, he poured out arrangements of works by Beethoven, Bizet, Dargomyzhskii, and Mussorgskii to be used at the front, and began work on a new symphony—his seventh. Most of it created in besieged Leningrad, this programmatic composition was fated to become not only the composer's most celebrated work, but the most famous single product of Soviet wartime high culture.

Shostakovich began composing the first movement of the Seventh Symphony in late July 1941 and completed it on September 3. Conceived on a scale so large (it lasts twenty-five minutes) that Shostakovich even considered presenting it as an independent symphonic poem, the first movement (*allegretto*) begins with a simple, heroic theme reflective, he later claimed, of peaceful domestic life.[23] Into this calm soon enter the distant sounds of an approaching army, first announced by a barely audible snare drum. Over this unvarying percussion accompaniment a seemingly innocuous marching tune arises, bouncing easily between the tonic (straightforward C-major) and dominant keys. As in Ravel's *Bolero*, the movement proceeds through an increasingly loud and violent series of twelve variations on this theme, building from a happy, care-free walking pace to a sinister, grotesque strut as the invader's malevolent nature becomes clear.

As the German bombing of Leningrad intensified in early September, forcing mass evacuations,[24] Shostakovich set to work on the second movement, an oddly ingenuous, even humorous scherzo that he completed in a mere two weeks. It took him only twelve days to finish the slow third movement, a solemn, requiem-like *adagio*. As he composed, bombs fell on the city like rain. Finally, on September 30, Shostakovich was ordered to evacuate. He and his family traveled first to Moscow, where they spent several uncomfortable weeks, then continued by train eastward to the evacuation center of Kuibyshev with a group that included composers and musicians from the Bolshoi Theater. It was in this Volga city (now called by its original name of Samara) that Shostakovich completed the symphony's final movement (*allegro non troppo*). At the top of the first page of the manuscript, in the left-hand corner, he scribbled in red ink: "Dedicated to the city of Leningrad."

On March 5, 1942, Shostakovich's Seventh—which had already generated considerable publicity in a country desperate for good news—received its premiere in the Kuibyshev Palace of Culture, a hulking concrete monument completed in 1938. It was performed not by Leningrad's own prestigious Leningrad Philharmonia, which had been evacuated to Novosibirsk, but by the Orchestra of the Bolshoi Theater under its conductor, the respected Samuil Samosud (1884–1964). Preceded by brief comments by Shostakovich, the performance (which lasts nearly 80 minutes) was broadcast on radio all across the USSR, provoking the most enthusiastic critical and public reaction both there and abroad. Listening in Moscow, where he remained throughout the war, violinist David Oistrakh wrote of his "enormous pride that our country has produced an artist capable, in the midst of such difficult times, of responding to the terrible events of war with such convincing strength and inspiration. . . . Shostakovich's music resounded like a prophetic affirmation of the victory over fascism, a poetic statement of the patriotic feelings of the people, and of their faith in the eventual triumph of humanism and light."[25] On March 7, the London *Times* published a report from its correspondent in Kuibyshev describing the premiere and urging a performance in England.

Realizing the propaganda and morale potential of Shostakovich's Seventh, Soviet officials moved quickly to arrange a Moscow performance. When it took place on March 29 in the historic Hall of Columns (the same hall in which Soviet leaders lay in state before burial), the Moscow premiere (given by the combined forces of the orchestras of the Bolshoi Theater and All-Union Radio) was broadcast worldwide. That the performance was punctuated by an air raid only heightened the drama of the occasion, and bestowed upon the symphony even deeper symbolism and significance. Before long, prominent European and American conductors were waging their own little wars over the rights to give the premiere of the Seventh in their respective countries.

In the United States publicity-conscious Leopold Stokowski, who was then sharing the conductorship of the NBC Symphony with Arturo Toscanini, had persuaded NBC to purchase the rights to the work as early as December 1941. Microfilmed in Kuibyshev, the score made its way by air and road to Teheran in Allied-occupied Persia, Cairo, and New York. After looking it over, Toscanini, for whom the NBC Symphony had been created in 1937, decided that he should be the one to conduct at such an important and newsworthy event. A strained exchange of letters between the two maestros ensued. "Don't you think, my dear Stokowski," wrote Toscanini, "it would be very interesting for everybody, and yourself, too, to hear the old Italian conductor (one of the first artists who strenuously fought against fascism) to play this work of a young Russian anti-Nazi composer. . . . Maybe I am not an intense interpreter of this kind of music, but I am sure I can conduct it very simply with love and honesty. . . . "[26] In the end, Toscanini (as usual) got his way—and the publicity. He conducted the NBC Symphony in the American premiere of the Seventh—which was also broadcast on radio to a wide and devoted audience—on July 19, 1942. This performance led to heightened feelings of solidarity between the USA and the USSR, still suffering staggering losses on the eastern front. It also led to many more performances of the Seventh by American orchestras—no less than sixty-two in the 1942–43 season—and under such famous conductors as Serge Koussevitzky, Eugene Ormandy, Pierre Monteux and others.[27]

But the most emotional and symbolically important performance of Shostakovich's new symphony—which had come to represent the survival not only of the Russian, but the human spirit—was its long-awaited premiere in Leningrad. Since there were few professional musicians left in the city, the orchestra that performed this demanding piece (which called for eight horns, six trumpets, five timpani and an expanded percussion section, as well as a large string section) had been gathered rather haphazardly. At the request of Karl Eliasberg (1907–78), the conductor and music director of the Leningrad Radio Orchestra, several dozen musicians had been summoned from the front to supplement his rag-tag ensemble in order to give the premiere. With such an uneven group of players, it was difficult for Eliasberg to achieve the polish and sound quality demanded by the Seventh. Surviving, in part, on food donated by the city's music-lovers, themselves near starvation, the orchestra rehearsed for five and six hours daily during the last week of July and the first week of August.[28] Meanwhile, Leningrad's commander-in-chief General Govorov was ordered to make sure that the enemy's artillery did not interrupt the performance.

As a ploy to boost morale in a city on the verge of extinction, the Leningrad premiere was scheduled for August 9, 1942—the very day that Hitler had designated to celebrate the city's fall with a victory celebration in the elegant Hotel Astoria (Hitler had even printed the invitations). Tickets for the performance were eagerly sought after. The audience that gathered on that Sunday evening in the Philharmonia included what was left of Leningrad's cultural elite, as well as leading party and military officials, infantry men with loaded weapons, sailors from the Baltic fleet and ordinary men and women in quilted jackets carrying gas masks. On the streets outside, bedraggled and hungry crowds gathered around loudspeakers to listen to a broadcast of the concert.

What mattered about the performance that day was not its artistic quality, which under the circumstances could hardly have been expected to be exceptional. What mattered is that the performance of this musical biography of suffering Leningrad happened at all. It was an emotional turning point in the battle to save the city, and the country. One of the many writers present at the premiere described it as a kind of collective municipal—and national—catharsis.

> Many people cried at this concert. Some cried because that was the only way they could show their excitement, others because they had lived through what the music was now expressing with such force, many because they were grieving for those they had lost, many because they were overcome by the mere fact of being present here in the Philharmonia. After all, not so long ago, they could not even have imagined ever seeing again this hall, these columns, these beautiful seats, the organ, the violins, horns and timpani.[29]

As a monumental *pièce d'occasion*, the Seventh enjoyed huge popularity in the USSR and in the countries of the anti-German alliance during World War II, but it quickly disappeared from concert programs everywhere except Russia after 1945. The Soviet propaganda machine made ample use of the legend of the heroic creation and early performances of the Seventh in subsequent years, as the cult of World War II grew to bloated proportions.[30] Eventually, however, even Soviet critics began to question its aesthetic merit, especially when comparing it to the composer's other symphonies. In her brilliant 1976 book on Shostakovich's symphonies, musicologist Marina Sabinina suggested that the Seventh suffered from a certain "excess of content and strong contrasts," and that its top-heavy construction left something to be desired.

> In the Seventh, it seems, we encounter—for the first time in Shostakovich's mature work—an undeniable failure of dramatic planning. The first movement takes the listener hostage with such huge force, and demands such an enormous release of nervous tension, that his attention inevitably drops and dulls towards the end of this symphonic giant.[31]

But no Soviet critic ever publicly called into question the sacred idea that Shostakovich's Seventh, which restored the composer to Stalin's good graces and for a time protected him from charges of ideological foot-dragging, was a musical attack upon German fascism and a glorification of the Soviet war effort. This situation changed, however, when *Testimony*, the composer's alleged memoirs, appeared in the West in 1979, four years after Shostakovich's death.[32] In one of the more sensational of the book's revelations, Shostakovich claimed that the Seventh was actually intended not as a denunciation of Hitler, but of Stalin.

> The Seventh Symphony had been planned before the war and consequently it simply cannot be seen as a reaction to Hitler's attack. The "invasion theme" has nothing to do with the attack. I was thinking of other enemies of humanity when I composed the theme.
> Naturally, fascism is repugnant to me; but not only German fascism, any

form of it is repugnant. Nowadays people like to recall the prewar period as an idyllic time, saying that everything was fine until Hitler bothered us. Hitler is a criminal, that's clear, but so is Stalin.

I feel eternal pain for those who were killed by Hitler, but I feel no less pain for those killed on Stalin's orders. I suffer for everyone who was tortured, shot, or starved to death. There were millions of them in our country before the war with Hitler began.

The war brought much new sorrow and much new destruction, but I haven't forgotten the terrible prewar years. That is what all my symphonies, beginning with the Fourth, are about, including the Seventh and Eighth.[33]

This revisionist view of Shostakovich's Seventh points out just how tricky the business of interpreting music can be. As a nonverbal and abstract medium, music (even when given titles) resists definitive programmatic "meaning." That Shostakovich understood the special power of music to express the composer's inner feelings and at the same time elude and even mislead less perceptive listeners (like the party censors) was clear from something he once said to his acquaintance and occasional collaborator, Soviet poet Evgenii Evtushenko: "I never lie in music, that's enough."[34] In other words, do not listen to what I say in those meaningless official pronouncements (or what others say about me); just listen closely to the music.

Not surprisingly, Shostakovich could never duplicate the unprecedented official and popular success of the Seventh Symphony. Indeed, its acclaim would come to haunt him in later years. When judged against it, his subsequent symphonies were found emotionally and ideologically wanting by the party bureaucrats and official critics whose job it was to monitor such things. They denounced his brooding Symphony No. 8 (completed in September 1943) as excessively gloomy and despairing in light of the improving fortunes of the Red Army after Stalingrad. The brief and unexpectedly frothy Ninth, finished in August 1945, soon after the German surrender, was received with even greater reservations.[35] After its premiere on November 3, 1945, by the Leningrad Philharmonia under Evgenii Mravinskii, the charming, Haydnesque Ninth was condemned as too frivolous and delicate to reflect the seriousness and enormity of the Soviet victory over Germany. It was also dismissed as thoroughly unworthy of the gravity inevitably accruing to any post-Beethoven "ninth" symphony.[36]

If Shostakovich reached the peak of his wartime career early, in 1941–42, Prokofiev took somewhat longer. It was, in fact, in the final months of the war that he presided over one of the greatest successes of his entire career: the premiere of his Symphony No. 5, Op. 100. Although it never attained anything like the acclaim or emotional charge of Shostakovich's "Leningrad" Symphony, Prokofiev's Fifth has proved a more lasting aesthetic contribution to the international orchestral repertoire. Having finally returned to Moscow with Mendelson after years of difficult traveling, Prokofiev set to work in 1944 on his first symphony in sixteen years. A moving distillation of his recent experiences, a statement of courage and endurance, the Fifth represented, he wrote, "the culmination of an entire period in my work. I conceived of it as a symphony on the greatness of the human soul."[37]

In his Fifth—which, unlike Shostakovich's Ninth, readily accepted the burden of significance that its number implied—Prokofiev finally found the orchestral equivalent of his highly successful ballet and film scores of recent years. Its musical style was sufficiently accessible and optimistic, appropriate for the depiction of "Soviet reality," and yet highly original and Prokofievian (especially in the inventive concluding *allegro giocoso*). Even as most twentieth-century composers were rejecting the symphony as an exhausted form, Prokofiev and Shostakovich, influenced by the inherent conservatism of Soviet culture, were exploring its undiscovered possibilities. Both Sviatoslav Richter and composer Dmitrii Kabalevskii later claimed that Prokofiev considered the Fifth his finest creation. At the same time, its remarkable dissimilarity to Prokofiev's most famous symphony, the brief, naughty, ironic, irreverent Symphony No. 1 ("Classical," 1917), starkly demonstrates how far the composer had traveled from his caustic pre-revolutionary beginnings.

The premiere of Prokofiev's Fifth on January 13, 1945, was another historic musical occasion, second only to the premiere of Shostakovich's Seventh, perhaps, in emotional significance. Prokofiev himself conducted, which was a rare event. One of those present in the Great Hall of the Moscow Conservatory was Richter, who later described what he saw and heard.

> The Great Hall was illuminated, no doubt, the same way it always was, but when Prokofiev stood up, the light seemed to pour straight down on him from somewhere up above. He stood like a monument on a pedestal. And then, when Prokofiev had taken his place on the podium and silence reigned in the hall, artillery salvos suddenly thundered forth. His baton was raised. He waited, and began only after the cannons had stopped. There was something very significant in this, something symbolic. It was as if all of us—including Prokofiev—had reached some kind of shared turning point.[38]

The salvos that delayed the performance came from Soviet cannons, paying tribute to the Red Army soldiers crossing the Vistula on their victory march toward soon-to-be-defeated Germany. Peace was near, only four months away.

But the intensity of his wartime existence had undermined Prokofiev's health and stamina. Only a few days after this triumph at the Conservatory, at the very pinnacle of his career, having finally attained his dream of becoming a Soviet composer, he experienced a sudden dizzy spell, fell, and suffered a brain concussion. He would never completely recover. While he lived for another eight years and produced more music, Prokofiev suffered numerous setbacks and was forced by doctors to work only in short, sporadic episodes.

Sadly, neither Prokofiev, Shostakovich, nor their musical colleagues got the rest and relaxation they needed when peace came to Europe in May 1945. After a brief period of cultural liberalization, Stalin launched another terrifying campaign of ideological persecution and xenophobic hysteria that would culminate in a full-scale inquisition led by Andrei Zhdanov at the infamous Conference of Soviet Composers in February 1948. Their invaluable and sincere contributions to the glorious Soviet victory over Hitler apparently forgotten, both Prokofiev and Shostakovich would again find themselves the targets of vicious attacks and slander that would result in isolation, discouragement, and the banning of their music. For both of them, and for their colleagues, this would be the real war.

## Notes

1. Dmitrii Shostakovich, *Testimony: The Memoirs of Dmitrii Shostakovich As Related to and Edited by Solomon Volkov* (New York, 1979), 136. Translated by Antonina W. Bouis. Although the authenticity of these memoirs was questioned when they first appeared (see Laurel Fay, "Shostakovich vs. Volkov: Whose Testimony?" *The Russian Review* [October 1980], 484–93), most scholars and those who knew the composer personally now accept them as fundamentally accurate. See also Ian MacDonald, *The New Shostakovich* (Boston, 1990).

2. Boris Schwarz, *Music and Musical Life in Soviet Russia*, 2nd ed. (Bloomington, Ind. 1983), 182.

3. Aram Khachaturian, "Muzyku nado pisat' serdtsem! . . . ", *Smena* 11 (1978), 26; and *Informatsionnyi sbornik* (Moscow: Orgkomitet Soiuza sovetskikh kompozitorov), 3–4 (1943), 5, as quoted in Viktor Iuzefovich, *Aram Khachaturian* (Moscow, 1990), 108–109. All translations in the text are mine unless indicated. Khachaturian also composed his Symphony No. 2 during the war.

4. G. Inozemtseva, "Put' sovetskogo baleta," *Sovetskie balety* (Moscow, 1985), 12.

5. Iraida Khrushchevich, ed., *Gosudarstvennyi teatr opery i baleta imeni S. M. Kirova* (Moscow, 1957), 72.

6. See my review of the 1990 American premiere in *Musical America* (July 1990), 55–56.

7. Schwarz, 188–89. See also Stanley D. Krebs, *Soviet Composers and the Development of Soviet Music* (London, 1970), 54–56.

8. Another example is Miaskovskii's Symphony No. 23, Op. 56 ("On Themes of the Songs and Dances of the Peoples of the Northern Caucasus"), completed in 1941. There is a tragic irony here in that Stalin uprooted many of these people in a brutal act during the war: see Stites, "Holy War," this volume.

9. B. G. Erzakovich, "Kazakhskaia muzyka," *Muzykal'nyi entsiklopedicheskii slovar'* (Moscow, 1991), 226.

10. "Shostakovich and the Guns," *Time* (July 20, 1942), 53–55; and "Composer, Soviet-style," *Time* (November 19, 1945), 57–58.

11. The attack began with the article "Sumbur vmesto muzyki" in *Pravda* on January 28, 1936.

12. During the war, *Nevskii* was shown repeatedly all over the USSR, both at the front and behind the lines, in an attempt to boost patriotic feeling and link the current struggle with the glorious Russian past.

13. Based on Valentin Kataev's 1937 novel *Ia, syn trudovogo naroda*, the opera deals with German military intervention in Ukraine following the 1917 Revolution. Eventually staged by Serafima Birman, it had its premiere at the Stanislavskii Opera Theater on June 23, 1940. The opera's negative portrayal of Germans also caused unanticipated difficulties for the composer.

14. Sergei Prokof'ev, "Khudozhnik i voina," S. I. Shlifshtein, ed., *S. S. Prokof'ev: materialy, dokumenty, vospominaniia* (Moscow, 1961) 243–44.

15. In general, the war years were not a particularly productive time for ballet. Only two notable ballets were composed: *Cinderella* (which received its premiere only after the war was over) and Khachaturian's *Gayane*, neither of which dealt with contemporary themes. It is true that the prolific Boris Asafiev (1884–1949), composer of the 1934 classic *The Fountain of Bakhchisarai*, churned out seven ballets during the war, mostly of an escapist nature, but none proved to be of more than passing interest.

16. This took place in Moscow on November 8, 1957. Because current events transfer poorly to the operatic stage, and because operas take a long time to compose and demand extensive rehearsals and scenic preparation, no memorable operas were created and staged during World War II. Among the composers who tried were Dmitrii Kabalevskii (*Pod Moskvoi*), Viktor Voloshinov (*Sil'nee smerti*) and Ivan Dzherzhinskii (*Krov' naroda*).

17. Shortly before the German attack, Prokofiev had left his first wife, the Spanish-born singer Lina Llubera, the mother of his two sons, to live with Mira Mendelson, a writer who was half his age. They married only in early 1948.

18. Ol'ga Lamm, "Druz'ia Pavla Aleksandrovicha Lamma. V evakuatsii (1941–43)," *Iz proshlogo sovetskoi muzykal'noi kul'tury*, 2 (Moscow, 1976), 99. See also Harlow Robinson, *Sergei Prokofiev: A Biography* (New York, 1987).

19. Sviatoslav Rikhter, "O Prokof'eve," *S. S. Prokof'ev: materialy, dokumenty, vospominaniia* 464–65.

20. Part I of *Ivan the Terrible* was screened publicly for the first time in Moscow on December 30, 1944, and won Prokofiev another Stalin Prize. Part II, however, because of Stalin's objections to its portrayal of Ivan as weak and indecisive, was withheld from distribution until 1958.

21. *S. S. Prokof'ev i N. Ia. Miaskovskii: perepiska* (Moscow, 1977), 459–60. See also O. P. Lamm, ed., *Stranitsy tvorcheskoi biografii Miaskovskogo* (Moscow, 1989).

22. For a more complete discussion of these films, see Harlow Robinson, " 'The Most Contemporary Art': Sergei Prokofiev and Soviet Film," *Studies in Comparative Communism*, 17, no. 3–4, 203–18.

23. Sof'ia Khentova, *D. D. Shostakovich v gody Velikoi Otechestvennoi voiny* (Leningrad, 1979), 36. This somewhat unreliable study contains a day-by-day examination of the composition of the symphony. Khentova also claims that the Seventh grew out of sketches made by the composer in the spring of 1941 for a projected symphony dedicated to Lenin. For a much more serious examination of Shostakovich's symphonies, including this one, see Marina Sabinina, *Shostakovich-Simfonist* (Moscow, 1976).

24. Among those evacuated during September was the Leningrad poet Anna Akhmatova, to whom Shostakovich allegedly entrusted a copy of the first movement of his Seventh. It was on her lap when she flew out of the city. Akhmatova later made reference to the symphony in her "Poema bez geroia." MacDonald, *New Shostakovich*, 273.

25. David Oistrakh, "Velikii khudozhnik nashego vremeni," *D. Shostakovich: stat'i i materialy* (Moscow, 1976), 25.

26. As quoted in Harvey Sachs, *Toscanini* (New York, 1978), 279.

27. Schwarz, 179.

28. Khentova, 96.

29. A. Rozen, "Razgovor s drugom," *Zvezda*, 2, no. 1 (1973), 81.

30. The Leningrad premiere of the Seventh was even the subject of a black-and-white Soviet feature film (*Leningradskaia simfoniia*) that embroidered the event, Hollywood-style, with a budding romance.

31. Sabinina, 162.

32. In a conversation with me, Solomon Volkov claimed that Shostakovich instructed him explicitly that because of their sensitive and controversial content, the "memoirs" on which they were collaborating could be published only after his death. Interview in Troy, N.Y., January 25, 1992.

33. Volkov-Shostakovich, *Testimony*, 155.

34. MacDonald, 252. See also Evtushenko, "Genius Is Beyond Genre: Dmitrii Shostakovich," in *Fatal Half-Measures: The Culture of Democracy in the Soviet Union* (Boston, 1991), 292–99.

35. See Sabinina, chaps. 3 and 4.

36. Volkov-Shostakovich, *Testimony*, 140.

37. Sergei Prokof'ev, "O moikh rabotakh za gody voiny," *S. S. Prokof'ev: Materialy, dokumenty, vospominaniia*, 252.

38. Rikhter, 470.

# 6

## Homeland, Home Town, and Battlefield

### The Popular Song

### Robert A. Rothstein

"ON THE twenty-second of June, at exactly four o'clock, Kiev was bombed" sounds more like a war communiqué than a song, but in fact these are the opening lines of what has been described both as the first Russian folk song and the first Russian lyric song of World War II.[1] Based on the prewar pop hit "Little Blue Kerchief" (Sinii platochek), it exemplifies the "interactive" character of the wartime repertoire: songs by professional composers and lyricists provoked responses and reworkings, and old melodies acquired new texts written by (often anonymous) amateur poets.[2] World War II was a time when the Soviet concept of "mass songs" (massovye pesni), songs for the masses, took on the new meaning of songs by the masses. It was also a time when epic, heroic songs gave way to lyrical ones, when what we shall call "songs of collective emotion" became secondary to "songs of individual emotion," and the nature of the Russian song repertoire was permanently changed.

The songs of World War II were not all born after June 22, 1941. During the 1930s Soviet songwriters had produced songs stressing the country's readiness against an unnamed foe:

If war comes tomorrow, if an enemy attacks,
If a dark force suddenly appears,
As one man the whole Soviet nation
Will rise in defense of the Motherland. . . .

The Union of Soviet Composers, organized in 1932, even had a "defense section" to encourage the creation of such songs, as did the Union of Soviet Writers. Maxim Gorky, for one, was not impressed with their efforts. In 1935 he criticized Soviet poets for their lack of interest in themes of defense and accused them of sounding like "political impotents" even when writing about "revolutionary erection[s]." He did not foresee that some of their war-related texts would become songs and live on to be sung at the front when war actually came.[3]

Not all of these songs were as explicit as "If War Comes Tomorrow" (Esli zavtra voina). In "Storm Clouds Have Risen over the City" (Tuchi nad gorodom vstali), also written in 1938, war is presented metaphorically, and the song is primarily about a young man imagining a farewell scene with his as yet unknown sweetheart. (The text does say that "dark forces are astir," thus recalling "If War Comes . . . "). Both songs were from films, which in the 1930s had become a powerful medium for popularizing songs. "Storm Clouds" owed its enduring success (through the war and beyond) as well to the fact that it was sung on the screen by Mark Bernes in his first singing role. Bernes, whose influence on Soviet song performance, according to one commentator, would be "hard to exaggerate," had long been a stage and film actor. His vocal qualities were supposedly not up to what was expected of singers, but once he was given a chance by director Sergei Iutkevich, his unpretentious, conversational style of singing won him and the songs he sang immense popularity.[4]

Probably the most famous Russian song of World War II was also written in 1938. It tells of the musical greeting sent by a young woman named Katiusha to her beloved, who is serving on an unspecified distant border. She asks him to protect their native land while she guards their love. It begins:

The apple and pear trees were in bloom.
Mists had floated out over the river.
Katiusha came out to the river bank,
To the high, steep bank.

The song was so popular that "Katiusha" became the nickname for the multiple-rocket-launchers used by Soviet forces during the war. An even more striking measure of the emotional impact of the song was the number of (mostly anonymous) musical responses it evoked. The literary scholar Ivan Rozanov collected more than fifty wartime texts (not counting variants) based on "Katiusha" and generally sung to its melody. These included "answers" from soldiers to Katiusha's message, songs portraying her as a guerilla fighter or frontline nurse, and songs about the Katiusha rocket. A frequent starting point was an allusion to the contrast between the idyllic prewar setting of Mikhail Isakovskii's song lyric and the bleak wartime landscape, in which the fruit trees had already lost their leaves or been destroyed by the Germans.[5]

The prewar songs were optimistic, intended to be uplifting and to build confidence in Soviet invincibility. Humor was an appropriate component and helped to keep songs like "Self-firing Samovars" (Samovary-samopaly)—a prize-winner in a contest for defense songs held in early 1941—popular during the war.[6] The song is about machine guns produced in the city of Tula, and it plays on the city's reputation for craftsmanship and especially for making samovars. These clever new "samovars" have

[A] special military spout:
It can scald the enemy a mile away
With fiery boiling water.

The tea from these samovars is not sweet for uninvited guests, the song continues; even if they put sugar in it or drink it Russian-style with a sugar cube in their teeth, it still burns through and through.

When the uninvited guests came on June 22, 1941, songwriters and performers enlisted for the duration. During the first few days of the war, in Moscow alone, some one hundred new songs were written.[7] Among them was "the musical emblem of the war," the song "Sacred War" (Sviashchennaia voina), which was published as a poem in *Izvestiia* and *Krasnaia zvezda* on June 24 and first performed by the Red Army Chorus on June 27 at the Belorussian Station in Moscow for soldiers leaving for the front. A member of the chorus reported that the soldiers were so affected by the song that it had to be sung five times.[8] It began:

Arise, vast country,
Arise for a fight to the death
With the dark fascist force,
With the cursed hordes.
Let noble fury
Boil up like a wave.
A people's war has begun,
A sacred war!

According to Aleksandr Aleksandrov, director of the Red Army Chorus and composer of "Sacred War," audiences always stood when it was performed and it often moved both listeners and performers to tears. Its role as an anthem of the war was secured by Soviet radio, which played it to open every broadcast day at 6 A.M.[9]

From the first months of the war there were intensive efforts to "expand the work of inculcating Russian fighting songs," as it was expressed in a September directive from the Central Political Command of the Red Army. As early as August the troops had been sent 150,000 copies of a newly published songbook and 12,000 accordions. (The military newspaper *Krasnaia zvezda* introduced the slogan: "An accordion to every company!") New songs were also introduced in regular radio broadcasts, in special films and in frontline concerts. The popular singer Klavdiia Shul'zhenko, for example, gave five hundred concerts for soldiers of the Leningrad front during the first year of the war (see Stites, this volume). They were recorded; printed as sheet music, postcards and broadsheets; and dropped as leaflets over occupied territories.[10]

Most of the early war songs, however, faded away after serving their initial function of mobilizing popular patriotic feeling. The wartime repertoire, especially that of the first two years, was dominated by older songs: popular tunes from the 1930s, songs from the Civil War and even pre-revolutionary folk and soldier songs. Often the old melodies were sung with new texts, as in the case of "On the Twenty-Second of June," with which we began. Some of the new texts were written by professional poets like Vasilii Lebedev-Kumach, who set a text about partisans to the melody of a Civil War marching song, "We Red Soldiers" (My krasnye soldaty) The new version, entitled "In the Midst of the Dense Forests" (Sredi lesov dremuchikh), may have owed some of its success to its connection with a nineteenth-century bandit song of the same title that was sung to the same melody. Lebedev-Kumach also "updated" some of his own lyrics, e.g., changing the future-tense forms of "If War Comes Tomorrow" when the "tomorrow" of 1938 became the "today" of 1941.[11]

Such updatings by professional poets rarely achieved the popularity of the familiar older versions. Much more successful in general were the completely new texts set to old melodies by anonymous authors at the front lines or among the partisans. One song, for example, recorded in 1943 on the Leningrad front and elsewhere, was widely sung to the melody of a late nineteenth-century song about a young man planning to run away with his beloved even if it means killing her elderly husband ("The Joy of My Life Dwells in a Terem [women's chamber]" [Zhivët moia otrada v vysokom teremu]). The 1943 text is about a young accordion player from the Vasilevskii Ostrov section of Leningrad who, despite a serious wound, leads the charge against a German machine-gun position. In the field hospital he amazes the nurses by asking for his accordion. The song ends:

> One morning a colonel
> Visited the wounded men.
> "Where are you from, you hothead?"
> He tenderly asked.
> The merry accordion player
> Answered him proudly:
> "From Vasilevskii Ostrov,
> From the Metallist Factory."[12]

Even old underworld songs were pressed into service during the war, among them one in which a thief sends greetings to his beloved from the Siberian prison camp of Kolyma. The wartime song changes the setting to the Belorussian front. The first and next-to-last stanzas of the older version are as follows:

> Far from the land of Kolyma
> I send you greetings, my beauty.
> How are you, my darling?
> Write me an answer as soon as you can. . . .

When my sentence ends,
I'll say good-by to the forests and the taiga,
And in a first-class railroad car
I'll race back to you, darling.

There is a striking resemblance between this text and that of a song described as being widespread during World War II. Here are the first and last stanzas:

From the distant Belorussian swamps
I send you my warm greetings.
How are you, my darling,
Write me an answer as soon as you can. . . .

When I finish the war with the fascists,
I'll say good-by to my machine gun
And in a military mail train
I'll race back to you, darling.[13]

One of the old melodies used most frequently was that of a late nineteenth-century sailors' song, "The Broad Expanse of the Sea" (Raskinulos more shiroko). It had been popularized in the late 1930s by the singer Leonid Utёsov, the leader of an influential jazz orchestra and star of the first Soviet musical film, *Happy-Go-Lucky Guys* (Vesёlye rebiata, 1934).[14] Perhaps the most popular new text set to its melody was about the death in battle of a sailor:

I met him near my native Odessa
When our company went into battle.
He was marching in front, with a tommy-gun on his chest,
A sailor of the Black Sea Fleet.

The battle is on land, and the sailor kills an enemy officer (referred to first as a "Teutonic Knight" [krestonosets] and then as a "fascist"), but is himself wounded and dies at a military first-aid station. As he lies dying he hums the old sailors' song and then, in an echo of many other old songs, asks a favor of the narrator:

"Perhaps you'll stop by in Akhtyrka?
Tell my wife 'farewell' for me
And give my sailor's cap to my son."[15]

The process of matching a new text to an old melody took various paths. In the summer of 1942 Lebedev-Kumach wrote a poem about a young partisan fighter derailing a Nazi transport train. The poem was published in *Pravda* and later printed as a broadsheet, which was dropped by air over the occupied Briansk region. Soon the text was being sung to the melody of a popular 1924 song about the Civil War, and with this melody it spread to Belorussia, Ukraine, Moldavia, the Baltic republics and beyond. The poem began:

> By a thick grove a young partisan
> Lay in ambush with his detachment.
> We will wait for the enemy in the autumn rain,
> We have no need to hurry or rush.

The song was often sung with the opening words "In a dark, thick grove" and with other lesser or greater departures from the poet's text.[16]

Another partisan song achieved similar popularity and variability. When Pëtr Mamaichuk, a soldier on the Leningrad front, learned about the death of a friend fighting behind enemy lines, he wrote a poem that began

> At the edge of the forest an old oak tree stands,
> Under that oak tree a partisan lies.
> He lies there, not breathing, as if sleeping.
> The wind rustles his golden curls.

The poet portrayed the partisan's mother grieving over her fallen son and the son's commander promising to avenge his death. When Mamaichuk later found himself in the same hospital ward as composer Leonid Shokhin, he asked the composer to set his poem to music, and the resulting song soon spread throughout the Briansk and central fronts and the country beyond and came to be regarded by many as a folk song. As is the case with "real" folk songs, its text and even its melody showed local variations.[17]

This process of folklorization, of changes in a song text (and sometimes in its melody) as the song spreads largely through oral transmission rather than through the duplication of printed texts, affected the work of other poets whose poems became popular wartime songs. In 1942, for example, Mikhail Isakovskii wrote a poem entitled "The Blue Ball Is Spinning and Turning" (Krutitsia, vertitsia shar goluboi) about a wounded soldier coming home on leave, only to find that his village has been burned and his beloved taken away by the Germans. The title, which also served as a kind of refrain, was taken from a turn-of-the-century waltz. Isakovskii's poem had a powerful effect on soldiers when read from the stage, and it was soon being sung on the front lines to the old waltz melody. Before long, variations appeared: in some the soldier's beloved has escaped from the Nazis and is a partisan fighter.[18]

Folklorization is one indication of a song's popularity; another, and one that was particularly striking during the war, is the phenomenon of responses or "answer songs," mentioned above in connection with "Katiusha." The phenomenon of answers to songs was not new in Russian popular music. Early in this century, for example, the popular hit "Coachman, Don't Race the Horses" (Iamshchik, ne goni loshadei) provoked the response "Race, Coachman" (Goni, iamshchik) and "Come Back, I'll Forgive Everything" (Vernis, ia vsë proshchu) was followed by "I Won't Return" (Ia ne vernus). Unlike the earlier examples, however, the wartime answers were usually sung to the melody of the song they were answering, and they were not composed by songwriters trying to capitalize on the commercial success of the earlier songs.[19]

One wartime song that provoked many responses was "The Burning Flame" (Ogonëk), Isakovskii's text about a soldier leaving his girl to go off to war and remembering the light that burned in her window:

> A girl saw a soldier
> Off to the front.
> She made her farewells
> That dark night on the front steps.
> And for a while the lad
> Could see beyond the mists:
> In the girl's window
> A little flame kept on burning.

Isakovskii wrote the poem in 1942 and someone, perhaps a navy accordionist named Nikitenko, started singing it to the melody of a Polish tango, "Stella." (The 1939 "reunification" of the previously Polish western regions of Ukraine and Belorussia with the corresponding Soviet republics had as a side effect the introduction of influences from Polish popular culture.)[20]

By 1953 folklorists had collected some twenty responses to "The Burning Flame," including one that condemned a girl for rejecting her fiancé when he returned from the war disabled, and others responding to that by portraying a girl who had remained faithful to a wounded soldier. Some of the texts set to the melody of "The Burning Flame" were in the form of "answers": the girl at home, for example, assuring her soldier that the light in her window was still burning for him.

There were also many responses to "In the Dugout" (V zemlianke), written in 1942 by Konstantin Listov to a text by the popular wartime poet Aleksei Surkov. It had its origins in a letter Surkov, a war correspondent, wrote to his wife during the defense of Moscow in November 1941. Initially some critics objected to the song as "defeatist" because of a line in the second half:

> You are now far, far away,
> The snows lie between us. . . .
> It's not easy for me to reach you,
> And death is only four steps away.

The song was, however, a favorite with the troops, "known on all fronts and by almost every soldier." A group of them wrote to Surkov that for the critics he could change the line to "death is four thousand English miles away." For soldiers he should "leave it the way it is—we after all know how far away death is."[21]

The soldiers also knew what it meant to be separated from their loved ones, and "In the Dugout" struck a responsive chord at the front and at home. The male voice of the song was answered by female words of empathy and encouragement:

I'm in that cold dugout with you,
And victory awaits us. . . .

In another text:

But our love, I know, is strong;
It will survive even the storm of war.

In a third:

Soon we'll meet again
And find the happiness that has gone astray.[22]

Like "In the Dugout," Konstantin Simonov's poem "Wait for Me" (Zhdi menia) was a kind of letter home from the front:

Wait for me and I'll return,
But really wait for me.
Wait for me when the yellow rains
Bring on melancholy;
Wait for me when the snow is driving;
Wait for me in the heat.
Wait for me when they forget about yesterday
And stop waiting for others. . . .

Simonov wrote the poem in the late summer of 1941 and it was published in *Pravda* (and then in local and frontline newspapers) in January 1942. An answer to it was published as early as March 1 of that year in the newspaper of the southern front, which explained that "many fighting men and commanders cut [Simonov's poem] out of the newspaper and sent it to their loved ones." This first published reply, like the dozens that followed it, was entitled "I'm Waiting for You" (Zhdu tebia).[23]

The process illustrated by "Wait for Me" was not unusual: soldiers would copy or cut out of the newspaper poetic texts that appealed to them and send them home. Circulated on the home front, the texts provoked answers, which were in turn sent back to the front and sometimes then published in frontline newspapers. All of this served, among other things, to popularize the original poem or song. In the case of the

Simonov text, at least ten composers set it to music, but the music that was most popular and that remained in the repertoire long after the war was by Matvei Blanter.[24]

Female answers to "Wait for Me" came not only from the home front but also from women serving as army nurses or in a medical corps and as partisan fighters. These roles were also reflected in songs. We have already mentioned, for example, folk variants of "Katiusha" that portray her at the front or fighting behind enemy lines. Among the innumerable variants of "Little Blue Kerchief" were texts in which the unnamed heroine had traded her "modest blue kerchief" for a helmet or for the "modest white coat" of a nurse.[25]

Professional lyricists also wrote songs about nurses, such as "Nurse Aniuta" (Medsestra Aniuta), a song that was said to have been "known to every frontline soldier without exception," despite the fact that it was neither recorded nor played on the radio.[26] It began:

> I can never forget
> Our meeting and that winter night.
> A cold, gusty wind was blowing
> And the water froze in my canteen.

(In many variants of the song the order of the first two couplets is reversed.) The song goes on to tell about a nurse risking her life to rescue a wounded soldier, a common theme in such songs—and a reflection of wartime reality. "Nurse Aniuta" was written in early 1942 for the first program of a newly-formed Black Sea Fleet ensemble by composer Iurii Slonov, who later recalled that at the time he had not heard any songs about nurses.[27]

Had Slonov been on the western front, he might have heard a popular song that made use of the two meanings of the Russian word *sestra*, "sister" and "nurse." In 1940 Evgenii Dolmatovskii wrote a "Song about a Sister" (Pesnia o sestre), which was published in *Komsomolskaia pravda* together with music by Nikita Bogoslovskii. The song was widely sung during the war in folklorized variants that in some cases improved on Dolmatovskii's text but kept his main image of the nurse, "the girl in the military overcoat and cap," who seemed like a sister. In most versions the first stanza of the song begins with the words "I remember," and the last one, with "I can never forget," phrases that occur in "Nurse Aniuta" and in several other contemporary songs about nurses.[28]

Another song written in 1940, "The Dark-Skinned Beauty" (Smuglianka), portrayed the Soviet woman as guerilla fighter. Although originally intended as part of a suite about Moldavian partisans during the Civil War, when it was finally performed by the Red Army Chorus in 1944, it seemed to be about contemporary events. Iakov Shvedov's text tells about a young man in love with a dark-skinned Moldavian girl, who leaves him to join the partisans. He is hurt that she does not ask him to come along, but he later meets up with her on the battle lines. The song begins:

> Once during the summer at dawn
> I looked in on the orchard next door.
> A dark-skinned Moldavian girl
> Was picking grapes there.

Anatolii Novikov's lively music for the song was based on Moldavian folk melodies. The song had not been performed in 1940, and when the composer proposed it for a radio broadcast in 1943, it was rejected as being too lyrical, not serious enough for wartime conditions. It was rescued from oblivion in 1944 by Aleksandr Aleksandrov, the director of the Red Army Chorus.[29]

Novikov and Shvedov were not the only songwriters who had to contend with a prejudice against lyricism. In August 1941 the composer Vasilii Solovëv-Sedoi, whose 1957 song "Moscow Nights" (Podmoskovnye vechera) would achieve international popularity, was unloading firewood in the port of Leningrad. The sounds of music coming from a ship at anchor in the roadstead got him to thinking about the sailors defending the city and inspired him to write a song about them, "Evening at Anchor" (Vecher na reide). Although in songwriting the text usually comes first, in this case Aleksandr Churkin wrote words to music already composed by Solovëv-Sedoi, who also supplied the first line of the refrain:

> Farewell, beloved city!
> Tomorrow we go out into the sea.
> And early in the morning
> We'll glimpse behind the stern
> A familiar blue kerchief.

The song, however, was not approved for performance; the times seemed to require dramatic, heroic songs like "Sacred War." It was only in early 1942, when the composer began to sing the song himself for soldiers on the Kalinin front that the immense popularity of the song began.[30]

Another song was written as an explicit polemic with the notion expressed in the Latin maxim *inter arma silent Musae* ("amidst [the sound of] arms the Muses fall silent"). Vasilii Lebedev-Kumach, disturbed by the comment of an army captain in 1943 that this was no time for singing songs, i.e., that the Muses should fall silent, wrote a poem that began:

> Who said that one should give up
> Songs in wartime?
> After a battle the heart needs
> Music twice as much!

With music by Anatolii Lepin, the song "Only at the Front" (Tol'ko na fronte) soon became popular.[31]

In a sense the battle for lyricism had already been won by the time Lebedev-Kumach wrote his song. As early as February 1942, Aleksei Surkov observed that in poetry publicistic and journalistic themes were giving way to lyric ones. Another poet, Tsezar Solodar, pointed out a few months later that "you sometimes don't want to sing a song at the top of your voice; [you just want] to sing it softly, privately."[32] At an April 1942 conference, members of the Union of Soviet Composers were encouraged to write lyrical songs, "songs about big human feelings." To be sure, they were also warned by a government official against getting carried away with "so-called intimate lyricism" and "sentimental lachrymosity."[33]

A song criticized the following year for its "tearfulness" nevertheless became one of the most popular and lasting songs of the war, "Dark Is the Night" (Tëmnaia noch'):

> Dark is the night, only bullets whistle over the steppe,
> Only the wind hums in the wires, the stars flicker dimly.
> This dark night I know that you, my love, are not asleep,
> And by our child's bed you secretly wipe away a tear.

Like "In the Dugout" and "Wait for Me," it was a kind of letter from the front, a letter that was somber in tone but optimistic in its ending:

> Death is not frightening; we've often encountered it in
>    the steppes.
> Even now it is hovering over me.
> You wait for me as you sit, awake, at our child's
>    bed,
> And that's why I know that nothing will happen to me.

Sung in the 1943 film *Two Warriors* (Dva boitsa; see Kenez, this volume) by Mark Bernes, "Dark Is the Night" got to the front lines before the film did and soon was being sung all over the country. Vladimir Agatov, who wrote its lyrics, recalled that when the song was being recorded for the first time, the initial batch of records was defective. It turned out that the recording engineer had spoiled the masters with her tears.[34]

In the same film Bernes, playing a soldier from Odessa, sang another song that won equal popularity and equal (or even greater) official criticism, "Kostia the Sailor" (Kostia-moriak):

> Kostia brought into Odessa
> Barges full of mullet,
> And all the longshoremen would rise
> When Kostia entered the beer hall.

The poet Evgenii Evtushenko, in reminiscences about Bernes, mentions the two songs alongside of "Sacred War" as defining the feelings of Soviet citizens during the war. At the other extreme, a postwar critic referred to "Kostia" as "nothing more than a trite (poshlaia) song in the spirit of pre-revolutionary Odessa 'folklore'." In 1963, at an evening celebrating the fiftieth birthday of the composer of "Dark Is the Night," Nikita Bogoslovskii, Bernes referred obliquely to the difficulties "Kostia" had caused. Addressing Bogoslovskii, Bernes recalled how during the war he and the whole country had sung "Dark Is the Night," which he called his favorite song. "But," he continued before singing a few lines of "Kostia," "we didn't only sing sad songs; we also sang happy ones. To be sure, they often made everyone happy but you and me."[35]

"Kostia" was a happy song in part because it had nothing to do with the war; it reminded listeners not of the Odessa that would be liberated only in 1944, but of the prewar Odessa—the home town of Bernes and many entertainers and songwriters. There were also songs that looked forward to happier times. As early as the fall of 1941, Ilia Frenkel wrote a poem in which he imagined the war being over:

> A warm wind is blowing, the roads are impassable,
> And on the southern front there's a thaw again.
> The snow is melting in Rostov, it's melting in Taganrog.
> Some day we'll reminisce about these days . . .
>
> I'll remember the infantry
> And my company,
> And you—for giving me a smoke.
> Let's smoke one, buddy,
> Let's have a smoke, my friend. . . .

Frenkel and his colleague on the newspaper of the southern front tried to sing the text; according to one account, the text was firm but the melody varied from day to day. Finally they enlisted the help of a professional musician, and the song "Let's Have a Smoke" (Davai zakurim) with Modest Tabachnikov's music was published in the newspaper. According to the writer Konstantin Simonov, who spent the entire war in the army, "there was no front on which [the song] was not sung." It was performed with great success by Klavdiia Shul'zhenko, who learned how to roll a cigarette frontline style in order to add some dramatic character to her rendition. She did it so convincingly that after concerts soldiers often offered to share their tobacco with her.[36]

Listeners also got caught up in another optimistic song from early in the war. "My Beloved" (Moia liubimaia) was originally written during the 1939 march into Western Ukraine and Western Belorussia, but became popular in a revised, 1942 version. The song ends with the lines:

In my small pocket
I have your snapshot,
So we're always together,
My beloved.

After Rina Bogopol'skaia performed the song for sailors of the Northern Fleet, the commander, Admiral A. Golovko, told her: "When you sang about the snapshot, I instinctively reached for the pocket of my tunic where I keep the photograph that is so dear to me."[37]

It is no surprise that Admiral Golovko reacted to the song as if Bogopol'skaia had been singing about him. What is striking in so many of the songs of 1941–45 is the prominence of individual feelings. Arnold Sokhor was on the right track when he wrote that "it was only in songs of the beginning of the war that the image of the whole nation rising to battle prevailed. It was soon replaced by the image of the fighting man, the direct participant of campaigns and battles. . . . "[38] When one examines collections of wartime songs, whether contemporary ones such as the 1944 *Songs of the Great Patriotic War* or later ones like those already cited from 1967 and 1975, it becomes clear that the repertoire contained many songs expressing the hopes and concerns, the anger and resolution of individuals, and relatively few expressing collective emotions.[39]

This does not mean that collective emotions could not be expressed well in song. At the very beginning of the war, fury and patriotic determination to drive the invaders out of the Russian Motherland had found very effective formulation in "Sacred War." Another composition of 1941, "Song of the Dnieper" (Pesnia o Dnepre), portrayed the same determination, combined with grief at having to abandon territory to the invading forces:

By the vines on your banks, by your steep cliffs
We loved and grew.
Oh, Dnieper, Dnieper, you are broad and powerful.
Cranes fly over you. . . .

The enemy attacked us, we left the Dnieper.
The mortal battle thundered like a storm.
Oh, Dnieper, Dnieper, you flow in the distance
And your water is like a tear. . . .

According to the author of the text, Evgenii Dolmatovskii, the first rehearsal of the song, with an ensemble performing for the southwestern front, was difficult because every time the singers began, they would start to cry.[40]

Later, in 1943, the commitment of the unsuccessful defenders of Sevastopol to return and liberate the city was expressed in a song about a sailor's oath to bring back the piece of granite (a fragment of a monument) that he had taken with him as he left the city. Although an individual took the stone, its return becomes a collective responsibility when he dies. The last verse of "Sacred Stone" (Zavetnyi kamen) began:

Through storms and squalls this stone will go
And will take up its proper place once again.

The song was popularized by Leonid Utësov, who had been moved by its expression of faith in an ultimate Soviet victory; when Sevastopol was finally liberated, he changed the future tense of the last verse to the past tense.[41]

Toward the end of the war, the first of several songs about the Red Army fighting beyond the borders of the Soviet Union gave voice to feelings of Russian patriotism, expressed in the first person plural. "Under Balkan Stars" (Pod zvezdami balkanskimi) ends:

We recall dark-brown eyes,
Quiet talk, ringing laughter. . . .
Bulgaria is a fine country,
But Russia is best of all.

All of these songs of collective emotion, from "Sacred War" to "Under Balkan Stars," evoked powerful feelings in their listeners and were popular during the war and afterward. Yet they were not the ones that provoked musical responses like the songs about Katiusha, the nurse, or the many "I Am Waiting for You" answers to Simonov's "Wait for Me." That kind of reaction was reserved for songs that spoke in the first- and second-person singular, or, as in the case of "Katiusha" or "The Burning Flame," portrayed an individualized hero or heroine. Such songs of individual emotion were not a new phenomenon in the history of Soviet popular music, but in the 1920s and 1930s they had often been attacked by Soviet critics as relics of bourgeois culture.

By the end of the war, however, musical expressions of individual feeling had won a legitimate place in the Soviet song repertoire. Despite an occasional recrudescence of ideological criticism, such as that leveled at the "tavern melancholy" of Nikita Bogoslovskii's songs for a 1946 film, songwriters continued to keep the lyrical "I" at the center of their compositions.[42] Even when a song about Leningrad refers to young years spent in the Young Communist League, it is "my Komsomol youth" (in the 1960 "Evening Song" [Vecherniaia pesnia]), or when thoughts about spring bring reminiscences of a home-town street with its "door of the regional Komsomol committee," this less than lyrical image is nonetheless in the context of things that are "dear and familiar to me" (in the 1956 song "When Spring Comes . . . " [Kogda vesna pridët . . . ]).[43]

Russian songs of World War II spoke of homeland, home town and battlefield, addressing the emotions of millions of Soviet citizens. They did so, by and large, from the point of view of the individual on the front lines, in the partisan movement or at the home front. Each of those millions of individuals could therefore feel that the songs were about him or her. As they listened to the wartime songs, sang them and wrote answers to them, Russians made these new songs of individual emotion a permanent part of the Russian song repertoire.

## Notes

1. As early as June 29, 1941, a soldier in Ukraine copied the text into his notebook. A month later it was collected from another soldier, this time in Central Russia. See S. I. Mints, O. N. Grechina, and B. M. Dobrovol'skii, "Massovoe pesennoe tvorchestvo," in V. E. Gusev, ed., *Russkii fol'klor Velikoi Otechestvennoi voiny* (Moscow-Leningrad: Nauka, 1964), pp. 103, 127–29.

2. The following songs (listed here together with their authors and composers, where known) are mentioned in this essay: "Sinii platochek," words by Iakov Galitskii, music by Jerzy Petersburski; "Esli zavtra voina," Vasilii Lebedev-Kumach, Daniil and Dmitrii Pokrass; "Tuchi nad gorodom vstali," words and music by Pavel Armand; "Katiusha," Mikhail Isakovskii, Matvei Blanter; "Samovary-samopaly," Sergei Alymov, Anatolii Novikov; "Sviashchennaia voina," Vasilii Lebedev-Kumach, Aleksandr Aleksandrov; "My krasnye soldaty"; "Sredi lesov dremuchikh"; "Zhivët moia otrada v vysokom teremu," Sergei Ryskin, Mikhail Shishkin; "Raskinulos more shiroko"; "Krutitsia, vertitsia shar goluboi"; "Vragi sozhgli rodnuiu khatu," Mikhail Isakovskii, Matvei Blanter; "Ogonëk," words by Mikhail Isakovskii; "Iamshchik, ne goni loshadei," Nikolai Ritter, Iakov Fel'dman; "Goni, iamshchik," Konstantin Basharin (Ostapenko), V. P. Semënov; "Vernis, ia vsë proshchu," Vladimir Lenskii, Boris Prozorovskii; "Ia ne vernus," Sergei Kasatkin (Krechetov), Boris Prozorovskii; "V zemlianke," Aleksei Surkov, Konstantin Listov; "Zhdi menia," Konstantin Simonov, Matvei Blanter (and a dozen others); "Medsestra Aniuta," Mikhail Frantsuzov, Iurii Slonov; "Pesnia o sestre," Evgenii Dolmatovskii, Nikita Bogoslovskii; "Smuglianka," Iakov Shvedov, Anatolii Novikov; "Podmoskovnye vechera," Mikhail Matusovskii, Vasilii Solov'ëv-Sedoi; "Vecher na reide," Aleksandr Churkin, Vasilii Solov'ëv-Sedoi; "Tol'ko na fronte," Vasilii Lebedev-Kumach, Anatolii Lepin; "Tëmnaia noch'," Vladimir Agatov, Nikita Bogoslovskii; "Kostia-moriak"; "Davai zakurim," Il'ia Frenkel, Modest Tabachnikov; "Moia liubimaia," Evgenii Dolmatovskii, Matvei Blanter; "Pesnia o Dnepre," Evgenii Dolmatovskii, Mark Fradkin; "Pod zvezdami balkanskimi," Mikhail Isakovskii, Matvei Blanter; "Zavetnyi kamen," Andrei Zharov, Boris Mokrousov; "Vecherniaia pesnia," Aleksandr Churkin, Vasilii Solov'ëv-Sedoi; "Kogda vesna pridët . . . ," Aleksei Fatianov, Boris Mokrousov. The text and music for most of these songs can be found in A. E. Lukovnikov, comp., *Druz'ia-odnopolchane: o pesniakh, rozhdënnykh voinoi* (Moscow: Voenizdat, 1975) and in volume 3 of A. V. Shilov, comp., *Slavim pobedu Oktiabria!* (Moscow: Muzyka, 1967). The last two songs are included in Tereza Rymshevich, comp., *Pesni 50-kh godov* (Moscow: Sovetskii kompozitor, 1986).

3. The newspaper *Sovetskoe iskusstvo* reported in its issue for December 11, 1935, that the Defense Section of the Union of Soviet Composers was organizing a "defense music week" (actually ten days: *dekada oboronnoi muzyki*) for early 1936. Gorky's comments can be found in his letter to Aleksei Surkov dated December 7, 1935, published in his *Sobranie sochinenii v tridtsati tomakh* (Moscow: Goslitizdat, 1954), 30: 411–14. A Red Army and Navy Literary Group, organized in 1929, was reorganized in 1932 into the Military Defense Commission of the Union of Soviet Writers (Aleksei Pavlovskii, *Russkaia sovetskaia poeziia v gody Velikoi Otechestvennoi voiny* [Leningrad: Nauka, 1967], pp. 10–12).

4. Recollections about Bernes, including N. I. Smirnova's comment about his influence, can

be found in L. M. Bernes-Bodrova, comp., *Mark Bernes: stati; vospominaniia o M. N. Bernese* (Moscow: Iskusstvo, 1980).

5. I. N. Rozanov, "Pesni o Katiushe kak novyi tip narodnogo tvorchestva," in Gusev, *Russkii fol'klor*, pp. 310–25.

6. The contest attracted some five hundred entries, according to Arnol'd Sokhor, *Russkaia sovetskaia pesnia* (Leningrad: Sovetskii kompozitor, 1959), p. 180.

7. Sokhor, pp. 249–50.

8. Sokhor, pp. 250, 274; Shilov, 3: 254; Lukovnikov, pp. 12–13. The musicologist Aleksandr Rabinovich coined the phrase "Muzykal'naia emblema Velikoi Otechestvennoi voiny" in his article of that title in the 1944 collection *Sovetskaia muzyka*, 4 (1944).

9. Maiia Sitkovetskaia, "Zvuchit kak gimn," in P. S. Darienko, ed., *Kogda pushki gremeli . . .* (Moscow: Iskusstvo, 1973), pp. 88–92.

10. Pavel Lebedev, *Pesni boevykh pokhodov: Soldatskoe pesennoe tvorchestvo Velikoi Otechestvennoi voiny* (Saratov: Privolzhskoe knizhnoe izdatel'stvo, 1986), pp. 16, 19, 84–88, 168–70, 172. On Shul'zhenko's front-line concerts see Darienko, p. 196, as well as Shul'zenko's autobiography, *Kogda vy sprosite menia . . .* (Moscow: Molodaia gvardiia, 1981), p. 98.

11. The song that Lebedev-Kumach reworked is called "a manly (muzhestvennaia) marching song of the Civil War" in Tat'iana Popova, *O pesniakh nashikh dnei* (Moscow: Muzyka, 1969), p. 260; Lebedev, p. 246, calls it "an old soldier song." They fail to point out that it was itself a reworking of the bandit song, which was in turn a folklorization of Fëdor Miller's 1848 translation of a German poem by Ferdinand Freiligrath (V. E. Gusev, ed., *Pesni russkikh poetov* [Leningrad: Sovetskii pisatel', 1988], 2: 36–38, 401–02). Part of the new version of "If War Comes Tomorrow" can be found in Lebedev, p. 244.

12. V. Iu. Krupianskaia and S. I. Mints, *Materialy po istorii pesni Velikoi Otechestvennoi voiny* (Moscow: Izd. ANSSSR, 1953), pp. 78–79. "Zhivët moia otrada" was a folklorization of an 1882 poem by Sergei Ryskin (Gusev, *Pesni*, 2: 244–45).

13. The underworld song can be found in Iakov Vaiskopf, *Blatnaia lira* (Jerusalem: n.p., 1981), p. 40. The wartime version is published in K. G. Svitova, ed., *Nezabyvaemye gody: russkii pesennyi fol'klor Velikoi Otechestvennoi voiny v zapisiakh K. G. Svitovoi* (Moscow: Sovetskii kompozitor, 1985), pp. 44–45, 97. S. I. Mints et al. cite "Far from the Land of Kolyma" as one of the several songs that served as the basis for whole cycles of wartime songs; the other songs mentioned are "Little Blue Kerchief," "Katiusha," "In the Dugout" and "The Broad Expanse of the Sea" (in Gusev, *Russkii fol'klor*, p. 127). Real prisoners, of course, brought songs with them to the punishment battalions.

14. On the film and on Utësov see S. Frederick Starr, *Red and Hot: The Fate of Jazz in the Soviet Union* (New York: Oxford University Press, 1983), pp. 153–55 and passim.

15. The old song, about the death of an overworked ship's stoker, was based on an 1844 literary translation of a Greek sailors' song (Gusev, *Pesni*, 1: 556 and 2: 397–400). The wartime song was often known under the title "Bezkozyrka," the Russian name for the sailor's cap mentioned in the last line, and became an unofficial anthem of the Black Sea Fleet (Krupianskaia and Mints, pp. 100–104). The end of "Bezkozyrka" is reminiscent of eighteenth- and nineteenth-century songs about coachmen dying in the steppe, such as "The Mozdok Steppe" ("Step Mozdokskaia"). See A. M. Novikova, comp., *Russkie narodnye pesni* (Moscow: Goslitizdat, 1957), pp. 92, 412–13.

16. The history of the Lebedev-Kumach poem (which he said he was inspired to write after hearing a speech by Stalin about the start of partisan warfare against the Germans), and of the resulting song is discussed in Lebedev, pp. 85–86, and Krupianskaia and Mints, pp. 184–86. The 1924 song ("Tam vdali za rekoi") can be found in Shilov, 1: 85–86. Its author, Nikolai Kool', had himself borrowed the melody of a nineteenth-century Siberian convict song, "Kogda na Sibiri zaimetsia zaria," the text of which is printed in Gusev, *Pesni*, 2, 350. The wide popularity of the song about the partisan is clear from a 1968 letter to *Izvestiia*, published under the title "S chego nachinaetsia Rodina" (October 24), p. 6, and responses printed a month later under the title "Soldatskaia sud'ba pesni" (November 23), p. 6.

17. A number of melodic variants of "Na opushke lesa" can be found in Popova, pp. 304–09. On the history of the song see also G. Pozhidaev, ed., *Muzyka na frontakh Velikoi Otechestvennoi voiny: stat'i, vospominaniia* (Moscow: Muzyka, 1970), p. 209, and Krupianskaia and Mints, pp. 182–83. Along with many other Russian songs, this one also made its way to what was then Palestine and acquired a new, Hebrew text (by A. Kletskin) as "Bearvot hanegev." See, e.g., Samuel Bugatch, ed., *Songs of Our People* (New York: Farband Book Publishing Association, 1961), p. 65.

18. Lebedev, pp. 210–11; Krupianskaia and Mints, pp. 154–55. The melody of the original "Krutitsia, vertitsia" had been revived through its use in the 1935–37 films of the Trilogy about Maksim. Isakovskii came back to the theme of the soldier returning to a destroyed home in a powerful song of 1945, "The Enemy Burned His Home" (Vragi sozhgli rodnuiu khatu).

19. The phenomenon is also known in American country and rock music, as was pointed out to me by my colleague Ron Story. Cf. Kitty Wells's "It Wasn't God Who Made Honky-Tonk Angels" as an answer to Hank Thompson's "The Wild Side," which begins with the line "I didn't know God made honky-tonk angels" (Bill C. Malone, *Country Music, U.S.A.* [Austin: University of Texas Press, 1985], pp. 223–24) or Damita Jo's "I'm Saving the Last Dance for You" in response to the Drifters' "Save the Last Dance for Me" (Arnold Shaw, *Dictionary of American Pop/Rock* [New York: Schirmer, 1982], pp. 14–15). Mints et al. (in Gusev, *Russkii fol'klore* p. 132) claim that the phenomenon was new and characteristic of the war period.

20. Shilov, 3: 266; Krupianskaia and Mints, pp. 120–22. One example of Polish influences is the case of Jerzy Petersburski, an internationally known composer of popular music, who found himself in the Soviet Union after 1939. An account of his career can be found in Tadeusz Matulewicz, *Skad ta pieśn* (Olsztyn: Pojezierze, 1987), pp. 145–50. The German-born jazz musician, Adi Rosner, who was active in Poland in the 1930s, was another "cultural import" from that country. His career is described in Starr, pp. 194–202.

21. A 1945 letter cited by Mints et al. (in Gusev, *Russkii fol'klor*, p. 130) testifies to the song's popularity. Lukovnikov, p. 102, quotes Surkov on the letter of support he got from the front.

22. Krupianskaia and Mints, pp. 127–28; Gusev, *Russkii fol'klor*, pp. 130–34. The last line is an allusion to the end of Surkov's text, in which the poet asks the accordion playing in the dugout to call "our happiness that has gone astray."

23. Lebedev, pp. 255–70.

24. Lebedev, pp. 255–70; Sokhor, p. 306.

25. V. Iu. Krupianskaia, *Frontovoi fol'klor* (Moscow: Goslitizdat, 1944), p. 117, speaks of "innumerable" variants. Several are cited in A. N. Vladimirskii, " 'Sinii platochek' na voine", in *Problemy izucheniia russkogo ustnogo narodnogo tvorchestva*, 2 (Moscow: Moskovskii oblastnoi pedagogicheskii institut im. N. K. Krupskoi, 1976) pp. 141–55. The original version of the song, written in 1940 by Jerzy Petersburski to words by Iakov Galitskii, was also extremely popular both at home and on the front. Klavdiia Shul'zhenko helped to popularize it with an updated text by Mikhail Maksimov; see the account in Shul'zhenko, pp. 93–95. The fullest and most recent account of the history of the song is in Matulewicz, pp. 136–53.

26. Lebedev, p. 369.

27. Lukovnikov, pp. 120–21. The text was written by Mikhail Frantsuzov, the director of the ensemble. One variant was published in Krupianskaia and Mints, pp. 118–19.

28. N. N. Grigorovich and S. I. Shlifshtein, comps., *Russkaia literatura v sovetskoi muzyke* (Moscow: Sovetskii kompozitor, 1975), 1: 245; Krupianskaia and Mints, pp. 115–17; Ia. I. Gudoshnikov, *Iazyk i stil' pesen Velikoi Otechestvennoi voiny* (Voronezh: Izd. Voronezhskogo universiteta, 1959), pp. 40–42, 78–79; Lebedev, pp. 367–68; Popova, pp. 342–43. Dolmatovskii's 1940 text actually begins with a stanza that sets the soldier's meeting with the nurse in the context of the 1939 Soviet invasion of what had been Polish territories east of the Bug River. Those four lines seem not to have been sung later and were omitted by Dolmatovskii when he reprinted the poem in a 1947 collection. A similar fate apparently befell an entire song connected with the Russo-Finnish war of 1939–40, "Red Army Nurses Have Arrived at the Front" (Voennye sëstry Krasnoi Armii pribyli na

front). The song was sung in a film about that war called (in the United States) *Girl from Leningrad* (*Frontovye podrugi*) and seems to have achieved some popularity, but the song and the film are almost never mentioned in postwar Soviet sources. An exception is the reference in Krupianskaia and Mints, p. 115; more typical is Novikova, who does not identify an anonymous wartime song about nurses as a variant of the film song (pp. 619–20, 695).

29. Lukovnikov, pp. 220–26.

30. Popova, p. 283; Lukovnikov, pp. 52–55; Pozhidaev, pp. 101–103.

31. Lukovnikov, pp. 155–58; Pozhidaev, p. 232; Sokhor, p. 324. A collection of memoirs and other materials about the role of the arts on the battlefronts of the war (Darienko) alludes to the Latin maxim in its title, *When the Cannons Roared . . .*

32. Surkov's comment, from *Literatura i iskusstvo* for February 12, 1942, is cited in Pavlovskii, p. 97. The quotation from Solodar ("Pesniu khochetsia ne tol'ko raspevat'. Pesniu khochetsia i napevat'. Napevat' vpolgolosa, naedine s soboi") comes from the April 18 issue of the same newspaper and is quoted by Sokhor, p. 240.

33. Pavlovskii, p. 122; Sokhor, p. 241. See also the account of the meeting and the closing address by M. B. Khrapchenko in the article "Kompozitory v dni voiny," *Pravda* (April 30, 1942), p. 4.

34. The recording incident is reported in Shilov, 3: 264. The song's popularity is described in Nina Zavadskaia, *Liubimye pesni voennykh let* (Moscow: Sovetskii kompozitor, 1987), pp. 90–91. A correspondent for the newspaper of the Second Ukrainian Front reported in November 1943 that the film was very much in demand on the front lines and that "frontline soldiers everywhere were already humming the melodies . . . so successfully performed by the actor M. Bernes" (quoted in Lebedev, p. 172). After the war it was occasionally criticized as "a gloomy blues tune" (A. Danilevich, *Muzyka na frontakh Velikoi Otechestvennoi voiny* [Moscow-Leningrad: Muzgiz, 1948], p. 21) or "an emphatically sentimental tango" (Sokhor, p. 305).

35. The criticism is by Danilevich, p. 21. Evtushenko's comments and Bogoslovskii's account of the evening in his honor are found in Bernes-Bodrova, pp. 156, 169–71. Unlike "Dark is the Night," which was published and frequently reprinted, "Kostia" long maintained its popularity without, apparently, ever having been published or recorded. (It was finally included on a Bernes long-play released in the late 1960s.) One measure of its wartime popularity is the existence of satirical, anti-German texts parodying "Kostia," e.g.: A German cruiser brought in/ Barges full of coffins/ Bells rang in the cathedral/ When it entered the port of Hamburg (Mints et al., p. 142).

36. Lukovnikov, pp. 33–7; Shilov, 3: 257–87; Shul'zhenko, pp. 100–101.

37. Shilov, 3: 261; V. I. Zak, *Matvei Blanter* (Moscow: Sovetskii kompozitor, 1971), p. 172; R. Bogopol'skaia, "Na Severnom Flote," in Pozhidaev, p. 179.

38. Sokhor, p. 278.

39. The collection *Songs of the Great Patriotic War* (*Pesni Velikoi Otechestvennoi voiny*), published in Moscow in six parts by the Union of Soviet Composers, contained the words and music for forty-four songs. Fifty-four are included in Lukovnikov and sixty-six in part 3 of Shilov. The individuals whose emotions are expressed are almost always men, at least in the songs by professional songwriters.

40. Evgenii Dolmatovskii, *Rasskazy o tvoikh pesniakh*, 2nd ed. (Moscow: Detskaia literatura, 1973), pp. 191–96. See also Lukovnikov, pp. 25–28.

41. Lukovnikov, pp. 140–45, contains the post-liberation version of the text and tells how the composer Boris Mokrousov was inspired to write the song by a newspaper article about the sailor and his oath to return the stone. A similar account can be found in Pozhidaev, pp. 100–101; the original newspaper story about the Sevastopol stone is reprinted in Pozhidaev, pp. 250–53. The pre-liberation version of the song text is contained in Shilov, 3: 83.

42. The criticism of Bogoslovskii was contained in a Central Committee resolution cited by Sokhor, p. 352.

43. See note 2.

1. Front page of *Pravda* reprinting Stalin's July 3, 1941 radio speech. *Illiustrirovannaia istoriia SSSR* (Moscow: Mysl, 1977), p. 358.

2. Citizens of Leningrad read the news from the front. *Podvig Leningrada: reportazh voennogo fotokorrespondenta D. Trakhtenberga* (Leningrad: Khudozhnik SSSR, 1966).

3. Boris Polevoi in the field: courtesy of Louise McReynolds.

4. Ol'ga Berggol'ts (Bergholtz), the poetic voice of Radio Leningrad: Harrison Salisbury, *The 900 Days: the Siege of Leningrad* (New York: Avon, 1970).

5. Woman listening to the radio during the Blockade of Leningrad in Harrison Salisbury, *The 900 Days: the Siege of Leningrad* (New York: Avon, 1970).

6. The three major composers, left to right: Sergei Prokofiev, Dmitrii Shostakovich, Aram Khachaturian, 1945: *Testimony: the Memoirs of Dmitri Shostakovich* as told to Solomon Volkov, tr. Antonina Bouis (New York: Harper and Row, 1979).

7. Dmitrii Shostakovich in civil defense garb on the cover of *Time* magazine, 1942.

8. Sergei Prokofiev receiving the Order of the Red Banner of Labor from Soviet President Mikhail Kalinin, 1943. Postcard (Moscow: Planeta, 1976), courtesy of Harlow Robinson.

9. Buying tickets for a performance of the Red Army Song and Dance Ensemble at the Leningrad Philharmonic. *Podvig Leningrada: reportazh voennogo fotokorrespondenta D. Trakhtenberga* (Leningrad: Khudozhnik SSSR, 1966).

10. Comedy team Iurii Timoshenko and Efim Berëzin entertaining the troops: *Russkaia sovetskaia estrada*, 3 v. (Moscow: Iskusstvo, 1976–81), II, 392.

11. Concert during a lull in fighting. *Illiustrirovannaia istoriia SSSR* (Moscow: Mysl, 1977), p. 381.

12. "We shall mercilessly crush and exterminate the enemy," a 1941 poster. V. V. Vanslov, *Chto takoe sotsialisticheskii realizm* (Moscow: Izobrazitelnoe iskusstvo, 1988), p. 25.

13. "Grandchildren of Suvorov and children of Chapaev, let's beat the hell out of them," poster by Kukryniksy, slogan by Samuil Marshak, 1941. Kukryniksy, *Po vragam mira!* (Moscow: Plakat, 1982), p. 17.

14. "Partisans! Wreak Vengeance without Mercy!" Poster courtesy of Beate Fieseler and Suzanne Conze, University of the Ruhr, Bochum.

**партизаны, мстите без пощады!**

15. Street art in besieged Leningrad. *Podvig Leningrada: reportazh voennogo fotokorrespondenta D. Trakhtenberga* (Leningrad: Khudozhnik SSSR, 1966).

16. Roman Karmen, wartime documentary cinematographer. Pacific Film Archive.

17. Partisan heroine seeks vengeance in film *She Defends the Motherland* (*No Greater Love*), 1943. Hungarian Film Archive.

18. German soldier takes aim on a child in the film *Rainbow*, 1944. Hungarian Film Archive.

19. Sergei Eisenstein's film *Ivan the Terrible*, part II, 1944–46. Pacific Film Archive.

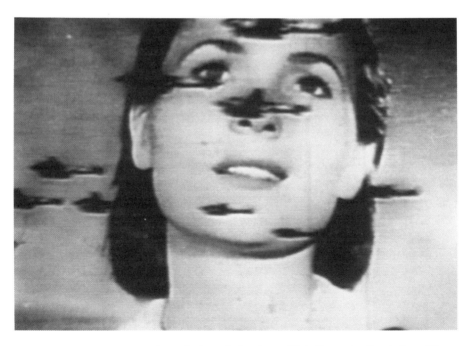

20. Victorious Soviet warplanes fly through the ghost of Zoia Kosmodem'ianskaia: a still from the film, *Zoia*, 1944. Photo by David Hagen.

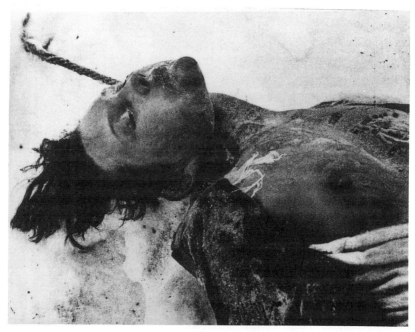

21. Photograph of the executed corpse of Zoia Kosmodem'ianskaia, 1941. Germany, Bundesarchiv, RO130/325, copy courtesy of Rosalinde Sartorti.

22. M. G. Manizer, monument to Zoia Kosmodem'ianskaia, 1942: V. V. Vanslov, *Chto takoe sotsialisticheskii realizm* (Moscow: Izobrazitel'noe iskusstvo, 1988), p. 27.

23. M. G. Manizer's sculptural
ensemble, "The People's
Avengers," 1944: V. V. Vanslov,
*Chto takoe sotsialisticheskii
realizm* (Moscow: Izobrazitel'noe
iskusstvo, 1988), p. 29.

24. Memorial Cemetery at Khatyn in Belorussia where an entire village was burned
alive by the German occupiers: Hans-Heinrich Nolte, ed., *Der Mensch gegen den
Menschen: Überlegungen und Forschungen zum deutschen Überfall auf die
Sowjetunion, 1941* (Hanover, 1992), p. 224.

# 7

# Drama of Struggle

## The Wartime Stage Repertoire[1]

### Harold B. Segel

T HE GERMAN INVASION of the USSR on Sunday, June 22, 1941, found the most prominent Soviet theatrical companies away on their usual summer tours of provincial
centers. The Moscow Art Theater, for example, was in Minsk, the capital of the Belorussian republic, while the Malyi was performing for the benefit of the coalminers of
the Donbass region.[2] Before theater, like other national resources, could be mobilized
in support of the war effort, the touring companies first had to be returned to Moscow
and Leningrad. The situation of the Moscow Art Theater was especially precarious in
view of the proximity of Minsk to the front lines, and all haste was required to get the
company out in time. Once back in Moscow, the theater resumed its rehearsals of
Nikolai Pogodin's "classic" 1930s play about Lenin, *Kremlëvskie kuranty* (The Chimes
of the Kremlin). Air raids temporarily interrupted the proceedings, but such was the
sense of the commitment of everyone involved in the production that they spared no
effort in resuming their work as soon as the all-clear signal was sounded. When the
dress rehearsal of the play was held in mid-October 1941, the German forces had already moved menacingly close to the capital.

The long siege of Leningrad and the real threat of the fall of Moscow to the invaders necessitated the relocation of the leading theater companies deep into the interior
of the country. Before reestablishing itself in still safer Sverdlovsk, the Moscow Art
Theater stopped for a while in Saratov where on January 22, 1942, it held its long-de-
layed premiere of *The Chimes of the Kremlin*. The Malyi Theater was dispatched to
Cheliabinsk; the Vakhtangov Theater, to Omsk; and the Leningrad Academic Theater
in the Name of Pushkin, to Novosibirsk.

When the threat to Moscow had been reduced about a year later, the majority of
the capital's theaters were able to return to home base. In the far harsher circumstances
then prevailing in Leningrad, the stage was kept alive mainly by smaller theaters such
as the Theater of Musical Comedy and the Theater of the Baltic Fleet. Responding to

the need to maintain a semblance of cultural normalcy in the siege-ravaged former capital for the sake of morale, a new company, consisting mainly of radio performers, was established on October 18, 1942. Not surprisingly, its first production was Konstantin Simonov's immensely successful war play, *Russkie liudi* (The Russian People).

Shoring up the morale of Soviet frontline troops quickly came to be regarded as a matter of no less urgency than heartening the spirit of the civilian population behind the lines. Toward this end, theaters organized actors' brigades to accompany various Red Army units.[3] The first of these was the brigade of Moscow actors drawn from different theaters that went off to the Vyazma district as early as July 1941. By the beginning of 1944, some twenty-five frontline theaters were in operation. Although conditions at the front during war would hardly seem propitious to anything but the most rudimentary entertainment, these theaters managed to mount full-length dramatic works in addition to the more modest, lighter theatrical fare that became their basic stock in trade. Eyewitness accounts attest to the extraordinary courage of actors performing amidst the nerve-shattering roar of heavy enemy bombardment. Of the many Soviet theaters and brigades so active at the front during the war, one that particularly distinguished itself was the branch of the Vakhtangov Theater. It was accorded special distinction at a review of the frontline theatrical companies held in Moscow in 1943.

War engaged not only the energies of theaters, but also those of playwrights. Before long an appropriate body of dramatic works came into existence. Now that a half century has passed since the war, and the Soviet Union itself has dissolved, the time may be ripe to reconsider how Soviet dramatic writers attempted to deal with the experience of the war. Our first instinct would doubtless be to shrug off this wartime drama as overwhelmingly ideological in nature and hence of little artistic consequence. To be sure, the plays were written to boost morale, to foster a sense of national pride, and to constrain defeatisim by emphasizing the heroic. The purposes for which the plays were written contain no surprises. In a general sense, the same can be said for style. Drama written during the war, and in circumstances of war, could not afford the luxury of innovation. Besides, the freewheeling Soviet artistic experimentation of the 1920s and early 1930s had been brutally repressed by the time the war broke out. Yet, for all its limitations, Soviet wartime drama is worth a retrospective glance, not for the purpose of reaffirming the obviousness of much of it, but to observe instead how dramatists used the resources of the dramatic idiom to transcend the demands of domestic propaganda.

The historical significance of the Great Patriotic War, as World War II came to be known in official Soviet parlance, has often deflected attention from the operations of the Soviet military prior to the German invasion in 1941—in Poland, Finland, and the Baltic. Although the Soviet occupation of eastern Poland was hardly the kind of military campaign Soviet artists would feel driven to immortalize, the production of plays on military themes in the period 1939–41 may be regarded as much an oblique reflection of this particular event as a response to growing Soviet apprehension over the rise of German military power as well as Japanese expansionist ambitions in the Far East. The international climate of the late 1930s in general offered ample rationalization of greater national preparedness. But the occupation of Poland in 1939 represented the potential for immediate military engagement, the more so in light of the bitter hostilities between Poland and the new Soviet state in 1920.

Two plays inspired by the heightened sense of national danger and the need for greater preparedness were Leonid Leonov's *Polovchanskie sady* (The Orchards of Polovchansk, 1938) and Vladimir Solovëv's *Feldmarshal Kutuzov* (1939). Although celebrated primarily as a novelist, Leonov also wrote several plays before World War II. These include dramatizations of his novels *Barsuki* (The Badgers, 1927) and *Skutarevskii* (1934); *Untilovsk* (1928), about a remote Siberian community; *Provintsial'naia istoriia* (A Provincial Story, 1928), a somber picture of rural life; *Usmirenie Badadoshkina* (The Taming of Badadoshkin, 1929), about a profiteer during the period of the New Economic Policy (1921–28); *Volk* (The Wolf, 1939), like *The Orchards of Polovchansk* also dealing with military preparedness; *Metel* (The Snowstorm, 1939), which in its original form was suppressed by censors during rehearsals by the Malyi Theater because of its unflattering portrait of a corrupt Soviet official; and *Obyknovennyi chelovek* (An Ordinary Person, 1940–41), Leonov's sole comedy, about the thwarted materialistic ambitions of a mother for her daughter. Leonov wrote two plays during the war: *Nashestvie* (Invasion, 1942), which has long been regarded as one of the best Soviet plays to come out of World War II; and *Lenushka* (1943), which, despite its similar celebration of Russian heroism, has never enjoyed the esteem accorded *Invasion*. Leonov's last play, *Zolotaia kareta* (The Golden Coach, 1946–55), also ran afoul of the authorities, like *The Snowstorm*, because of its frank depiction of the problems of readjustment to postwar life among residents of a devastated provincial town.

Leonov's *The Orchards of Polovchansk*, though written in 1936, revised, and first staged in 1939, buzzes with the electric atmosphere of imminent war and resonates with themes of patriotism, heroism, obscure political intrigue, and impending conflict that awkwardly contend for balance with ingredients of Chekhovian style. An ominous aura of impending military collision is given weight by two brothers in uniform: one who is killed in the line of duty, and another who is on military maneuvers in the vicinity of Polovchansk, scene of the drama. The sounds of tanks, artillery, and rockets reverberate throughout the play, underscoring in a sense the fragility of the calm reigning at Polovchansk. It is also made clear against whom the military precautions are being taken. The Germans and Japanese are mentioned directly on a few occasions and, as if to emphasize the point, a principal character frequently recalls his fighting against the Germans (possibly in the First World War and most probably in the "intervention" during the Civil War). *The Orchards of Polovchansk* captures the sense of evil encroaching on a calm, orderly way of life. The sounds of war games are distant at first, but they continue to draw menacingly nearer. In trying to strengthen the underlying meaning of his play, Leonov may have been operating symbolically with both the death of one character and the ironically juxtaposed arrival of a villain. If the untimely death foreshadows the death of many heroic young men in a great conflict looming on the horizon, then the villain's reappearance seems to suggest the impossibility of ever fully eradicating evil from life.

Unlike Leonov, who has been admired more for his prose fiction than his plays, Vladimir Solovëv was mainly a dramatist who specialized in historical subjects. An erstwhile collaborator of Meyerhold's, he built his reputation as a dramatist mainly on such plays as *Velikii gosudar* (The Great Sovereign, 1943–55), about Ivan the Terrible; *Feldmarshal Kutuzov* (Field Marshal Kutuzov, 1938–39); *Denis Davydov* (1953–55), about the Russian hussar poet who distinguished himself as a partisan fighter during the war against Napoleon; and *Pobeditelei sudyat* (The Victors Are Judged, 1953), which is set in the time of the Franco-Prussian war of 1870–71. For Solovëv, the gathering clouds of war in the late 1930s awakened recollections of past threats to Russian sovereignty. The historical parallel of richest dramatic potential was, of course, Napoleon's invasion of Russia in 1812. Solovëv consequently used the event as the basis for his most highly regarded historical drama, the verse play *Field Marshal Kutuzov*. Produced by the Vakhtangov Theater in 1939, and later awarded a Stalin Prize, the play proved immensely popular and continued to be performed in a number of Soviet theaters throughout the war years.

The popularity of *Field Marshal Kutuzov* rests mainly on its old-fashioned patriotism and on the titular character who was conceived as a repository of traditional Russian wisdom. No matter how great the pressures on him, Kutuzov cannot be swayed from his decision, once taken, to avoid engaging the French forces until the possibility of victory is greatest. The troops under him and several of his highest-ranking officers yearn for the chance to give the French battle, and regard the strategy of retreat as a blemish on the honor on the Russian army, and indeed on Russia itself. But Kutuzov will not be deterred. Once his plan has been formulated, he will see it through to the end. So admired and respected is he by his men that, even where doubts exist, no active opposition emerges against him. When his strategy ultimately succeeds, Kutuzov's wisdom—the wisdom of a Russian patriot and leader whose thoughts for the well-being of his country are not predicated on the glory of a single battlefield success—is vindicated.

Apart from some rearrangement of scenes, it was principally the character of Kutuzov that Solovëv revised most in a later version of his play. In the original version, Solovëv emphasized both the doubts of others (especially Tsar Alexander I) concerning the elevation of Kutuzov to the head of the Russian armies over General Barclay de

Tolly; and the reluctance of Kutuzov to assume the responsibility, in view of his own uncertainty about the best course of action to pursue against Napoleon. However, in the revised version of the play, the heroic stature of Kutuzov is magnified by the total elimination, or reduction, of those scenes devoted to the politics behind Kutuzov's appointment, and the old warrior's doubts as to strategy. Moreover, in the later version, Solovëv intensifies the ideological conflict engendered by Kutuzov's strategy. Tsar Alexander's appointment of Kutuzov—in the earlier version of the play—comes as a reluctant submission to the will of the Russian people, to whom Kutuzov appears the only Russian military leader capable of driving the French from Russian soil. Alexander's personal choice—one aggressively supported by Sir Robert Wilson, the English military attaché—is General Bennigsen, the commander of the Russian cavalry. In the revised version, the lines are even more sharply drawn between the conflicting interests represented by Bennigsen and Kutuzov. Bennigsen became unequivocally a tool by which Wilson hoped to put the Russian military to the best service of English interests. Wilson pushes hard for an immediate battlefield encounter with the French. Kutuzov opposes this on the grounds that the Russians should not meet the French in battle until a reasonable chance for victory exists; that can come only when French supply lines are stretched and bad weather and partisan raids have begun to take their toll.

Kutuzov similarly opposes Wilson's insistence that the Russians continue the war against Napoleon in the west, once the French have been driven from Russia. The issue of the possible Russian pursuit of the French across Europe assumes such significance in Solovëv's play that the closing words are those of a dying Kutuzov again admonishing Tsar Alexander to hold Russia's interests paramount and avoid the temptation to extend the war beyond the Russian frontier.

The opposition of conflicting ideologies in the later version of the play turns on the now elevated issue of loyalty and patriotism. As a *native* Russian, a true son of Russia, Kutuzov must place the well-being of his country and its people above all other considerations. But in the case of Bennigsen, there are mitigating circumstances. Because of his German origin, Bennigsen is presented as more susceptible to the influence of the English military attaché and therefore capable of taking positions ultimately harmful to the Russian cause. It is interesting to observe how this ethnic "taint," above all with repect to military officers of German origin, has been carried over from the Soviet Civil War literature of the 1920s.

The danger of the influence represented by Wilson is spelled out in no uncertain terms in the later version of the play. In act I, scene 7, Kutuzov declares at one point to Prince Bagration, the commander of the Second Russian Army, that Wilson is a spy. Earlier, Solovëv had been content merely to imply that Wilson's advice to the Russians was guided by English self-interest. Tsar Alexander's confidence in Wilson and his support of Bennigsen are likewise contrasted with the confidence in and support of Kutuzov by the Russian people and the masses of the Russian armed forces. The implication, present in the first version of the play, that the tsar's enthusiasm for Bennigsen is motivated largely by the desire to see the popular Kutuzov humbled by the failure that Alexander sees as inescapable, is also less muted in the later version. Shortly after labeling Wilson a spy, Kutuzov adds that Wilson's spying serves not one but two courts, suggesting that the second court is that of Tsar Alexander, whose motives in advancing Kutuzov to the command of the Russian armies are tied to interests incompatible with those of the Russian people. Hence, in the later version of the play, dramatic conflict assumes a primarily ideological dimension. Kutuzov and the Russian people, whose support propels him to the command of the armies over the objections of many, assume the collective role of defender of the Fatherland against enemies from without and within. The external enemy is Napoleon, plainly visible, portrayed at times convincingly as clever and cynical. Less obvious, though hardly less dangerous, is the internal enemy represented in the later version by Wilson, the emissary of an ally who seeks to promote only the interests of his own country, England, and by Tsar Alexander himself, whose jealousy and desire for vengeance on Kutuzov cast him in the role of an enemy of the Russian people, whose collective will Kutuzov embodies.

The element of ethnic "taint" (Bennigsen) and the dimension of class conflict (Kutuzov and the Russian people versus royalty and nobility—Tsar Alexander and Sir Robert Wilson) are more sharply delineated in the later version of *Field Marshal Kutuzov*. The significance of this extends beyond Solovëv's play. The more imminent war appeared to the Soviet Union in the late 1930s, the more intensified became the spirit of Russian nationalism. This is reflected in two aspects of the play in particular. The first is the exaltation of Russianness represented by the figure of Kutuzov himself and by the heroic Russian peasant partisans welded into an effective fighting force by the hussar poet Denis Davydov (whom Solovëv made the subject of his next historical drama). By weighting the role of the partisans (their harassment of the French is presented as a major factor in the success of Kutuzov's strategy), Solovëv not only pays his due to ideology (the heroic people, the *narod*, are the backbone of the campaign against the enemy). He also completes the equation of conflicting forces within the Russian camp, since Kutuzov emerges as the expression of the will of the Russian people and eventually triumphs because he has the support of the people. The other expression of Russian nationalism is the shadow cast over the intentions of foreigners and the loyalty of non-Russians or people of non-Russian origin living within the borders of the state, especially Germans. Nationalism mates with xenophobia to produce suspicion even of potential allies.

Like Solovëv's other historical dramas, *Field Marshal Kutuzov* is written in verse. But even though he subtitled his work a "historical chronicle," which obviously brings Shakespeare to mind, Solovëv made no serious attempt to revive the neo-Shakespeareanism of, for example, Pushkin's *Boris Godunov*. The basic meter of *Field Marshal Kutuzov* is not the iambic pentameter "blank verse" of *Boris Godunov*, but the twelve-

syllable iambic line used for most Russian tragedy down to the middle of the nine-
teenth century. However, to avoid the monotony of a completely regular metric pattern, Solovëv introduced lines of shorter length and imperfect rhymes in different patterns. The play also has frequent (though less abrupt) changes of scene, reminiscent of
*Boris Godunov*, as well as substantial monologues and soliloquies situated at key junc-
tures. But Solovëv's language, while in verse, is essentially unpoetic and functional.
The sense of the historical past is conveyed by the use of verse, an older metric pattern,
and certain devices of the traditional chronicle-drama genre, such as soliloquies, a
large cast of characters, and a number of scene changes. The result, however, is an
occasionally interesting historical drama in verse, but not poetic drama.

Plays written after June 22, 1941 were of course more clearly oriented to the present, but some remained sensitive to the aptness of historical analogy as shown in
Solovëv's *Field Marshal Kutuzov*. An example is Aleksandr Afinogenov's *Nakanune*
(On the Eve), which was actually written after the German invasion, in August 1941—
the playwright himself was killed in an air raid on November 5, 1941—but was set in
the June days immediately preceding the outbreak of hostilities and in the first month
of the war.

The three-act play is not one of Afinogenov's best and should be regarded as an
exercise in devotional drama. Its aim, at the very outset of the war, was to inspire
courage and a belief in ultimate victory. The first scene of act 1 introduces the principal
figures, particularly Andrei Zavialov, an agronomist in his middle thirties, and his Turk-
men wife, Dzheren. The gathering clouds of war cast a long shadow over the party
being held in the country house of Andrei's father, the old smelter Timofei Zavialov,
on the outskirts of Moscow to celebrate the arrival of Andrei's older brother, Ivan, a
major-general in the Red Army. The late June evening, the sounds of music, and the
effort of the guests to savor the remaining days of peace create a distinctly lyrical aura.
But the drone of planes, the rumble of tanks, and war bulletins over the radio at the
beginning of the second scene of act 1 shatter the mood. Caught up in the conflict, the
Zavialovs and their friends quickly adapt to the altered circumstances of their lives.
When the German advance can no longer be halted, they make the painful decision
to torch the nearby wheat field around which so much of their lives has revolved. The
action costs Dzheren her life. At the end of the play, when she is being carried in near
death, her last words are: "The wheat is burning, Andryusha, I know. . . . My darling,
I'm fine."[4] The silence that follows is soon filled with the growing roar of bombers
flying overhead. The play could have closed appropriately at this point. But to translate
Dzheren's heroic death into the appropriate patriotic finale, Afinogenov brings Ivan
forward to declare: "Sister, we vow to avenge ourselves for your death, for the burned
villages and cities, for the earth trampled by German boots, for our tears and grief . . .

for everything! We swear on your death to scorn death and to show no mercy in battle. We swear to destroy pity in ourselves and to hate the enemy as fervently as we love life and our Fatherland. Blood for blood, and death for death; our vengeance will be terrible. We swear it!" As all the other characters now assembled on stage repeat the vow, the drone of the bombers changes into a mighty symphony of battle.

The scorched-earth policy symbolized by the torch put to the wheat field in *On the Eve* reiterates the Russian tactics of Napoleonic times. In *Field Marshal Kutuzov*, Solovëv emphasizes Russianness and the transformation of civilians, especially ordinary people, into guerrillas. These emphases reappear in Afinogenov's play. Once caught up in the war, the Zavialovs and their friends swiftly transform themselves into heroic guerrilla fighters. The Russianness empasized by Solovëv, above all through the figure of Kutuzov, expresses itself in *On the Eve* by means of an insistent cultural continuity. To celebrate Ivan's homecoming, one of the characters is asked to recite poems by Maiakovskii and Bagritskii; but the greater preference is more classical—Lermontov's romantic poem with a Georgian setting, *Mtsyri*. It is also more appropriate in view of Dzheren's eastern background. Classical Russian literature again appears as a link with the past in act 2, scene 3, when the actress Garaeva reads selections from Tolstoy's *War and Peace* to the men of an antiaircraft battery now located on land adjacent to the Zavialov property. When Ivan, the Red Army general, continues the reading, he chooses, significantly, a passage from the novel in which Kutuzov expounds the rationale behind his strategy of allowing the invader to advance as far as necessary until, like a ripe fruit, he is ready for the picking.

The years 1941 to 1945 produced, expectedly, a rich crop of plays about the war. Most were schematic exercises in the propaganda of heroism and nationalism. A few, however, rose above the ordinary. These include, by common consensus, such works as *Dym otechestva* (Smoke of the Fatherland, 1942), a joint effort by the Tur Brothers (the collective pseudonym of Leonid Tubelskii, 1905–61, and Pëtr Ryzhei, 1908–?) and Lev Sheinin (1905–?); *Russkie liudi* (The Russian People, 1942), by the best-known Russian writer of the war period, Konstantin Simonov (1915–79); *Nashestvie* (Invasion, 1942), by Leonid Leonov; and *Front* (1942), by the popular Ukrainian playwright, Aleksandr Korneichuk (1905–72). Perhaps it is no mere coincidence that the best Soviet plays about the war date from the early years of the conflict. Impressions were then the strongest and the need to create a war repertoire so urgent that dramatists seemed able to enjoy a somewhat greater latitude in their treatment of events than was true later.

The Tur Brothers, as a team or in collaboration with other dramatists, began their career in the late 1920s and early 1930s. Together with Iakov Gorev and Aleksandr Shein, Pëtr "Tur" wrote *Neft* (Oil, 1929), about workers in the Baku oil fields, *Utopia* (1930), about the construction and launching of a vessel named Utopia and used here to symbolize the Soviet Union, and *Sem' volny* (Seven Waves, 1935), about imprisoned criminals. With the minor playwright Iosif Prut, who specialized in military subjects, the Tur Brothers wrote *Vostochnii batalion* (The Eastern Battalion, 1935), which deals with a foreign legion composed of various nationalities. The collaboration with Lev Sheinin, a coroner who had won some literary renown with his detective fiction, proved the most productive. Several melodramas about the adventures of spies in Russia and of Soviet diplomats abroad were written by the Tur-Sheinin team in the late 1930s. The best of these was *Ochnaia stavka* (The Confrontation, 1938). Their collaboration continued through the war years and resulted in three plays: *Smoke of the Fatherland*, *Chrezvychainyi zakon* (The Extraordinary Law, 1943), and *Poedinok* (The Duel, 1944).

More substantial a war play than Afinogenov's *On the Eve*, *Smoke of the Fatherland* is particularly striking for its heavy dosage of melodrama, attributable no doubt to Sheinin's collaboration. The scene is again the grim days of the invasion in 1941, but before much time elapses, a novel element appears in the form of a somewhat quixotic "White" Russian, a former landowner's son who returns to his father's estate in the village of Viazovka in the uniform of a German officer. He reclaims the family property and promptly sets about restoring the old order. His own cruelty and that of the Germans, in relation to whom he is a mere puppet, ultimately bring him and his fantastic vision of a resurrected pre-revolutionary Russia to ruin. But before his just deserts as the villain of the piece are meted out with all the inexorable logic of traditional melodrama, he remains the central focus of interest through much of the play. The brave partisans led by Kasatkin, and even the stereotypical Russian traitor—Lisovskii—are little more than devices of conflict and contrast until melodrama completely dictates the tempo of the last two scenes (the play is divided into seven) and interest shifts from character to incident.

The Tur Brothers and Sheinin strive for a high degree of excitement early in the play and use traditional melodramatic techniques to achieve their goal: scene endings coinciding with peaks in the action or loaded with suspense, withheld information, and onstage physical confrontations and violence. Because of its pervasive melodramatic character, *Smoke of the Fatherland* is a rather effective, even interesting, play despite its share of such commonplaces of Soviet war drama as brutal Germans, heroic Russian partisans, the prank-loving but colorful and endearing guerrilla hero (Petia Zabudko), the traitor Lisovskii, who stays behind to throw in his lot with the Germans, and the eventual Soviet victory.

As the returned "White," Zhikharёv commands attention more because of his novelty as a character in the drama of the period than for his intrinsic worth as a dramatic portrait. In writing plays about the war, during the conflict, Soviet dramatists had obvious expectations to fulfill. The enemy had to be uniformly portrayed as cruel and evil, and the Russians, courageous and heroic. In the forefront of Russian valor stood peasants, workers, and other Soviet "little people" transformed into brave partisans. The inevitability of a Soviet victory always had to be held before the audience. The virtues of Russian nationalism and the continuity of Russian culture also had to be emphasized. But Soviet dramatists, like dramatists anywhere, were anxious to make their plays as theatrically viable as possible and sought ways of accomplishing this despite the ideological demands placed on them. This seemed even more the case in the early years of the war. For a greater sense of verisimilitude, dramatists introduced the figure of the disloyal Russian who seeks to feather his own nest by collaborating with the Germans.

But a bizarre character such as Zhikharëv in *Smoke of the Fatherland* is less an acknowledgment of the existence of the type than a reflection of the dramatist's desire to make his work exciting and even suspenseful notwithstanding the demands of ideology. This is particularly evident in the last scene of *Smoke of the Fatherland*. The peasants of Viazovka are being positioned for the filming of a German propaganda documentary. They will appear at the bottom of a staircase ready to present the traditional Russian bread-and-salt greeting to their returned master, Zhikharëv, who will emerge at the top of the staircase wearing a black suit laid out for him by the peasant Efim. At the crucial moment, when everyone's gaze is directed to the top of the staircase, illuminated now with klieg lights, and the cameras have begun whirring, a German military band playing stirring music all the while in the background, it is not Zhikharëv who appears, but Efim. Moving slowly down the staircase with a swaying motion, he announces to the incredulous onlookers that he has just taken the life of Zhikharëv.

The kind of theatrics manifest in such a scene were by no means extraordinary in Soviet drama of the 1930s. But their appearance in the usually conservative Soviet war plays comes as something of a surprise and must, in the final analysis, be taken on an individual basis. Even when writing about the German invasion, the Tur Brothers and Lev Sheinin were loath to abandon their melodramatic habits. The result was that their plays about the war, while generally schematic, were nonetheless composed with a keen sense of theater.

Beyond doubt, the most celebrated play to come out of the war was Konstantin Simonov's *The Russian People*. So well known was the work in the United States that no less distinguished a figure in the contemporary American theater than Clifford Odets prepared an "American acting version" of it for the Theatre Guild of New York.

Simonov's playwriting began in 1938 when he wrote his first dramatic work, *Obyknovennaia istoriia* (A Familiar Story), about an Arctic explorer. It was revised and produced two years later in Moscow under the new title *Istoriia odnoi liubvi* (The Story of One Love). It fared badly with the critics, but Simonov more than made up for it not long after with his very successful *Paren iz nashego goroda* (A Lad from Our Town, 1940–41), about a tank driver, for which he was awarded a Stalin Prize of 100,000 rubles. Certain of the play's characters became virtual household names in the Soviet Union and reappear in *The Russian People*. Simonov's other wartime plays were *Zhdi menya* (Wait for Me, 1942) and *Tak i budet* (So Will It Be, 1944). The first, about the heroic escape from behind German lines of a downed Russian pilot, driven, above all, by the desire to return to the wife he left behind, was a dramatization of an immensely popular poem from a collection written by Simonov for his wife and titled *S toboi i bez tebia* (With You and without You; see Rothstein, this volume).

*The Russian People* is a fairly predictable Soviet war drama. Set in August 1941, in a town already occupied by the Germans, it creates a sense of excitement from the exploits of heroic Russians, men and women alike, the touch-and-go struggle with the Germans, the daring and danger of secret missions behind enemy lines, and chance encounters. The romantic love of hero and heroine, the death of a noble comrade, and the heroic transformation of ordinary people make for the inevitable sentimentality. For dramatic interest as well as verisimilitude, the Russian ranks also include cowards, defectors, and traitors. For the sake of historical continuity, some vestige of pre-revolutionary Russia is introduced, overt party propaganda gives way to Russian patriotism and nationalism, and the drama concludes with a Russian triumph. The familiar ingredients are all there, to be sure, in Simonov's play, but they hardly define the great appeal of the work and the theatrical presence behind it.

Although similar in some respects to *Smoke of the Fatherland*, *The Russian People* is better constructed and broader in its appeal. In the Tur-Sheinin play, dramatic interest is divided between Zhikharëv and Kasatkin's partisans. In Simonov's work, it is more concentrated. A young partisan girl, Valia, slips back and forth on secret assignments between the German-held town on one side of a river and the Russian forces on the other side. Her dangerous exploits, and the constant threat of capture, maintain a high degree of suspense and serve not only as a link between the two opposing camps but, more importantly from a dramatic point of view, as a useful means of relating figures on both sides of the river to the central action. In the occupied town, Valia is sheltered by the wife of the German-appointed mayor who in effect collaborates with the invaders by meekly doing their bidding. The cruel death of the mayor's soldier son, his wife's revenge, and her calculated involvement of her husband in her own noble death—all occurring at a fast pace in act 2, scene 1—justifiably rank among the more powerful episodes in Soviet World War II drama and are as theatrically effective as the staircase scene in *Smoke of the Fatherland*.

The Russian military in Simonov's play, including Valia's romantic partner, Ivan Safonov, are a gallery of familiar Soviet wartime dramatic types. But one figure in particular stands out: Vasin, a former tsarist officer in his early sixties. He and Zhikharëv from *Smoke of the Fatherland* both represent a common type in Soviet war drama—the individual with pre-revolutionary associations. In the Tur Brothers-Sheinin play, Zhikharëv is the former "White" who returns to Russia with the German army in the hope of restoring the old order. He represents a sequel, as it were, to a figure such as Colonel Talberg in Bulgakov's Civil War play, *Days of the Turbins*. From the "White" who flees revolutionary Russia with the Germans, we now have in Zhikharëv the "White" who returns to Soviet Russia with an invading German army some twenty years later, obsessed again by the dream of a Red-free Russia. Vasin is the other side of the coin—the tsarist officer who makes common cause with the Soviets. The favorable treatment of an old tsarist officer such as Vasin who sides with the Soviets, even to the point of sending his own nephew to certain death, has a lineage in Russian post-revolutionary drama going back to the 1920s and the figure, specifically, of Captain Bersenev in Boris Lavrenëv's play *Razlom* (Breakup). The ideological rationale behind a figure such as Vasin is clear enough. Common cause against a traditional enemy (the Germans) takes precedence over partisan antagonisms rooted in the Civil War. In the face of a *German* invasion, there are only Russians, not "Reds" or "Whites"; and the defense of the fatherland far outweighs the defense of a political system.

It is also interesting to observe here the extent to which plays about World War II followed certain patterns of the drama of the 1920s dealing with the Civil War. This was natural in view of the fact that the campaigns of the Civil War represented the weightiest military engagements of the Red Army up to the German invasion of 1941. Moreover, the events of the Civil War generated a dramatic literature which would obviously have suggested itself as a model for playwrights during World War II.

Just as there are pro- and anti-Soviet former tsarist officers in the World War II drama, so are there Soviet defectors as well as heroes. In Simonov's play, the defector is Kozlovskii (alias Vasilenko), whose role parallels that of Lisovskii in *Smoke of the Fatherland*. Kozlovskii is a pivotal character in the play. A German spy, he infiltrates the Russian camp by following Valia's route across the river. His mission is to collect intelligence and to lay a trap for Valia. The trap, and the response of the Russians to Valia's eventual capture and imprisonment, trigger much of the melodramatic intensity of Simonov's play. Kozlovskii is also used to define the ideological significance of Vasin. In his one major contrivance in *The Russian People*, Simonov makes Kozlovskii Vasin's nephew, whom the older man has not seen in a long time. After revealing his identity to Vasin, Kozlovskii discloses his true loyalties and attempts to enlist Vasin's support. Not only does Vasin refuse to assist Kozlovskii, he turns him over to Safonov, thereby setting in motion the ultimately successful plan to rescue Valia and the play's optimistic conclusion.

Familiar ingredients reappear in Leonid Leonov's best-known and most frequently performed war play, *Invasion*: a small Russian town in the early days of the war; stock types such as the anti-Red former Russian émigré (Mosalskii), the heroic Communist (Kolesnikov), compromising Russians anxious to save their necks at any cost (Faiunin and Kokoryshkin), exemplary Russians (Dr. Talanov and his family), brutal Germans (Wiebel, Spurre, and Kuntz); and a happy ending (the final-curtain liberation of the occupied town by Soviet parachutists). But the presence of such commonplaces in Leonov's play is misleading since it is anything but an exercise in Soviet World War II dramatic topoi. If partisan resistance and heroics dominate the action in such plays as *Smoke of the Fatherland* and *The Russian People*, *Invasion* was conceived along different lines. War is the inescapable fact of Leonov's play, the background against which everything in the drama must be viewed and, indeed, measured. Yet within this context, the dramatist's concern shifts from the epic to the lyric, from the drama of the group to the drama of the individual. This shift enabled Leonov to write a play which certainly has flaws (the *deus ex machina* victorious ending, for one), but which deserves consideration as one of the most provocative to come out of the war. It also reflects a sincere desire on the part of the dramatist to transform the experience of war into something intellectually more engaging than the rousing patriotism to be found in the plays of most of his peers.

At the core of *Invasion* is an inquiry into the psychologically transformative power of war's suffering, a power sufficient to turn an arrogant, self-centered, young ne'er-do-well into a man possessing the courage to sacrifice himself so that a better man (in a civic sense) might live. The subject of this transformation is the erring son, Fëdor, of the town doctor, Talanov. In the first draft of the play, the cause of Fëdor's break with his family was his innocent involvement in a political crime. In the final version, it is because of a sordid love affair about which—perhaps wisely from a dramatic point of view—Leonov is sparing of details. After an absence of three years and a temporary parting from the woman, Fëdor returns to his father's home. Shortly thereafter, the town is overrun by the Germans. The residents begin to adjust to the new circumstances of their lives and it is this adjustment that Leonov dramatizes rather than the more conventional heroics of resistance.

Fëdor's restlessness and recalcitrance seem impervious to change until the play's pivotal episode—the brutal assault by the Germans on a teenage girl, Aniska, the granddaughter of the Talanovs' servant, Demidevna. Typical of Leonov's low-keyed approach throughout *Invasion*, the assault on Aniska, like other brutalities in the play, is relegated to an offstage action only the effects of which are shown onstage. Aniska's assault becomes the turning point in Fëdor's life. The horrible violation of innocence succeeds in cracking the wall of arrogance and self-interest narcissistically nurtured over several years. A compulsion to atone, to reestablish contact with the collective, arises in Fëdor and needs just the proper catalyst to be realized. This comes when a local Communist official, Kolesnikov, wounded and presumably a partisan, is sheltered in the Talanov home after he is brought there by Fëdor's sister. Fëdor's earlier relationship with Kolesnikov (in act 1) was marked by a kind of resentful acrimony. But now the wounded and hunted Kolesnikov becomes the instrument of Fëdor's regeneration.

When it becomes apparent that the Germans have traced Kolesnikov to Dr. Talanov's house and will arrest him the moment he leaves it, Fëdor takes Kolesnikov's place. Since neither man is known to the Germans by sight, the ruse goes undetected. The possibility of disclosure arises in the third act of the play, during the interrogation of Fëdor, at which his parents are present. But at the crucial moment, when they perceive what is happening, the Talanovs resist the natural impulse to reveal their son's true identity and thereby save his life, perhaps intuiting Fëdor's spiritual need. The final act of Fëdor's personal drama, when he at last attains self-fulfillment, comes at the end of the play. In a prison cell awaiting execution, Fëdor is not immediately accepted by his fellow Russians as Kolesnikov's surrogate, worthy of being executed as Kolesnikov. The inmates debate the matter and finally accept Fëdor in recognition of his undeniable heroism. He and two other prisoners die before the others are rescued in a daring surprise raid by Soviet parachutists.

The ending of *Invasion*, and the few, doubtless obligatory, references to Stalin's military leadership preceding it, sound the only really discordant notes in the otherwise subdued psychological drama almost wholly devoid of heroics, strident patriotism, and overt political propaganda. The more understated quality of Leonov's play, which sets it apart from most Russian wartime drama, is carefully developed, from the outset with the lack of hysteria among the townspeople in the face of the German occupation, to the moment when Fëdor quietly confronts his death. The actual occupation of the town by the Germans is not dramatized, as the focus shifts entirely to the process of adjustment by the townspeople and their efforts to preserve some degree of normal life despite the occupation. The assault on Aniska occurs offstage and produces no emotional excesses onstage. The murder of German officers by Kolesnikov and his guerrillas is never seen by the audience. The seizure and death of Fëdor are also kept offstage, as is the arrival at the end of the play of the parachutists who appear out of nowhere in the sky.

If there is less overt physical action in Leonov's play than in other Russian war dramas, it is also true that significant character interaction and transformation are shaped by action rather than by words or by the confrontation of opposing personalities. Leonov's technique is nowhere better demonstrated than in Fëdor's metamorphosis and the emotion-charged (if emotionless) interrogation scene in act 4, where his parents are faced with the agonizing decision whether to reveal his true identity to the Germans. The lack of any "soul searching" on Fëdor's part may create the impression that his metamorphosis lacks sufficient motivation. But this is not the case. The change is neither arrived at suddenly nor theatricalized, as it might easily have been. It springs instead from the circumstances of Fëdor's private life and his psychological state the moment he beholds the battered body of Aniska. Rather than being thrust suddenly upon the audience, Fëdor's transformation is disclosed piecemeal, unobtrusively, and only through action.

On the formal level, one further aspect of *Invasion* merits comment—Leonov's extensive use throughout the play of long, detailed stage directions. These not only provide information on attire, gestures, props, and so on, but at times are so literary and narrative as to seem aimed principally at a reader. This reflects, one suspects, not just the dramatist's concern for the manner in which his work is brought to the stage, but a certain dissatisfaction with the limitations of the dramatic form on the part of a writer essentially more comfortable with the expansiveness of the novel. Some of the best examples of such stage directions occur in the dramatically effective third act in which Fëdor, impersonating Kolesnikov, is interrogated in the presence of his parents, and at the very beginning of act 4. Viewed more closely, these stage directions, especially in act 3, create the distinct impression that Leonov was striving for something even beyond narration. The room in which the interrogations are conducted is filled with a variety of characters, Russian and German alike. When the Germans are first introduced into the scene, the stage direction calls for their moving in a rigid, wooden manner reminiscent of pasteboard figures, or puppets: "Now guests of a secondary significance are visible. They are pasteboard, with the restricted movements of mannequins. Hearing the non-Russian speech of the new arrivals, Kokoryshkin peeped out and then seemed even to shrink in size."[5]

In light of other directions in the same act, it is apparent that Leonov sought not only to convey the impression of something nonhuman about the Germans through their physical movements, but also to introduce an element of the grotesque into the scene. Consider, for example, the directions governing the movements of the German officer, Spurre, and the Russian flunky, Kokoryshkin. Spurre has just come into the room and Kokoryshkin begins to greet him. But before he finishes, Spurre mistakes him for the prisoner Kolesnikov. Kokoryshkin barely perceives what is happening when the German grabs him by the collar and rushes him out of the room. The first part of the stage direction reads: "Like a little feather, he turns Kokoryshkin around with his back to the door and leads him with his arm extended. They exit rhythmically, as though dancing, leg to leg and face to face. Kokoryshkin offers no resistance and is just very afraid of stepping on Spurre's toes. . . . "[6] For stage directions such as these, employed, above all, to heighten through movement the already grotesque character of the entire act, one has to go back to the comic art of Gogol or Sukhovo-Kobylin whose inspiration—at least for the act—should not be discounted.

The acclaim with which such plays as Simonov's *The Russian People* and Leonov's *Invasion* were greeted was paralleled by the controversy touched off by the play *Front*, also dating from 1942, by the prolific and well-regarded Ukrainian dramatist, Aleksandr Korneichuk. The esteem in which Korneichuk was long held in the Soviet Union is reflected in the inclusion of his name in virtually all accounts of Soviet *Russian* drama, despite his Ukrainian background. Although several of his plays such as *Pravda* (The Truth, 1937), *Bogdan Khmelnitskii* (1939), and a few war dramas are set in Ukraine and feature Ukrainian characters, his most successful works are more general in nature and avoid figures with distinct regional association. The best examples of this prior to *Front* are his first important play, *Gibel' eskadry* (The Sinking of the Squadron, 1933), about heroic Red seamen during the Revolution, and *Platon Krechet*

(1934, revised 1953), a popular work in its day featuring a self-effacing surgeon who performs an important operation while under suspicion of professional malpractice. So widely were Korneichuk's plays published and staged in Russian, he has, to all intents and purposes, been regarded as a Russian dramatist and has usually been treated as such by Soviet theater historians.

*Front*, Korneichuk's major wartime drama, owes much of its fame to the nature of its conflict. As a play, it is capably crafted, like most of Korneichuk's works for the stage, but it is less gripping than Simonov's *The Russian People* or Leonov's *Invasion*. It contains no noteworthy structural or stylistic features, no memorable moments, no characters developed beyond types. But it is bold in an ideological sense, and it was this boldness that attracted so much attention to the play when it first appeared on the pages of *Pravda* in the fall of 1942.

In Russian drama of the 1930s especially, conflict often revolved around the figure of a person who, in one way or another, becomes an obstruction in the path of Soviet progress. In Korneichuk's *Front*, the antistate theme has simply been updated and adapted to the circumstances of World War II. The *diversant*, or "wrecker," is now a stubborn, inflexible old general of Civil War fame, who holds a position of immense importance as a frontline commander against the Germans. General Gorlov's "wrecking" consists of a total inability to assimilate the methods of modern warfare. He believes that his way is best, but his faulty planning results in a series of blunders which eventually contribute to the death of his son, Sergei, who serves in his command. Through Gorlov and the sychophantic flunkies who surround him, Korneichuk attacks the ineptitude and outmoded thinking of older officers whose military experience was acquired in the Civil War, and who obstinately refuse to recognize that any changes in the concept and technique of warfare have taken place since then. Although he exhibits at times a genuine feeling for the heroism and sacrifice of men serving under him, Gorlov adds to his old-school complacency and unpardonable vanity a contempt for younger officers whose skills far surpass his. Having distinguished himself in the Civil War, Gorlov assumes that there is nothing more for him to learn about warfare, especially from younger men who lack his experience.

Predictably, the negative portrait of Gorlov is balanced by the positive figure of a brilliant younger officer named Ognëv. Ognëv chafes under Gorlov's obstinacy and stupidity, and in a decisive campaign countermands Gorlov's orders and turns a potential disaster into victory. Angered over such a challenge to his authority, Gorlov tries to break the younger man. By this time, however, higher military authorities and presumably Stalin himself as commander-in-chief have learned of both Gorlov's blunders and Ognëv's brilliance. They remove the older man and replace him as commander with Ognëv. Also opposed to Gorlov is his own brother, Miron, the director of an airplane factory. The conflict between Gorlov and Ognëv is of sufficient plausibility to sustain the play without the addition of Miron Gorlov, whose role is gratuitous.

When a military assignment brings Miron to his brother's theater of operations, he soon learns of the "crisis of command" and himself urges his brother to step down. In so adding a family dimension to the conflict of his play, Korneichuk was following an old path in Soviet drama. Husband and wife were on opposite sides in Konstantin Trenëv's "classic" Civil War drama, *Liubov' Iarovaia* (1925), and sisters in different political camps were similarly contrasted in Lavrenëv's *Breakup* and Isaak Babel's *Mariia* (1935). Korneichuk invests Miron with the function of a *raisonneur* through whom he voices his own (and the party's) attitude concerning obstructionist figures out of the past such as General Gorlov. Apart from this function, the character has little significance in the drama.

*Front* may possess relatively little value as dramatic literature, but there is no denying its importance in 1942 as a vehicle for thinly veiled criticism of older members of the military establishment such as the Civil War heroes Budënnyi and Voroshilov. Despair over early Soviet defeats in the second year of the war and the agonizing search for causes created a climate in which the appearance of a play such as *Front* would have aroused considerable controversy. Obviously, much of what Korneichuk portrays in *Front* struck a sympathetic chord, and opinion swung in favor of the play. But Korneichuk's boldness was also tempered by prudence. While exposing the anachronistic outlook of a General Gorlov, *Front* is careful to indicate the possibility of a younger officer such as Ognëv circumventing orders he considers ill-conceived and the speed with which a Gorlov is removed from a position of command when higher authorities become aware of the true state of affairs. In the end, in the manner of all didactic drama, evil is punished and good rewarded. General Gorlov is made to pay for his vanity, intransigence, and blundering with the twin loss of his son and his command. Through the vindication of Ognëv, and his elevation to Gorlov's command, virtue is once again rewarded. Keeping Korneichuk's high party connections in mind, *Front* can be read as a calculated endeavor to prepare public opinion for the replacement of outmoded but popular military leaders of Civil War vintage by younger, better-trained, and more up-to-date generals such as Konev and Zhukov whom Ognëv undoubtedly represents in the play.

Soviet World War II drama harbors few surprises. It is a drama intended to inspire hope in the inevitability of a Soviet victory by presenting audiences with portraits of heroism and courage. It weaves its conflicts out of familiar material. Yet despite the constraints of ideology and didactic purpose, a few dramatists sought ways to breathe the spirit of living theater into their plays. Whatever their shortcomings, the Tur Brothers' and Lev Sheinin's collaborative efforts and works by Afinogenov, Simonov, Leonov, and Korneichuk reflect an obvious desire to satisfy the demands of ideology without betraying the theatrical imperative to engage an audience. Reading, or rereading,

Soviet World War II drama over half a century after the events themselves provides keen insight into those issues theatrical writers at the time sought to emphasize, in order to instill a sense of national pride and purpose in a people of whom extraordinary demands were being made.

## Notes

1. The present chapter draws heavily on chapters 9 and 10 of my book, *Twentieth-Century Russian Drama: From Gorky to the Present* (New York: Columbia University Press, 1979).

2. For a fuller discussion of the activities of Soviet theaters in the early days of the war, see *Teatr*, 5 (May 1975), 5–10, 18–20, 48–53; *Stranitsy istorii sovetskogo teatra* (Moscow: Iskusstvo, 1965); and *Istoriia sovetskogo dramaticheskogo teatra*, V (Moscow: Nauka, 1969).

3. For a more detailed account of these, see ibid., pp. 80–93. See also Stites, this volume.

4. This and the following quotation are from the original text of the play as it appears in Aleksandr Afinogenov, *Pesy, stati, vystupleniia* (Moscow: Iskusstvo, 1977), vol. 2, 464.

5. Leonid Leonov, *Teatr*, 2 (1960), 57.

6. Ibid., 58.

# 8

# Frontline Entertainment

## Richard Stites

THE FRONTLINE CONCERT brigade (*kontsertnaia frontovaia brigada*) was a particular kind of performance vehicle that fit perfectly into the wartime design for reaching the troops with art that was entertaining, uplifting, morale-building, and of course politically correct. In it one finds a mix of virtually all the performing arts as well as a close interlock with nonperforming arts (cartooning, fiction). Neither its content nor its form was novel. The mixture of genres on stage goes back to European and prerevolutionary Russian traditions of variety show and cultural evening (called in Russian *vecher* or *kontsert*) that were preserved in Soviet performance art. Revolutionary spectacles, *estrada* (popular stage) concerts, workers' club entertainments, and even Kremlin command performances—all featured a blend of "high" and "middlebrow" numbers, verbal texts, music, and dance. The men and women who staffed the brigades in World War II came from theater, concert hall, ballet, opera, the world of popular music (stage, recording, and radio), folk ensembles, circus, puppetry, standup comedy, literature, and the movies. The cultural offering was correspondingly eclectic: at one end the light genres; at the other, the classics. Like Soviet radio, the brigades offered a mix; and to add to that mix, troops frequently performed for the performers: singing their own songs or "delivering" shells and bombs, autographed by entertainers, to the enemy after the concert.[1]

In form, the wartime brigades were a revival of the mobile agitation units sent to the front on trucks, trains, and riverboats during the Russian Civil War. In the 1920s, mobile culture was practiced with great vigor by youth, women's, and godless organizations, though entertainment was often subservient to numbingly dull political messages. During the stormy years of collectivization and cultural revolution, more organized cultural "crusades" were unleashed on the countryside. Once artists came under full centralized control in the early 1930s, they were expected not only to avoid certain themes and cleave to certain aesthetic rules (those of "socialist realism"), but also to carry out tasks assigned to them by the state, to mount concerts in factories and military units across the country, and to forge formal links (called *sheftsvo*) with the armed forces, enterprises, and institutions. Theaters and orchestras toured the peacetime barracks, camps, and naval bases; and when sporadic fighting broke out in the Soviet Far East with Japan in the late 1930s, companies were sent there as well. This activity was upgraded for the wars in Eastern Poland, Bukovina, and Finland in 1939–40 and greatly amplified after the German invasion of 1941.[2]

The production of popular culture during the war was a result of both voluntarism and mobilization, but the latter occurred to a degree undreamed of in other belligerent states, even Nazi Germany. This was especially true of live performance. The main organs of control and deployment were the Committee on the Arts, the Central Committee of RABIS (the Union of Art Workers—a startling formulation in itself). These committees, composed of thoroughly politicized art bureaucrats, received orders from military authorities and other organs and carried them out with great vigor. That mobilization of the arts began on the very first day of the war, June 22, 1941, is not such a remarkable thing given the long experience alluded to (see Kenez, this volume, for cinema mobilization). On day two of the invasion, RABIS sent out a circular to embarkation points, recruiting offices, and railroad stations informing troops that "wherever units of the army or navy can be found, art workers will be sharing their lives. Now as never before, art will be a mighty and warlike means of victory of communism over fascism."[3]

The organizational, numerical, and geographical scope of this operation was enormous by the standards of the time. To the front lines, the rear areas, and the towns were dispatched local branches of theaters, whole theater companies, and mixed brigades. RABIS was assisted by the Moscow TsDRI (Central House of the Arts), the Chief Political Administration of the Army, and other groups. Artists and performers of every kind could be seen lining up at TsDRI, waiting for assignments: the soprano A. V. Nezhdanova, the composer Dmitrii Kabalevskii, the architects A. V. Shchusev and Lev Rudnev, the painter Pavel Konchalovskii, and the pianist, Vladimir Sofronitskii. A typical order mandated on July 16, 1942, that the students in the fourth year at the State Institute of Theatrical Arts, Russia's main drama school, were to evacuate along with the Moscow Arts Theater to Saratov, there to form frontline theatrical brigades. A few scattered figures will give a sense of the tempo and density of activity. By October 1941, the government had sent out forty-two *estrada* brigades; by May 1942, sixty-one. At the local level, in Moscow Oblast during the first week (June 22–July 2), 450 concerts involving 700 artists were performed; and by early September, 3,000 concerts and fifty spectacles were mounted in the city of Moscow alone. As the Germans were approaching Leningrad, the authorities sent out Agit-Trucks with speakers and performers, including the noted film actor Nikolai Cherkasov, star of the 1938 anti-German film, *Aleksandr Nevskii*. In Rostov Oblast, thirty-six brigades with 992 artists gave over five hundred concerts. Odessa during the first ten days presented 250 concerts; Ordzhonikidze, 140, Irkutsk, 184.[4]

Various flat and probably inflated claims have been made about the total picture.

About 3,800 theater-concert and circus brigades were formed and deployed in the first year of the war, 700 from Moscow, 500 from Leningrad, and the rest from elsewhere. One participant claims that some 45,000 artists serving in 3,720 brigades performed over 400,000 concerts at the front. A similar claim puts it at 42,000 artists in around half a million performances. Another, more modest estimate, talks of more than 100,000 performances given at the front in the war years. Six hundred stage artists were decorated. Real totals may never be known, since many performances were unnoted or uncounted. Because of the huge numbers of troops and their vast dispersion, the brigades could never have saturated the armed forces. What impresses is the variety of places visited and the sheer mobility of civilian entertainment brigades in a war and a country noted for transport hunger. Although older and infirm artists and those needed to perform for the bigwigs stayed at home, a large number of the prewar stars of stage and screen appeared in front of the soldiers and sailors. How many troops were reached? If official figures were exaggerated, they may have been balanced by the fact that concerts were given in shifts—to dragged-out troops just relieved, pilots back from raids, ships pulling in to ports—thus extending the outreach that was recorded.[5]

The brigades made their way to every front on warplanes, boats, trains, and wagons, by cutter through mined waters, along a front bombed and shelled, across mine fields, arriving at trenches, bathhouses, and foxholes. Sometimes they got lost or were stopped by sentries and sent back. Impromptu forest theaters with stage and dressing rooms were organized; more often the "theater" was a glade, an open field, a truck bed, the deck of a warship, a hangar (see fig. 11). The comedienne M. Mironova, dressed in a light blue ball gown and silver slippers, regaled her audience from a float in the middle of a swamp. Standup comedian Vladimir Khenkin did his routines right on an airfield: the concert would stop, pilots would mount up, fly off and drop bombs, and then return to yell for a continuation of the show. Conversely, German air raids or offensives often provided "intermissions"—lasting as long as three hours. Actors sometimes had to help build defenses. In battle, some were caught in the fire, killed, or wounded. One touring company captured by the Germans was thrown alive into a well. Artists traveled light, usually without sets or costumes, though the troops preferred realistic re-creations of the original sets, theater, and costumes. Memoirs of performers cite audience size ranging from three to 1,000.[6]

Performances were held on all points of the compass: Vladivostok, a monastery in the Carpathian Mountains, Murmansk, Northern Norway, the polar seas, the Black and Baltic Seas—and hundreds of points between. Asians from warm climes wrapped in fur hats and quilted jackets found themselves in snowy north Russia in the fall of 1942 when the First Tadzhik Frontline Brigade put on national songs, dances, and comedy. Ethnic variety prevailed in the brigades: Jews, Poles, Asians, Caucasians, even recently vanquished Balts. Between jaunts to the front, artists raised morale in the rear-area cities. In Moscow, the popular big-band leader, Leonid Utësov, on learning about the invasion, quickly abandoned a concert of music adapted from Ivan Dzerzhinskii's 1935 opera *Quiet Don* to a program of patriotic songs. Satirist Nikolai Smirnov-Sokolovskii quickly invented the monologue, "Hitler will be Beaten." Actors' groups known as "Living Newspaper" offered poster-like crudity to induce high emotional responses. In beleaguered cities like Odessa, the *politotdel* (political arm) of the Communist Party ordered the formation of a brigade which gave five or six concerts every day during the seventy-three agonizing days of the siege. These concerts offered local patriotic and Jewish motifs in their songs and comedy acts: as the siege ended the entertainers boarded one of the last evacuation ships to the Northern Caucasus, where they continued to entertain. Leningrad witnessed 25,000 performances during the three-year blockade. When the only remaining theater in the city, the Musical Comedy, opened, it was filled every night in spite of cold, hunger, shells, and sale of tickets for bread rations (400 grams per ticket).[7]

What kind of cultural offerings did the brigades bring with them? Music, readings, poems, dance, one-act plays, scenes, lectures, circus acts, comedy routines. The very first artists to hit the frontline circuit represented in miniature the shape of the coming enterprise: literary readers Sergei Balashov and N. Efros; comedians Mikhail Garkavi, Vladimir Khenkin, Lev Mirov, E. Darskii, V. A. Dykhovichyi, M. Raskatov; singers Lidiia Ruslanova and Klavdiia Shul'zhenko; dance team Anna Redel and Mikhail Khrustalëv. To urban Russians (or those ruralists who possessed a radio), these were household names from the world of contemporary entertainment. Soviet performers thus brought not only cherished songs, poems, and plays—but also the pleasure of live celebrities who needed no more introduction to the Russian combatant than did the names of their American counterparts to GIs: Eddie Cantor, Al Jolson, Bing Crosby, Judy Garland, Jack Benny, or Bob Hope. Differences in style were significant, to be sure: there were no poetry readers or folk ensembles in the American armed forces entertainment network.

Poetry and prose readings had long been part of the Russian scene in public events. Russians adore the music of their language and the expressiveness of verse and rhyme; they listen with rapture to public readings live or on the radio. In choosing material to be uttered to the troops, it became apparent at once that the defiant and declamatory hoorah-patriotic themes of the immediate prewar period and the early months of the war struck a dissonant chord. Readers and reciters—mostly actors from stage and radio—had to find the right voice and tone in order to avoid the ring of falsity. They culled the classics with great care. Pushkin's epic poem, "Battle of Poltava,"

could easily be applied to the hope for another decisive victory over a foreign invader.[8]
The verse of the revolutionary poet Vladimir Maiakovskii inspired Sergei Balashov, a
theater actor and dramatic reader for the stage and radio. He gave live one-man readings of Russian, Soviet, and foreign prose and poetry replete with gestures, costumes,
and music. In the war, he declaimed Maiakovskii's verses on a submarine and among
tankers and—a habit of many—wrote some verses on a torpedo to be "delivered" to a
German ship hull. From Mikhail Lermontov, Lev Tolstoy, and Maxim Gorky, actors
drew well-quoted passages memorized by Soviet schoolchildren as well as fresh works
by the Soviet writers Mikhail Sholokhov, Konstantin Simonov, Aleksei Surkov, and
Aleksandr Tvardovskii. Foreign classics were sometimes used to unmask the difference
between "good Germans" and Nazis. Heinrich Heine's satire helped to explain German barbarism. (The use of a Heine monument in the Soviet occupation zone of Germany for this contrast can also be found in the famous postwar film, *Meeting on the
Elbe.*) Nonfiction readings of essays, newspaper articles, and pamphlets were occasionally offered as a way of giving voice to journalism.[9]

The whole idea of comedy on the Soviet warfront may come as a surprise to West-
erners who have been led (by misunderstanding and distortion emanating from both
sides) to see Russians as fundamentally humorless, and to those who see nothing funny
about war. The latter assumption also disturbed some Soviet critics in the early months
of the war, until it was shown that soldiers—even those who lay dying in hospital—
wanted to laugh at the old familiar foibles of everyday life as well as at the German
enemy. Stage comedy, though constricted by political censorship, had never disappeared from public life in the USSR, and a whole generation of radio and stage per-
sonages were at hand to generate cathartic laughter. Humor of another time and place
may not travel well over the decades, but a stretch of the cultural imagination may
help explain why soldiers guffawed to this rich and cruel ditty recited by comedians
at the front after the German defeat at Stalingrad:

> Frau Greta hasn't slept for days.
> Her Fritz does not respond
> To all those letters she has sent
> To the back of the beyond.
> "Mein Gott, what's happened to my Fritz
> Who's fighting on the Volga,
> And battling near some Stalingrad,"
> Thinks poor, distraught Frau Greta.
> It's time to realize, dear Frau,
> Your letters will not reach him now.
> Fritz is gone and simply is:
> "No Longer at This Address."[10]

On the same theme, Stalingrad, a comedian acted out a famous wartime poster showing Hitler in a wedding dress, weeping because he lost his "ring", i.e., the twenty-two German divisions encircling Stalingrad. Stand-up performers from the capitals like Arkadii Raikin, later to be the king of the Soviet comedy stage, maintained a certain level—hilarious but correct—of urban amusement. Others, like Iurii Timoshenko and Efim Berëzin had worked together before the war and, when drafted, began to do shows based on their invented characters, Galkin the Cook and Mochalkin the Bath Attendant (see fig. 10). Their skits, dialogue, ditties, dances, and routines were drawn from life on the company street, dugout, and front line. It was loose, unstructured, improvised, and coarse, resembling village fun-making, wedding parties, toasts, and jokes as well as prerevolutionary folk fair entertainment. Timoshenko used an exaggerated Ukrainian accent and vocabulary to project a bumpkin image—in a way that was, at the time in many places, nonoffensive. The down-to-earth quality of this entertainment was also found in the numerous adaptations of Tvardovskii's picaresque farce, *Vasilii Tërkin*, one of the most popular wartime writings, but probably known better to the troops in its acted versions than in the original written one.[11]

The warring nations of 1939–45 showed an extraordinary tendency to exalt and revere classical music and, through media promotion, turn it into something like a popular art (see Robinson, this volume). The occupied nations treasured their own musical heritage, particularly the romantic productions of the previous century. The music of Dvořák, Chopin, Rachmaninov, and Grieg on American radio and in movies was associated with the heroic struggles of beleaguered peoples. In war-racked Russia the most mournful strains of Chopin, Beethoven, and Chaikovskii filled the concert halls and airwaves. Liudmila Shaposhnikova, a drama student touring the front, thought that many of the troops were unprepared for classical music, and indeed had never heard any. But in fact, they received it well, although some of the pious accounts of audience reception—like accounts of the masses in 1917–18 hearing their first concerts—ought to be taken with caution. Most of the classical offerings were art songs, arias, or solo instrumental selections—usually squeezed in beside popular entertainment. For obvious logistical reasons, no one had to sit through Beethoven's *Eroica Symphony* or Wagner's *Ring*. For example, after a violinist at the front played Chaikovskii's "Sentimental Waltz" accompanied by a guitarist, the latter then played the famous popular wartime song, "Dark Is the Night," from the movie *Two Warriors*. The dancer Tamara Tkachenko—later famous as a folk choreographer—recalls giving fifty-one performances in seventeen days in the region of the old Napoleonic invasion route. Her company included *estrada* and radio stars and the extremely popular folk singer Lidiia Ruslanova.[12]

What about martial music at the front? This was, perhaps not surprisingly, less popular than it had been in the period of military buildup and war scares of the late

1930s. Songs about the armed forces (such as the famous "Katiusha") were important as self-entertainment when sung by the troops; and "patriotic songs" about love of the land had wide appeal. Big bands—jazz or pop orchestras—used them regularly in frontline concerts. But those about combat—fighting, action, violence—were avoided by the brigade performers. Viktor Belyi and Iakov Frenkel (a proletarian composer and a mass-song lyric writer) wrote "Song of Five Heroes," about "five sons of the Motherland" who are killed in a tank battle. But combatants did not care to hear this kind of song when being entertained, though they did sing them themselves (see Rothstein, this volume). Military bands were of course ubiquitous, as in all armies, and the big ones went on tour. The giant Red Army ensemble split itself into four detachments and went off to different sectors (see fig. 9). Half of their 1,500 concerts were given at the front. But their repertoire was as much "folkish" as it was martial.[13]

The explosion of officially promoted and spontaneously organized folk performance art in the Patriotic War is one of the most visible signs—of which this volume speaks so many times—of the deepening nationalism, traditional nostalgia, and collective emotionalism of those who fought and suffered in it. It is also a prime example of how the goals of the regime and popular feelings could be temporarily fused in cultural forms. The folk revival had begun in the mid-1930s as part of Stalin's cultural legitimation program, and the folk ensemble with peasant costumes and balalaikas became a familiar part of the cultural landscape. In wartime, these ensembles were sent to the front; and by 1944 the folk revival had erupted into a major cultural wave of festivals in Moscow, recently liberated Leningrad, Rostov, Gorky, Sverdlov, and Saratov; at the last concert nine hundred singers from thirteen choirs joined forces. The most popular folksinger of the era, Lidiia Ruslanova, was among the most wanted entertainers in the frontline brigades. Military units with no access to the mobile brigades put on their own amateur folk productions. However it may have been exploited for political purposes in other times, the groundswell of folk music reflected the depth of national feelings ignited by the struggle for existence.[14]

The bandleader Leonid Utësov once claimed that song had more instant emotional power than mere verse, in that the music added feelings to the words. There can be no question that song, especially what is loosely known as popular song, held the greatest emotional sway for the audiences of the entertainment brigades. The range of requests by the troops was very wide, but tilted toward love songs, nostalgic romances, and the light and frothy melodies of prewar days, including those from musical comedy films sung by Liubov' Orlova and written by Russia's foremost popular songwriter, Isaac Dunaevskii. Frontline fighters did intone solemn hymns such as the emotion-packed "Sacred War," but preferred hearing other things from the brigade entertainers. Pop and jazz reigned supreme.[15]

Among the songbirds who delivered what was desired at the front, by far the most famous—then and in memory—was Klavdiia Ivanovna Shul'zhenko. Caught in Erivan when war broke out, she and her colleagues in the Jazz Ensemble of Vladimir Koralli entrained to Leningrad and volunteered to tour the front. They went straight from the train station to headquarters and were enrolled in the army—Shul'zhenko holding the rank and uniform of a private. She recalled her first sortie to the front on a bus through the city drenched in autumn rain, past deserted buildings with windows like blinded eyes, empty trams arrested on their tracks like frozen cattle, monster-like flak balloons rising from frozen bridges and canals. Sharing the hunger, fatigue, and fear of the massing troops, she and her comrades gave concerts in the morning for departing units, in the afternoon for the wounded, and in the evening to those in the rear—all accompanied by crashing shells and bombs. Shul'zhenko gave five hundred performances in one year alone. Like other artists, she worried about the appropriateness of her "light" prewar fare—love songs, tangos, and foxtrots—given the somberness of front life. And like those others, she was persuaded by the warriors themselves who begged her to sing "the old songs" of love. A pilot, on seeing Shul'zhenko in uniform, asked her to put on a peacetime dress "so that things will be as in the prewar days."

So Shul'zhenko—or Klava, as the troops called her—sang her 1930s hits about old love letters, about "fiery Chelitas and ornery Lolitas," about sadness and lost affection. These were sentimental, eminently personal and intimate romances that had once been assaulted by sturdy "proletarians" as counter-revolutionary. Like her counterparts Vera Lynn of England, Zara Leander (a Swede by birth) of Germany, and Edith Piaf of France, Shul'zhenko's appeal was in her style: the gestures, the clarion voice, and the unabashed but skillfully deployed emotionalism made her a national icon. Lt. General of the Air Force Vasilii Golubev said later, in the pious rhetoric of postwar recollection, that her songs were as necessary as bombs and shells in the war. Women and men combatants alike saluted her, wrote to her, shared meals with her. Soon she became the most celebrated entertainer in the country. An airman about to bail out of his crippled plane heard her voice on the radio and flew in on "one wing." Her biggest hit was "Little Blue Kerchief," which became her theme song. In February 1942 she sang it in the film, *Concert for the Front Lines* (*Kontsert—frontu*), a morale-builder starring among others the actor Igor Il'inskii, Raikin, Utësov, Ruslanova, and the clown Karandash. As a film it was a show about show people, roughly equivalent to Hollywood's *Stage Door Canteen* and to the German UFA Studio's *Wunschkonzert*. Shul'zhenko was named Meritorious Artist of the RSFSR in September 1945.[16]

The success of big-band jazz was the result of three things: the genuine popularity it had achieved during those years in the 1920s and 1930s when it was not being persecuted; the concessions to popular taste that differentiated the years 1941–45 from those before and after; and the American alliance. Without discounting the power of emotional memory, one reason that millions looked back (and some still do) with nostalgia to the war years was the looser cultural milieu of the time. Soviet jazz of the 1930s, like that in Nazi Germany, had been curtailed and smoothed out in the manner of American "high-society" bands who promoted the sweet over the hot. The big bands of Boris Renskii, Iakov Skomorovskii, Aleksandr Tsfasman, Utësov, and others played American tunes such as "All of Me" and "Sunny Side of the Street." There was so much demand for jazz music by the troops that railwaymen, aviators, cooks, and the NKVD formed their own outfits. A group of students at the Leningrad Conservatory formed the Sympho-Jazz Ensemble and toured the front. When the American film *Sun Valley Serenade* appeared on Soviet screens in 1944, the popularity of Glenn Miller's style rose to new heights.[17] The best wartime jazz leader was "Eddie" (Adolph, but called Adi or Edi) Rosner, a Berlin-born son of a Polish-Jewish emigré. Rosner fled into Soviet territory at the beginning of the war and ended up in Moscow, from where he toured the front with his band. An admirer of the American trumpeter and bandleader, Harry James, Rosner banished the balalaika and concertina from his orchestra and played straight American jazz.[18]

If Rosner was the most "authentic" jazz-band-leader, Leonid Utësov (Vaisbein, or Weissbein, 1895–1982) was certainly the most eclectic and popular. Born in Odessa, he had made a career in prerevolutionary Jewish vaudeville and became a jazz pioneer in the 1920s and then the star of a zany but spectacularly successful musical-comedy film of the 1930s. When war began, he mobilized his band and, with Moscow as his base, ventured to the Urals, Siberia, the Soviet Far East, the front near Kalinin (Tver), and to the Volkhov front, with his daughter Edit as vocalist. His touring cycle, totaling more than two hundred concerts, resembled those of the Agit-Trains of the Civil War period. His band appeared in Leningrad and in his home town, Odessa, after these cities were freed from German occupation and blockade.

Utësov's shows were pure *estrada*: a synthesis of big-band music, pop and patriotic songs, comedy, and dance. His slapstick humor, which owed much to the Marx brothers and Ted Lewis, but had been curbed in the late 1930s, was now permitted full scope. Utësov had an ear for the currently popular. He staged the immortal "Wait for Me" with a reply sung by a female voice "I'll Wait for You;" and when his band played "Dark Is the Night" at a Moscow theater, the audience stood up to sing along. A careful impresario, he could bow to official solemnity by composing the "Knight's Fantasy" (Bogatyrskaia Fantasiia), blending themes from the Battle of Poltava and victory over Napoleon in 1812, and by playing Dunaevskii's anthem-like "Song of Motherland," Shostakovich's Leningrad Symphony, and the exalted "Sacred War". But he could also combine a tribute to Russia's allies with the desires of his audience in songs like "It's a Long Way to Tipperary" and "Bombardiers" (sung in English and Russian by Edit Utësova), a straight adaptation of the American hit, "Comin' in on a Wing and a Prayer." Even anti-Nazi novelty tunes about Baron Zilch and Fieldmarshal Filthy were reminiscent of Spike Jones's once-famous "Right in der Führer's Face." During the siege of Odessa, Utësov sang "Mickey [Mishka] of Odessa" over the airwaves:

> You're Mickey of Odessa and you know what that means.
> That terror, fear, and sadness are absent from your soul.
> You're a seaman, Mickey, and sailors never cry.
> And never lose their courage or lose heart.

Utësov's great success lay in merging sweet-jazz elements with the wartime mood and employing the kind of topical pathos that the American Al Jolson did at about the same time by adding a generous portion of "heart" to every song he sang.[19]

The theater world did not remain stationary. The All-Russian Theater Society called for a "defensive anti-fascist repertoire of modest format performances." In practice this meant Russian and European classics and Soviet prewar and wartime pieces. Mounted on stage also were special pastiches of Lenin's life and wisdom from plays and from movies such as *Man with a Gun*, a Civil War political melodrama of the 1930s. Some entire theater companies toured the front and the rear; others sent part of their staff as itinerant acting brigades to perform selected scenes—often flanked by musical and comedy shows. The Red Army Theater in Moscow vacated its mammoth star-shaped edifice, was evacuated to Sverdlovsk, and from there radiated teams to front or rear. The Malyi Theater actress, forty-one-year-old Elena Gogoleva, along with Igor Il'inskii and others, was dispatched to the west and south of Moscow to put on scenes from Aleskandr Ostrovskii, Shakespeare, Gorky, and others for about three weeks in the winter of 1942, doing forty shows at fifteen different points along the front. Bomber pilots in their audience thanked the brigade as they set out to give their own "concert" to the Germans. On the eve of its departure for the front in August 1942, a brigade from the world-famous Moscow Art Theater debated the relevance in wartime of a classical repertoire but were soon convinced by the soldiers' enthusiastic reception of Pushkin's *Stone Guest*, Dostoevskii's *Brothers Karamazov* (a dramatic reading), Chekhov's *Three Sisters*, and Satan's monologue from Gorky's *Lower Depths*.[20]

Light entertainment on stage receded in the rear area for a while; due to the harsh psychology of the moment and the need for blackouts. But it too was soon enlisted for the war. Circus and *estrada*, with their traditions of mobility and variety, were perfectly suited to frontline entertainment. In Moscow, a theater of light satire, Little Hawk (named after the Soviet pursuit plane), was launched by veteran actor David Gutman, who persuaded the authorities that a "fighting theater" was needed. Staffed by well-known writers, comedians, and musical figures, it offered barbed verses, sketches, and one-acters relevant to the war. Axis politicians were presented as losers: Vichy French leader Pierre Laval fell off a high wire; Romanian dictator Marshal Antonescu sang off key; strongman Mussolini could not lift his weights; and the boxer Hitler was knocked out. Front-theater troupes freely adopted these themes. In the circus, the great clowns Karandash, Vitalii Lazarenko, and the Durov brothers had only to re-costume their old political targets Kerenskii, Lord Curzon, and Makhno into Nazi villains. Karandash introduced a dog dressed as Goebbels to bark out a report to the Führer. The Durovs put on The Three Gs: Gitler (Hitler), Gimmler (Himmler), and Goebbels, all played by dogs. These characterizations, along with the perpetually freezing and miserable "Winter Fritz," were inspired by political cartoons and posters.[21]

Puppet theater, an art designed primarily for children in most Western countries, was a popular adult entertainment in Russia—before the war, and before the revolution. The Obraztsov Central Puppet Theater was divided into two teams at the start of war; one in Moscow, the other in Vladivostok, where it entertained sailors of the Pacific Fleet. The Far Eastern company returned to Moscow for a few days and then were off on a five-river journey which took the evacuated theater (hit by a bomb) to Ufa and then to Novorossiisk, which became its home. The puppeteers put on more than four hundred shows in towns and villages, army camps and hospitals, frontline dugouts and partisan forest encampments. Among their acts were a mini-operetta, "On the Rooftops of Berlin," with cats as the main characters and "Meeting of Dogs," with Hitler as a shepherd dog and Admiral Horthy, the political chief of Hungary, as a black mongrel who bites Antonescu.[22]

Operetta was another great night-out favorite of the Soviet urban population and had been since the turn of the century. By nature frothy and apolitical, it had suffered bumps in the early cultural revolutions but was legitimized by the mid-1930s. Grigorii Iaron, a longtime performer in the Moscow Operetta Theater, described the dilemmas of his art in time of war. On July 22, 1941, the company was giving a summer performance of the Viennese operetta *Silva* in the Mirror Theater of the Hermitage Garden in Moscow. In mid-performance, Iaron yelled "air raid" and although the audience wanted the show to continue, it was stopped. In October the theater was evacuated along with many others to the Volga. On returning to the capital the company resumed its work in early 1942 with *Wedding at Malinovka*, a 1937 farce about the Bolshevik struggle against the Ukrainian anarchist Nestor Makhno. Iaron claims that the audience felt a rare moment of identification with the present when the singing hero, surrounded by choristers from the Red Army Choir, promised revenge on the German occupiers of 1918.

War was no easier to blend into operetta than had been revolution. A few dealt directly with a wartime theme: *A Tale of the Forest*, about partisans; *The Ocean Covered Vast Expanses*, about sailors; and *Girl from Barcelona*, a fantastic concoction about a communist refugee to Russia from the Spanish Civil War menaced in 1941 by her ex-fiancé, who serves with the invading Spanish fascist Light Blue Division. An attempt to adapt the nineteenth-century nationalist popular fiction of Mikhail Zagoskin was not a success. Laughter, melody, and—yes—froth is what the public still wanted.

*Silva* remained the undying favorite. *Maritza* by the same composer (Imre Kalmán) had not been done since 1915; when revived, it had to be purged of such lines as "I will dream about her belly button and her short transparent skirt."[23]

A word about self-entertainment at the front: this was encouraged by some commanders as a morale builder when there were no brigades and in the long hours and days between combat engagements. A talented performer would take the initiative or be ordered by an officer to organize shows from among the troops. Song and dance, accompanied by assorted instruments—guitar or accordion—were the staples. Since women served within or alongside many units in this war, sometimes the genders were mixed on stage doing dance styles of the time and of past time: hopak, waltz in a tap-dance manner, or the long-forgotten "Crimean Tatar Girl." Witnesses also describe spontaneous readings out loud from Ehrenburg, Simonov, Surkov, Tvardovskii, and Gorky or couplets, jokes, rhymes, sayings, and anti-fascist ditties. Iurii Nikulin, later a famous clown and then director of the Moscow Circus, got his first performance experience in the front lines as an amateur in the ranks.[24]


Did the Soviet experience with frontline entertainment differ in any substantial way from that of other belligerents? The only country to match it in scale was the United States, through the agency of the United Service Organizations (USO). Formed in 1941, it coordinated the voluntary efforts of Christian, Jewish, youth, and other private welfare agencies to provide various social and spiritual services to the armed forces. Its most visible function was troop entertainment provided by volunteers from radio, movies, the night club circuit, and even the legitimate stage. Like Soviet brigade members, American performers put on shows of mixed genres; unlike them, they offered very little in the way of classical selections and very much in the way of leggy females. USO troupes had to travel immense distances—Africa, Europe, the Pacific—to reach the fighting forces and, like the Soviet show-people, sometimes endured the danger of enemy fire. In both cases, they represented expressive links to the home front, supplemented by radio (see Von Geldern, this volume) and an occasional film. Verbal and photographic evidence of Soviet soldiers laughing at comedians recalls footage of the reaction of GIs in the Pacific to Bob Hope; and there is no reason to doubt that the catharsis of real laughter was authentic for both armies in the lull between battles.

We know very little about tensions between civilians and the military, audience and actors, officers and men, women and men, or ethnic groups. The brigades drew from all major nationalities; a fairly large percentage of the entertainers were Jewish, reflecting their prewar prominence in the arts and particularly in popular and mass culture.[25] Was there a hierarchy that determined who got to be entertained, such as officers, certain units, branches, proximity to front? Did privilege and power deter-mine which performers served in brigades, as opposed to those who remained in the rear or those who got drafted and lost their lives as soldiers? (The circus aerialist, Ivan Shepetkov, was one of the twenty-eight Panfilovites who perished before Moscow in 1941.)[26] Recollections of both performers and veterans about the relations between brigades and troops are bathed in mutual affection. Their descriptions of heroic men and women combatants are couched in folkloric and pious terms. Almost all the brigade entertainers recall the days of war with solemn joy. According to some, they were well fed and clothed, certainly better than most soldiers and most civilians too. One natural offshoot of the prewar *sheftsvo* relationship between the military and the entertainment world was fraternization and even intermarriage of elite officers and celebrities.[27]

On the content of entertainment and its impact on the troops we can speak with some certainty. Some of it was orchestrated from the center. Political officers, on orders from above, could manufacture spontaneities; and the programs, routes, and repertoires were closely screened, if not planned, much more than in other wartime societies, where censorship was more defensive and passive than active. This does not mean that their was no heart, no emotion, no room for ad-libbing in the relations between performer, genre, and audience. Soldiers were not averse to contemporary war themes, even though some performers wanted to delete the death of Arkadii in Simonov's play, *A Lad from Our Town*; evidence of repertoires shows that home-related themes were the most wanted and the most offered. In the case of jazz, it is clear that soldiers' own desires were considered. The troops wanted laughter, satire, and fun, song and dance; and they were happy to take small doses of high culture along with it. They were no more interested in seeing enacted battle scenes after a day of fighting (even if such scenes could be done believably) than had been workers in hearing industrial machinery concerts mounted during the Civil War.[28]

Wartime entertainment spread and deepened culture among the population. The evacuation of orchestras and theaters and the concerts and performances in out-of-the-way places was the cultural counterpart of the relocation of industry, which brought new kinds of markets and employment opportunities to far-flung regions. Even allowing for exaggeration and patriotic posturing and the nostalgia of the aged, one is struck by the glow of memory among the entertainers—for each other, for the men and women at arms, and for the general population in a bonding that few nations experienced in that war. This memory partly accounts for the vast and enduring popularity of those who performed at the front. About long-term influence upon the arts themselves one can speculate that performance styles changed and actors' understanding of life deepened. Many interrupted studies to go to the front, a move that delayed but did not hurt careers. The most historically interesting facet of wartime entertainment was that it expressed something like real values of millions of people on certain matters: not purges or executions or party politics; but on homeland and friendship, love and loyalty, gender roles and recent traditions. It showed a public resurgence of the "personal life, intimate feelings, deep emotional authenticity, and even quasi-religiosity" of which I spoke in chapter 1. The most terrible of all wars, for all its frantic cruelty and devastation, had revealed a closer glimpse of the heart and soul of a nation than had been seen for some time.

## Notes

1. For tsarist and revolutionary roots of military entertainment forms, see E. M. Kuznetsov, *Iz proshlogo russkoi estrady* (Moscow, 1958); Richard Stites, *Russian Popular Culture: Entertainment and Society since 1900* (Cambridge, Eng., 1992), chap. 1; Hubertus Jahn, *Patriotic Culture in Russia during World War I* (Ph.D. diss., Georgetown University, 1989); James Von Geldern, *Bolshevik Festivals, 1917–1920* (Berkeley, 1993); Peter Kenez, *The Birth of the Propaganda State* (Cambridge, Eng., 1985); *Russkaia sovetskaia estrada*, ed. E. Uvarova, 3 vols. (Moscow, 1976), 1 (1917–30), 2 (1930–45), to be cited as RSE.

2. *Ocherki istorii russkogo sovetskogo dramaticheskogo teatra*, 3 vols. (Moscow, 1954–61; to be cited as OIRSDT); 2, 528–31.

3. O. A. Kuznetsova, "Estrada v period velikoi otechestvennoi voiny," RSE, 2, 371–97 (372).

4. *Iskusstvo v boevom stroiu: vospominaniia, dnevniki, ocherki* (Moscow, 1985), to be cited as IBS, pp. 15–26, 98; OIRSDT, 2, 529.

5. Kuznetsova; Irina Vasilinina, *Klavdiia Shul'zhenko* (Moscow, 1979), p. 60; on transport problems, see Holland Hunter, "Successful Spatial Management," in Susan Linz, ed., *The Impact of World War II on the Soviet Union* (Totowa, NJ, 1985), pp. 47–58.

6. Kuznetsova; IBS, pp. 23–24, 72; OIRSDT, 2, 533–34.

7. IBS, pp. 47–56, 72; Leonid Utësov, *S pesnei po zhizni* (Moscow, 1961), p. 176; Kuznetsova, p. 6 and passim. I. Zim, "Raskinulos more shiroko," *Sovetskaia kul'tura* (April 13, 1965): 1. Living Newspaper was a proletarian drama form that had risen in the 1920s.

8. At Poltava in 1709, Peter the Great inflicted a major defeat upon the Swedish invading forces.

9. IBS, pp. 8, 24; Kuznetsova; Sergei Balashov, "Slushaite, tovarishchi potomki," *Iskusstvo estrady: sbornik* (Moscow, 1964) pp. 13–78; OIRSDT, 2, 533.

10. G. Terikov, *Kuplet na estrade* (Moscow, 1987), p. 125; Lev Mirov and Evsei Darskii performed their entire routine before a burned and bandaged soldier in hospital: *Mastera Estrady* (Moscow, 1964), p. 108.

11. For the constant interchange between poster art and theater, see N. I. Smirnova, *Sovetskii teatr kukol, 1918–1932* (Moscow, 1963), pp. 322–41; IBS, pp. 108–11; Iurii Dmitriev, "Dvadtsat' s gakom," *Teatr* 5 (1965): 105–109. For the comic roots: A. F. Nekrylova, *Russkie narodnye gorodskie prazdniki, uveseleniia i zrelishcha: konets XVIII-nachalo XX veka* (Leningrad, 1988) and Kuznetsov, *Iz proshlogo*. On Tërkin, see: *Sovetskie pisateli na frontakh Velikoi Otechestvennoi voiny*, vol. 78 of 2 parts *Literaturnoe nasledstvo*, (Moscow: Nauka, 1966), 1, 563–601.

12. IBS, pp. 20, 26–29, 249. On *Two Warriors* and its hit song, see Rothstein (this volume) and Stites, *Russian Popular Culture*, pp. 113–14.

13. *Pesni Velikoi Otechestvennoi voiny* (Moscow, 1945), a songbook published by the defense ministry, p. 14, for "Song of Five Heroes." General treatments: Rothstein (this volume); Suzanne

Ament, "Soviet Songs of World War II" (ms.); Arnol'd Sokhor, *"Katyusha" M. I. Blantera* (Moscow, 1960).

14. Frank Miller, *Folklore for Stalin: Russian Folklore and Pseudo-folklore of the Stalin Era* (Armonk, N.J., 1990); Stites, *Russian Popular Culture*, pp. 78–79, 108–109. On Ruslanova: S. Frederick Starr, *Red and Hot: the Fate of Jazz in the Soviet Union* (New York, 1983), p. 186; Leningrad Radio documentary on her life, January 19, 1990; *Muzykal'naia zhizn'* (May 1975): 18–19; and *Poët Lidiia Ruslanova*, record sleeve notes.

15. Rothstein (this volume); Ament, "Soviet Songs of World War II"; Al. Romanov, *Liubov' Orlova v iskusstve i v zhizni* (Moscow, 1987), p. 192; P. F. Lebedev, *Pesni rozhdënnye v ogne* (Volgograd, 1983), p. 6; L. Danilevich, *Muzyka na frontakh Velikoi Otechestvennoi voiny* (Moscow, 1948) p. 22.

16. V. V. Dementev, *Pesni i sud'by soldatskie* (Tashkent, 1982); Vasilinina, *Klavdiia Shul'zhenko*, pp. 60–79.

17. As they occupied cities of Eastern Europe, Soviet authorities found and confiscated many movies—local and foreign, mostly German and American. "Chattanooga Choo-Choo" from *Sun Valley Serenade* became a virtual anthem for jazz fans. These were called "trophy films" and became very popular in postwar Russia: Starr, *Red and Hot*, pp. 193, 237–38; Stites, *Russian Popular Culture*, pp. 125–26; Kenez, *Cinema and Soviet Society, 1917–1953* (Cambridge, Eng., 1992), pp. 213–14. For jazz in Nazi Germany, see Michael Kater, *Different Drummers: Jazz in the Culture of Nazi Germany* (New York, 1992) and Detlev Peukert, *Inside Nazi Germany* (New Haven, 1987).

18. Starr, *Red and Hot*, pp. 183–94; IBS, p. 330.

19. Stites, *Russian Popular Culture*, pp. 103–110; ; Utësov, *S pesnei*, pp. 173–88; Dmitriev, *Leonid Utësov*; Starr, *Red and Hot*, pp. 183–94; *Leonid Utësov: Recordings of the Forties and Fifties*; *Leonid Utësov: zapisi 40-kh-50-kh godov*.

20. OIRSDT, 2, 528–43; IBS, pp. 7–26, 59–66, and passim.

21. M. Krimker, "Pervyi frontovoi: k 25-letiiu moskovskoi bitvy," *Sovetskaia estrada i tsirk*, 12 (Dec. 1966), 3; Kuznetsova; S. M. Makarov, *Sovetskaia klounada* (Moscow, 1986), pp. 93–119.

22. Sergei Obraztsov, *My Profession* (Moscow, 1981); IBS, pp. 89–97. Hungarian and Romanian troops participated in the invasion of Russia and still nurtured mutual hostility over Transylvania.

23. Grigorii Iaron, *O liubimom zhanre* (Moscow, 1960), pp. 193–206.

24. IBS, pp. 213–20, 271–84.

25. Jack Miller, *Jews in Soviet Culture* (New Brunswick, N.J., 1984) pp. 65–106.

26. OIRSDT, 2, 542–48; *Tsirk: malenkaia entsiklopediia* (Moscow, 1979), p. 373.

27. IBS, pp. 22, 25. On the military-theater linkup, see Stites, *Russian Popular Culture*, pp. 69–70.

28. OIRSDT, 2, 535–39. For those concerts, Stites, *Revolutionary Dreams: Utopian Vision and Experimental Life in the Russian Revolution* (New York, 1989), p. 136.

# 9

# Images of Hate in the Art of War

## Argyrios K. Pisiotis

Few events leave as strong an imprint on culture as do wars. During the Great Patriotic War, the popular arts and especially state propaganda targeted the Nazi invaders and often identified them with the German people. Soviet culture from 1941 to 1945 became predominantly Russian, as the initial German onslaught put many of the major non-Russian peoples behind the Wehrmacht's lines, and as the Stalinist leadership deemed the revival of Great Russian traditions and symbols necessary for carrying out the war successfully. Here I will examine various Russian images of the Germans, primarily in posters, press cartoons and films, and secondarily in articles, editorials and news pieces of the periodical press, in the material of circus and variety shows (*estrada*), theatrical plays, and songs.[1] The official propaganda of the Stalinist state, when combined with popular feeling, yielded an exceptionally negative image of the enemy that contributed to the ferocity of Russian war against the Germans. The main cause of that ferocity, of course, was the behavior of the German occupying forces on Soviet soil and the consequent sufferings of the country's inhabitants.

The Nazis had been portrayed in Soviet propaganda since the late 1920s as lackeys of German industrialists and enemies of culture and peace. After Hitler came to power, the "German fascists," as the Nazis were labeled, became increasingly identified with the entire German people.[2] Traditional anti-German feelings among Eastern Slavs, and the memories of World War I offered a fertile ground for an escalating demonization of the Germans that was briefly interrupted by the Ribbentrop-Molotov Non-Aggression Pact.

The first official presentation of the war of 1941–45 conformed to the ideological imperatives of Marxist-Leninist ideology. Announcing the outbreak of the war on radio, Molotov drew a clear distinction between the leaders and the people of Germany:[3] "This war has not been inflicted upon us by the German people, or by the German workers, peasants, and intellectuals, of whose sufferings we are fully aware, but by Germany's bloodthirsty rulers. . . . " Thus, the People's Commissar of Foreign Affairs did not depict a war between conflicting nationalisms, but a war against *a class enemy at the international level*. Stalin reinforced the class-struggle message at the

*141*

beginning of the war by claiming that the enemy wanted to "restore the power of land-owners, reestablish Tsarism, destroy national culture, and turn Russians into slaves of German princes and barons."[4] The official position on radio and in the press changed, however, within the first week of the war. Exhortatory anti-German posters started to appear and by 1945 they would amount to thousands. Russian cartoonists filled the pages of popular magazines with dehumanizing caricatures of the enemy, while *estrada* and circus artists created and performed skits that ridiculed and demonized the Nazi villains. Each of the visual and linguistic means used to portray the Germans has particularities related to the identity of the creators and the receivers. Nevertheless, there was a common typology of recurring phraseology, themes, and imagery.

## Thematics of the Images

Though Soviet images of Germans did not shy away from an ideological interpre-tation of the war, they stressed its national aspects.[5] Germans were traditional con-querors (*zakhvatchiki*), invaders (*okkupanty*); their goal was to enslave the world as they were doing in other countries and in parts of the Soviet "Motherland." Newspaper and magazine articles as well as posters called upon the Red Army to liberate their en-slaved brothers. A category of posters features children, old men, and women behind barbed wire or performing forced labor under the surveillance of a Nazi guard, and the posters command the Soviet soldier to hurry and free them. In the film *Rainbow* (*Raduga*), a child is separated from his mother, who is held captive behind barbed wire.

Russian propaganda viewed the Germans as destroyers of everything that the peaceful Russian and Soviet people had built in the past, as well as of everything beau-tiful and wholesome. Newspapers and the documentary films *Stalingrad* and *Moscow Strikes Back* emphasize the destruction of hospitals, factories, schools, museums, and libraries (see Kenez, this volume). In the film *She Defends the Motherland*, scenes of happy rural family life are harshly disrupted by German guns and bombs. Another film, *Zoia*, lists the major works of infrastructure the Germans destroyed. In the play *On the Eve* (*Nakanune*, Aleksandr Afinogenov, 1941), the drone of German planes and the rumble of tanks covers the sound of music in a provincial Russian home. In the film *Vanka*, German soldiers shoot little birds for amusement.

Nazi hostility to culture is also amply stressed in the press, cartoons, and shows. The most frequently criticized early Nazi practice was the burning of books. According to Soviet propaganda, the Nazis were barbarians, uncivilized rogues, plunging the world into a new Dark Age. In *Zoia*, her teacher ("Owl") reads about the burning of books and calls the Germans "vandals," "idiots," "savages," "scoundrels," and "crimi-nals." *Moscow Strikes Back* stresses German vandalism, too: "They blew up the home of Chaikovskii. . . . They know of a single artwork: destruction." In the film *Three in a*

*Shell Hole*, the wounded Soviet soldier complains that he had wanted to be a student, but that the attack by "German scoundrels" prevented him.[6]

Soviet films, posters, and press presented German atrocities as breaking the all-time record of bestiality. *Stalingrad* identifies all Germans with "Nazi cutthroats," who commit acts of "lunacy," "monstrosities," "unbelievable butchery." The SS are called the "cream of Germany's cesspool of crime." *Moscow Strikes Back* refers to German soldiers as "brutalized young men, drunk with success," "hordes of invaders" and "a generation trained in murder," whose "bestiality is a dark page from the blackest and bloodiest record in human history." In the documentary *The Kharkov Trial* the narrator says that the deeds of the "Hitlerite butchers exceed the horrors of barbarism," and a German war criminal pleads for mercy "because the whole German army is like him."

Both German officers and soldiers starve the occupied population, stealing animals and clothes from them. In *Rainbow*, a German goes into a house looking for a cow to milk, and a small boy informs him that their cow has already been taken by the "Fritzes."[7] In *Lieutenant Hopp's Career* (*Kariera Leitenanta Goppa*), the Germans steal a pig from the villagers. An officer in *She Defends the Motherland* and a soldier in *Vanka* wear eye-patches, alluding to piracy, looting, and killing. Accordingly, the Germans' most common epithets in the Soviet press and posters underscore their atrocious nature: *killers* (*ubiitsy*) and *child-killers* (*detoubiitsy*), *butchers* (*palachi*), *man-eaters* (*liudoedy*), *cannibals* (*kannibaly*), *vermin* (*gada*).

One of the less frequent but nevertheless powerful attributes of the German character was debauchery, and the related theme of sexual violation, literary and allegorical. German lustfulness, which had been incarnated by Franz von Kneischütz in the prewar film *Circus* (1936), was particularly stressed in *Rainbow*. Interestingly enough, and perhaps out of Bolshevik puritanism, newspapers and magazines did not make frequent references to rape, something that featured constantly in a formulaic way in the crime lists of Germans in other occupied countries. However, posters count on the enormous suggestive effect that the violation of females had on (male) soldiers as defenders of the society. A few posters depict beautiful, helpless women with hands tied, in an obvious sensual pose, and appeal to the soldier (in the second person singular) not to let the conqueror "ravage his loved one".[8] Other posters feature monstrous Nazi officers drooling over the bodies of young women.

German warriors were presented as perfidious and depraved. In the short film *Three in a Shell Hole*, a Russian nurse takes care of a German officer and a Soviet soldier, both wounded. The German reaches for his gun to kill the nurse, but is shot in time by the Soviet soldier who gives the moral lesson of the story: Germans are "wolves" and "rats." In *She Defends the Motherland*, a German draws a knife and kills the Soviet soldier who had spared his life. In the play *On the Eve*, a Russian Jew who gives blood to save a German officer is later killed by the same man.

German soldiers, more often than officers, are visually depicted as stupid, docile and brainwashed cowards who do not know what they are fighting for. Magazines are full of cartoons in which silly-looking German soldiers are beaten by the Red Army or by partisans. In the comedy *Lieutenant Hopp's Career*, a few old peasants manage to capture the German commander and his detachment. Germans allegedly attacked only the defenseless population, not the Red Army or partisans. In posters, German soldiers oppress and harass old men, children, and women. They require the peasants to bow their heads in subordination; they kill undernourished children and keep old women in concentration and hard labor camps.[9] In *Rainbow*, there are no male adults in the occupied village, except for old men. The German soldiers push around a pregnant woman, make her walk barefoot in the snow, beat, interrogate, and torture her; and when she finally bears her baby, the German commander shoots it in cold blood. In the end they kill her too. Another small boy is shot and killed for no reason as he runs to his mother. In the main streets of the village, women and old men are hanged from telephone poles. A German soldier terrorizes children with his rifle.[10] All these things and worse were of course actually happening.

Even before German defeats began, depictions of shabby, unshaven, undernourished Nazis, with blackened eyes, bandaged heads and legs, and dressed in frayed uniforms and rags, attempted to divert attention from the Red Army's own difficulties and shortages of equipment. Another partial distortion of truth is the juxtaposition of old, toothless German soldiers to young, virulent, slick Soviet soldiers or partisans, male and female, as in *Zoia, Vanka*, and *She Defends the Motherland*. In some caricatures, films and *estrada* sketches, Germans are repulsive beings with thick, dark spike-like hair on their faces and legs, narrow foreheads and elongated chins, resembling apes.

Numerous cartoons illustrate the brainwashing of the German people. Nazi ideology is inserted in young people's empty skulls as they are sent off to war. When news from the Eastern front is bad, skeptical Germans enter Goebbels's barbershop "Optimism" and come out with literally "new brains," saluting the Nazi way. The director of the film *Rainbow* shows the degree of Nazi indoctrination when the German commander writes to his wife that although they are in a "wild, harsh, and barbarian country, the order of the Führer motivates" them.

Some themes of anti-German propaganda reflect the continuity between Soviet perceptions of the war and Russian modern history and tradition.[11] Posters, cartoons, *estrada* sketches and couplets consider Napoleon's defeat in Russia as a premonition of the Wehrmacht's fate. In caricatures, Napoleon's ghost derides Hitler for his attack on the USSR.[12]

Alexander Nevskii's fabled victory against the Teutonic Knights in 1242, as well as the Russo-Polish victory in Grünwald (1410) were invoked by Soviet artists as harbingers of the defeat of the Nazis, the racial descendants of the Knights. Posters feature

Alexander Nevskii leading the Russian troops against the hated enemy. Other Russian national heroes, such as Dmitrii Donskoi, Suvorov, and Kutuzov, appear in posters to exhort the Red Army to victory, and illustrate the continuity of the struggles of Russian people against invaders from the West (see fig. 13).[13]

Russian memories of World War I revived an image of the Prussian officer, which filled posters, cartoons, films, and circus farces. Usually fat and round-faced (well fed), with the indispensable monocle in the eye, the old Wilhelminian officer represents the perfect merger of the national and class enemy, who put on the Nazi uniform to attack and pillage Russia once more.[14] His arrogant look alludes to alleged class inequities in the Wehrmacht. The stout colonel in *Lieutenant Hopp's Career*, as well as the captured German general in the film *She Defends the Motherland*, wear monocles. The latter's name, von Falk, betrays his social origin. In the same film, the officer who interrogates the partisan leader Pasha carries a swagger stick and white gloves.

The Prussian aristocratic officer's figure was borrowed from World War I posters, while the same image had been applied during the Russian Civil War to White generals and to personifications of the Western interventionist countries.[15] In the 1920s and 1930s, the same fat, arrogant, dark-clad figure had been employed to symbolize capitalism, Wall Street, monopolies, the military-industrial complex and industrial captains.[16] This continuity is due not only to the Soviet propaganda's attempt to draw parallels between all those enemies, but also to the fact that some of the best artists of the early Soviet period were the ones who produced the majority of the anti-German posters and cartoons, as well as the later cartoons of the Cold War.[17]

Contrary to the general physical characteristics of Germans, both officers and soldiers in films like *Lieutenant Hopp's Career* almost always have dark hair and often a dark complexion, whereas Soviet soldiers are fair.[18] This distortion not only symbolizes the association with Evil and Good respectively, but it may also reflect traditional Russian feelings of superiority over the dark-skinned peoples of Central Asia and Transcaucasia.

Germans are often rendered "faceless," particularly in films.[19] The foe becomes impersonal, a tool of destruction rather than a thinking and feeling human being. In *Rainbow*, there are practically no outdoor scenes in which the facial features of the soldiers are visible. The Germans have wrapped their faces in strips of cloth, to protect them from the cold. Emotional agitation cannot be detected in the dark spaces between the soldiers' collars and the metallic shells of their helmets. The camera zooms in on black, impenetrable holes, which occupy the place of the eyes.[20] In indoor scenes Germans are sparsely lit and remain in the dark so that their faces are barely visible. The Soviet skiers who liberate the village sweep swiftly through the snow in their white camouflage uniforms, like angels who rush in to break the evil spell as a rainbow shines above them. This messianic scene is repeated in *She Defends the Motherland*, where Russian planes suddenly appear in the sky at the most critical moment, as well as in the play *Invasion* (*Nashestvie*, 1942), where a little town is liberated by parachutists. Films and *estrada* skits simulate the allegedly mechanical, inhuman way German troops march, thus alluding to the (Prussian) militaristic tradition. This further reduces Germans to inanimate, or at least, unthinking beings.[21] As most warring peoples do, the Russians targeted their enemy's voice and language, which is usually incomprehensible and therefore sounds meaningless. Soviet films and skits represent the German language as pompous and militaristic and often akin to barking. *Zoia* and other films include long scenes of Germans shouting orders to Russians.

Soviet artists ridiculed Germans by depicting them either as extremely thin, exceptionally fat, or having a combination of thin and stocky body parts. Bloated bellies together with long noses, gaunt faces and skinny legs not only generate hilarity, but also make the enemy look unreal. Distortions of size also aim at creating a visual impression of "denial of reality." Germans are given dwarfish, smaller-than-life dimensions and are reduced to insignificance next to the much bigger Soviet soldiers and partisans (the relative size of other objects such as trees shows that the latter are of normal and not gigantic size). By being blatantly unrealistic, these representations imply that the enemy is not a real being, or, in any case, not a human being. In circus, too, Hitler, Goebbels and other Nazis' roles were often acted by dwarves or represented by small effigies.

Germans are often depicted as animals or machine-like beings, or as combinations of creatures made up of mechanical and animal parts, such as a spider with metallic claws. Dogs,[22] jackals, wolves, hyenas, pigs, sheep (symbols of imbecility), crows, and other black rapacious birds are the most frequent animal forms of Wehrmacht soldiers in magazine caricatures, circus and *estrada* acts. Posters and cartoons concentrate on the Nazis' low intellectual abilities and their barbarity and hostility to culture by characterizing them as apes or cavemen. However, the most frequent animal images of Germans in posters are rats and other rodents, spiders and sludgy insects, snakes, dragons, and worms. *Estrada* actors, recycling a World War I pun, called Germans *prusaki* (cockroaches; *Prussak*=Prussian).

## Press, Entertainment, Posters, and Their Targets

The tools of state propaganda and means of popular entertainment reveal slightly varying preferences to particular targets among the invading Germans. These different emphases and images reflect Soviet perceptions of who was responsible for the war and the destruction, provide a hint as to the identity of those who produced and consumed these images, and sometimes help the researcher to distinguish between the product of pure propaganda and the views and feelings of the people.

The single most often targeted individual by far is Hitler. Several posters and hundreds of cartoons in magazines, dehumanize him more severely than any other Nazi leader.[23] Soviet propaganda presented Hitler as the incarnation of the Nazi regime and the scourge of war, and it heaped anger and scorn upon his beliefs about Slavic racial inferiority. Most people usually focus attention on visible, tangible enemies, and thus Russians found it easy to concentrate their hatred and efforts on Hitler. Caricatures depicted him with a big belly, small legs, and an exaggerated tuft of hair flying out from his little head. Cartoons and posters also rendered him as a dog, a wolf, a snake, a worm, a spider, and called him a bloodthirsty man-eater. In circus, Hitler was the main target of comical songs and couplets. Actors presented Hitler as a lunatic dressed in rags (to symbolize the military defeat and bankruptcy of National Socialism), as a power-hungry dictator, or simply as a dog.

Very often, in *estrada* acts, cartoons and posters, Hitler is accompanied by Goebbels, who is depicted as a dwarf, or as the Führer's puppy or monkey, running behind him. Although more powerful Nazi leaders such as Göring and Himmler appear occasionally in magazine caricatures and in *estrada* and circus acts, Soviet propagandists and artists reserved second place for Goebbels. Soviet soldiers who played dominoes called the double-six Hitler and the double-five Goebbels.[24] His daily war announcements on the radio, which concealed the advances of the Red Army, and his attempt to present the German attack as defense of Western civilization against Bolshevik Asiatic barbarity made Goebbels a natural opponent of Soviet government spokesmen, journalists, artists, and playwrights who were trying to rebut Nazi propaganda.[25] Russian people were urged to despise his voice, described and parodied as raving and incomprehensible. Posters depicted Goebbels as a dog barking in a microphone, while circus farces featured real dogs doing the same thing.

The official—albeit rarely emphasized—Soviet interpretation of war causalities held German capitalists accountable first and foremost, an interpretation that we find primarily in the official press, as well as in a few cartoons. Although *Pravda* and *Izvestiia* editorials often castigated the Nazi leadership and German capital more than the people, news items referred to the Germans or German fascists collectively, and considered every German soldier to be a killer.[26]

The treatment of Germans was mildest in the theater. Artistically superior plays used symbols and techniques of visual representation similar to those of the more popular *estrada* acts, but their plots were usually devoted not to the dehumanization of the Germans, but to the reconciliation of all Russians in face of the enemy, as in *The Russian People* and *Invasion*.[27]

In poems, songs and couplets in *estrada*, as well as in circus acts and films, all the Germans were reduced to criminals, irrespective of rank or office.[28] Moreover, these genuinely popular ways of entertainment boldly implicated the noncombatant German population in the Wehrmacht's and the SS's crimes. All Germans were seen as accessories to those crimes, not only because they put Hitler in power but also because they profited directly from the maltreatment of the occupied population.[29] Perhaps for this reason, *estrada* couplets and sketches wish the worst to the German women and children: the death of their spouses and fathers on the Eastern Front. *Estrada's* sarcasm and a delight in the pain and sufferings of the enemy permeated songs and couplets, and probably reflected widespread military and civilian feelings:[30]

| | |
|---|---|
| Frau pisem zhdët s Kavkaza, | The Frau awaits a letter from the Caucasus, |
| No molchit eë kumir. | But her idol remains silent. |
| On vchera ostavil srazu, | Yesterday he suddenly departed |
| Armavir i bozhii mir! | From Armavir and from the world! |

Caricatures in humor magazines, because of their comical nature, more often ridiculed than demonized the Germans. Soldiers were usually portrayed as stupid and officers as more malicious. Posters were issued by the state, and therefore displayed similarities to the newspapers' portrayal of the Germans, though they are occasionally comical. Posters treated Germans in separate categories (Nazi leaders, officers, soldiers, armaments industrialists, ordinary civilians) but dehumanized all of them with the same severity.

The content and message of a total of 222 Russian-language posters included in a representative collection at the Library of Congress (excluding those congratulating and glorifying the Soviet Army and people for the victory and those urging the population to rebuild the damages) show how Soviet propaganda defined the German nation as the enemy, and suggest that the tens of thousands of posters it circulated helped to instill this view among the population.[31] Of those posters, 62.1 percent (138) display German atrocities and bestiality (*zverstvo*); or exhort the Soviets to crush, annihilate, exterminate the "enemy," the "Germans," or the "German-fascists," to avenge murder, pillage, and rape, and to liberate women and children in captivity (see fig. 12, 14). Another 8.5 percent (19) feature heroes from Russian history, or contemporary heroes of the military and the resistance, who also urge the Soviet soldiers to crush the enemy. Other categories include posters devoted to Hitler, other Nazi leaders and Allies (8.1 percent), to the increase in production of foods and war materials (12.6 percent),[32] and to security and safety instructions (5.8 percent).[33] Though the Soviet government had defined as its ultimate task in the war, together with the other peace-loving nations, to liberate the world from "fascist slavery," posters that celebrate the common cause of the Allies are confined to a meager one percent.

The frequent identification of the *Nazi* with the *German* is important, due to the massive distribution and particular nature of posters, which were possibly better indicators of popular feelings than other media of expression. Theater, *estrada*, circus, and the press were all closely controlled by the government. They may be popular even when their propaganda messages do not coincide with the popular feeling because they also offer entertainment and information. On the contrary, posters may have to approach more closely the popular psyche and to elaborate ideas that the viewer already has in mind in one form or another. Posters have to be convincing to be effective, or they lose their *raison d'être*. In this sense, the posters of the Great Patriotic War illustrate very well the dialogue between Soviet propaganda and the people. What did Soviet propaganda add to the existing Russian stereotypes and negative images of Germans?

In the poster captions the enemy was defined by impersonal terms that deprived him of the last shred of humanity. Soviet propaganda called on soldiers and people to exterminate the Germans mercilessly, and to avenge their nation: "Death to the fascist conquerors" (*Smert' fashistskim zakhvatchikam*), "Death to the fascist invaders" (*Smert' fashistskim okkupantam*), "Death to the fascist villains" (*Smert' zlodeiam fashistam*), "Death to the child-killers" (*Smert' detoubiitsam*), "Blood for blood, death for death" (*Krov' za krov', smert' za smert'*), "Death to the fascist viper" (*Smert' fashistskoi gadine*), "Do not let the fascist beast escape retribution" (*Ne uiti fashistskomu zveriu ot rasplatu*), and "We shall mercilessly crush and exterminate the enemy" (*Besposhchadno razgromim i unichtozhim vraga*).

Furthermore, the iconography of posters reveals not only the total identification of the Nazi and the German, but also an unusually frequent depiction of Germans as low forms of life, especially rodents and insects. The fact that such images are rarer in the anti-German propaganda of other nations in World War II and have very limited precedents in Russian anti-German depictions from World War I shows vividly how different the German-Russian struggle of 1941–45 was from other wars, warfronts, and theaters involving Germans. But part of the explanation rests in official ideology. During the Great Patriotic War, Germany and the USSR were ruled by National Socialists and Bolsheviks respectively, each with their own *Weltanschauung*. Both regimes were very familiar with each other's ideology; and they responded to each other's propaganda on a daily basis, through the radio, press, posters, and the theatrical arts. Images of rodents and parasitic insects are most prevalent in the National-Socialist and specifically in Hitler's depiction of the Jews and later in Goebbels's portrayal of Bolshevism, a brand of "spiritual Jewishness."

Hitler referred to the Jew as "a maggot in a rotting corpse," "a plague," "a noxious poison," "a germ carrier," "a drone," "a spider," "a bloodsucker," "a parasite," "a harmful bacillus," "a hydra," "a vampire," "a pack of rats."[34] Soviet posters abounded with similar images applied to the Germans. Soviet propaganda represented Nazism as a disease, a virus that contaminated peoples, and a corpse in decay; and it portrayed German troops as a pack of rats. The observed enormous suggestive power of the ideological vigor and absoluteness of Nazism might have certainly tempted Soviet propagandists to imitate it. It has been shown how much Nazi ideology influenced the

terminology and practices of the main anti-fascist forces, the Communists of the Wei-
mar Republic, as well as factions of the contemporary extreme Left in Germany and
other European countries.[35]

However, Soviet propagandists, being Bolsheviks and mostly Russians, drew on
other influences. Lenin had made use of parasitical terminology to describe class enemies such as kulaks, the bourgeoisie, part of the intelligentsia, and the clergy, whom
he often referred to as "bloodsuckers, spiders, leeches, parasites." Lenin defined the
single most important objective of the Revolution as "the cleansing of Russia's soil of
all harmful insects, of thieving fleas, bedbugs—the rich, and so on."[36] In his explica-
tions of the need for terror, one finds all the expressions used by World War II posters
to urge the extermination of the Germans, while his "Lessons of the Commune" is
credited with the first use of the term "extermination" with reference to human beings.
Lenin's inability to tolerate dissent, as well as his relative indifference to human suffering, has also been forcefully argued.[37] Similarly, Trotsky castigated in his speeches the
enemies of the Revolution as "cockroaches," "parasites and spongers," "weeds," and
"scum."[38] A similar lexicon was in use during the Stalinist purges of the 1930s. Wartime broadcasters, poster artists, and songwriters employed the terminology of intol-
erance and destruction embedded in vulgarized Marxism for decades.[39]

This "parasitology," and the metaphors from the medical profession (fashionable
among an entire generation of European demagogues), did not become a permanent
feature of popular outlook,[40] even though official images of parasites, disease, and
decay became very prevalent in the portrayal of the American "ruling circles" during
the first years of the Cold War. Inasmuch as posters, caricatures, and other sources
represent a juncture of popular and state-imposed cultural values, this last observation
indicates the potential influence and limitations of state propaganda, ideology, and
perception.

## Conclusions

The Soviet dehumanization of the German foe was understandably ardent and
profound. Other continental European peoples produced similar images of the Germans, but few cases approached the severity of the Soviet portrayal. Moreover, the
German-occupied European peoples did not have the technical means—posters, newspapers, magazines, theater, cinema—to disseminate those images among large numbers
of people. The demonization of Germans by the Soviets, on the other hand, presents
three particularities: the dehumanization of the enemy in images was exceptionally
intense; state propaganda disseminated these images to extraordinarily large numbers
of people; and, more problematically, the Soviets were exhorted to destroy invaders
in language that could sometimes be interpreted in more sweeping terms of national

annihilation by the highest level of their governments. Stalin's speech on the radio, after the German armies approached Moscow in October 1941, illustrates this point:[41]

> . . . these people without honor or conscience, with the *morality of animals*, who have the effrontery to call for the *extermination* of the great Russian nation, the nation of Plekhanov and Lenin, Belinsky and Chernyshevsky, Pushkin and Tolstoy, Gorky and Chekhov, Glinka and Tchaikovsky, Sechenov and Pavlov, Suvorov and Kutuzov. The German invaders want a *war of extermination* against the peoples of the Soviet Union . . . they will have it. Our task now will be to *destroy every German to the very last one, who had come to occupy our country. No mercy for the German invaders. Death to the German invaders.* [My emphasis]

The last phrases could be taken to mean that only Germans who invaded Russia should die. However, as the ferocity of the war revealed, many Russians saw all Germans as invaders, which meant that they should all be punished. How much public urging, hate propaganda and imagery, and popular misreading added to the already inflamed anger of the soldiery by the realities of this war is an open quesiton.

The Great Patriotic War was a war of nations, like many that preceded it.[42] As such, it led to a revival of Russian nationalism. Propaganda and popular culture drew heavily on older symbols, images, and artistic techniques to describe the enemy. The war pitted Russians against Germans, although Marxist-Leninist ideology was also successfully drafted to give Russians greater unity of purpose and to predicate the fall of German capitalist-driven imperialism.

Despite minor differences, all the Soviet mass media and ways of entertainment used more or less the same symbolism and disseminated similar images of the enemy during the war. Leadership and people were consonant in perceiving the Nazi threat as a German threat. The difference is that the more popular cultural manifestations, such as circus and *estrada*, did not clothe national hatred in ideology.

Official propaganda and elite culture have an option of amplifying or attempting to control justified popular wrath and instinctive violence. The ordeal of war, particularly of total war, tends to barbarize soldiers and civilians alike in all warring nations and propaganda exacerbates the barbarization. How different were the Russians from the other Allies? The Hollywood director, Frank Capra, who produced American propaganda films for the army in World War II was ordered not to be too harsh on the Germans because the US government "did not want the American people to start hating Germans."[43] On the other hand, the American popular mythology of the Japanese superhuman warrior and the adverse fighting conditions in the Pacific led to many battles of ruthless extermination in some theaters of that war, such as Guadalcanal.[44] It is true that neither the American president nor the high command nor the war posters urged American soldiers to annihilate every single Japanese (technically, neither did the Soviets do so for the Germans); but this did not prevent the U.S. from inflicting mass extermination by the dropping of atomic bombs on Japan. The main reason of course for the relatively—but only relatively—lesser American demonization of the Japanese enemy compared to the Soviets' demonization of the Germans is that that the United States suffered neither the occupation nor the mass sufferings and human losses incurred by the Soviet people in the war.

Soviet propaganda was successful in registering the feelings of the people and, subsequently, in magnifying and directing them in a way that facilitated the immense war effort. At the same time, the mixture of official propaganda and popular instinct had an explosive effect. The Soviet soldier, who for four years was being in essence admonished by his supreme leadership to "take revenge" and, by implication, to take no prisoners, did precisely that when his unit entered German-populated areas. This along with the record of German occupation policies in the USSR offer a much more credible explanation of Soviet atrocities in Germany than the bestial, uncivilized nature of Russians that German memoirs sometimes allege.

## Notes

1. For radio broadcasting, see Von Geldern, this volume.

2. In the prewar period Germans were demonized not only in posters and caricatures but also in works of high artistic quality, such as the film *Alexander Nevskii* (Sergei Eisenstein, 1938) and the plays *The Orchards of Polovchansk* (Leonid Leonov, 1938) and *Field Marshal Kutuzov* (Vladimir Solovëv, 1939). See Kenez and Segel, this volume.

3. *Izvestiia*, June 24, 1941, 1. Molotov uses the word *germanskii/nemetskii* eleven times and the phrase *germanskie fashistskie praviteli* only twice. Within days this terminology changed drastically and the war correspondents of *Izvestiia* called Germans "*fashistskie zakhvatchiki*," or simply "*fashisty*" or "*gitlerovtsy*" (*Izvestiia*, June 23–27, 1941). "*Fashist*" derives from the prewar Soviet criticism of the political system of Germany and "*gitlerovtsy*" emphasizes Hitler's role in that system.

4. Alexander Werth, *Russia at War, 1941–1945* (New York, 1964), p. 160.

5. In films, Germans pursue Communists and partisans more vigorously than others. In *Rainbow*, the Nazis call the heroine "*Bolshevichka*," while a German soldier who wants to intimidate a boy calls him "*partizan*." In *She Defends the Motherland*, a Russian who voiced the belief that Nazis can be tolerated, because they were only after Communists and Jews, is shot dead by the heroine.

6. In articles published in the American press, the Soviets portrayed themselves as education- and culture-loving people who were invaded by barbarians.

7. The most common stereotypical names for Germans were *Frits* (Fritz) and *Gans* (Hans), used in other occupied countries, too. In *estrada*, *Frits(y)* is used at least as often as *nemtsy*. See Georgii Terikov, *Kuplet na estrade* (Moscow: Isskustvo, 1987), p. 138. *Gans* is sometimes accompanied by a common German last name, usually *Miller* (*Müller*). The prefix of nobility, *von*, was used

in excess even where it did not originally exist, e.g., *von* Paulus, or *von* Göring in poetry, *estrada*, songs, and cartoons. See *Pravda*, July 7, 1945, 1. The English narration of *Moscow Strikes Back* uses the derogatory *von Butcher* several times. Sometimes, the above stereotypical names were combined, to create even more "German-like" names, such as *Gans von Frits*. See Terikov, *Kuplet*, p. 128. Soviet artists were resourceful with puns, and made up comical names that sounded German but derived from Russian words, such as *Frits Zimler* (*zima*=winter). Other puns derived from German terms, such as *Blitzkrieg*, which Russian clowns turned to *blitskrik* (*krik*=scream). See Elizaveta Uvarova, *Russkaia sovetskaia estrada, 1930–1945* (Moscow, 1977), p. 109.

8. Love themes are quite strong in some films and plays, such as *She Defends the Motherland*, and *Zhdi menia* (*Wait for Me*, 1942), a dramatization of Konstantin Simonov's popular song "Zhdi menia i ia vernus."

9. The theme of revenge is manifest at the end of *Rainbow*, where the heroine gives a speech to her fellow-villagers about how they should treat the captured enemy and how they should fight. In many posters partisans and armed peasants stand proud and exclaim: "We swear to take revenge against the fascist vermin." Other posters are titled "We shall avenge the atrocities of the butchers," "The hour of retribution is near," or "We shall hold accountable all fascist criminals" (in which a stern-faced Soviet soldier apprehends a German who is setting Russian homes afire). Identical phrases can be found in songs and poems recited in circus and plays. In Afinogenov's *On The Eve* all the Russian people assemble onstage, facing the audience, and amidst the noise of Nazi bombers and the rattling of German machine guns, they vow to avenge the death of a female character. In *Rainbow*, a mother holds her murdered child in her arms and curses the Germans, a picture we find in several posters with the caption: "*Otomstim!*" (We shall take revenge).

In another poster, a Russian woman with her emaciated child in her arms, calls upon the Red Army soldier to save her. The enemy is represented by a German bayonet, pointing at the helpless mother. When the heroine of *She Defends the Motherland* is taken to the gallows, the camera temporarily freezes, showing Pasha from the breast up. She is wearing a shawl similar to that of the mother in the poster, and a bayonet penetrates the screen from the left lower part, exactly as in the poster. In the last scene of *Rainbow*, the heroine stands on a hill and admonishes the people. Her gestures as well as her face are strikingly similar to "*Rodina Mat'*", the female figure that calls the Russians to arms in an early, well-known poster. The actress symbolizes Russia. The same poster hangs on the wall of a partisan recruitment office, where the heroine of *Zoia* goes. A poster and a film by Ivan Pyriev in 1944 had the same title: *V shest' chasov vechera posle voiny*. State propaganda reiterated identical phrases and images to ingrain a strong impression in the consciousness of the Soviets, by following principles which Goebbels, as the propaganda theoretician, referred to as "utmost simplicity and ceaseless repetition."

10. In *Zoia*, German soldiers mock the heroine, burn her face with a candle, beat her, and make her walk in the snow. In *She Defends the Motherland*, the Germans shoot POWs in cold blood.

11. In *Moscow Strikes Back*, the narrator says that "if the Nazis had read *War and Peace*, they would have anticipated their fate." In *On the Eve*, numerous references to Russian tactics in the war of 1812, as described by Tolstoy, serve to justify the Red Army's retreat as part of a wise plan, similar to Marshal Kutuzov's.

12. Original caricature forms from the Napoleonic wars had been used also in World War I for Kaiser Wilhelm II, who was sometimes depicted as a monkey, as was Hitler later.

13. The caption of one such poster lists Russian victories in 1242, 1760, and 1918 (Ukraine), and exclaims: "*Bili, bëm i budem bit'*" (We won, we are winning, and we will win).

14. For this reason, German officers in posters tend to be more repulsive than soldiers: fat, ugly faces, serpent eyes, sharp protruding teeth like those of a shark or a vampire, porcine noses and sharp, erect, hairy ears like a hyena's.

15. Similar White officers appear in the films *Chapaev* (1934) and *Karo* (1938). Even if Soviet film directors were not directly inspired by older films, it is true that the Soviets tended to attribute

the same traits to their enemies and drew linkages between them. In *Invasion*, a former anti-communist emigré collaborates with the Germans. However, in the play *Russian People* (Konstantin Simonov, 1942), an old Tsarist officer makes common cause with the Soviets and turns over his nephew, who is a spy, to the partisans. The triumph of Russian nationality over political and family affinities shows the wartime vigor of Russian nationalism. See Segel, this volume.

16. In *Zoia*, placards of the enemies of the regime appear in a May Day parade, some time in the 1920s. Some of them are fat, tuxedo-clad industrialists with vampire teeth. The play *Oil* (P. Tur, Ia. Gorev, and A. Shein, 1929), features a fat German capitalist with cigar, monocle, thick moustache, tuxedo and a black top hat, bearing a swastika on his chest. The same figure can be found in prewar and wartime posters, wearing a Nazi uniform.

17. Most prominent among the poster artists and cartoonists were Kukryniksy (Mikhail Kuprianov, Porfirii Krylov, Nikolai Sokolov), V. Deni, V. Ivanov and A. Kokorekin.

18. In cartoons, the percentage of dark-haired Germans nears 100 percent. Films like *Rainbow* allow for more verisimilitude. However, in *Lieutenant Hopp's Career*, Lieutenant Hopp and his aide have dark hair. In *Vanka* all the Germans have dark hair. Traitors, too, are dark-haired, as in *Alexander Nevskii*, *Rainbow*, and *She Defends the Motherland*. In *Rainbow* the male collaborator has long hair and a beard that remind one of depictions of kulaks in the 1920s and 1930s.

19. The beginnings of the tendency to obscure the face of the enemy in the Soviet cinema can be traced back to the early years. In a scene from the film *October* (1927), the camera follows Kerenskii (who is called a dictator) in the Winter Palace, showing only his military boots and his back. In *Alexander Nevskii*, the Teutonic knights' bodies and faces are hidden inside armor and helmets. In *She Defends the Motherland*, the camera shows a German army unit only from the knees up to the neck, dwelling on their boots and shiny bayonets, the tools of destruction.

20. Imitating Eisenstein's prolonged zoom on the helmets of the Teutonic knights as they gallop against the Russians, Mark Donskoi, the director of *Rainbow*, focuses repeatedly on the German helmets and their two small protrusions (bolts), perhaps to associate them with the devil's horns.

21. The play *Invasion* dwells on the rigid, wooden manner in which the Germans move. In motion pictures, the concept first appeared in *Battleship Potëmkin*, where peaceful crowds are shot down by Tsarist troops on the Odessa steps. The camera shows only the boots of the soldiers, as they move down the steps in perfect synchronicity, as if parts of a mechanical device. Innocently bystanding women, children, babies, and beggars are shot down. The same device is used during the "psychic attack" by the Whites in *Chapaev*.

22. *Estrada* and circus in particular, used real dogs for Hitler, Goebbels, Göring, and Himmler. In a sketch, a dog is offended because it was named Hitler. Uvarova, *Estrada*, p. 98, records the circus act *Young Fritz* (*Iunyi Frits*), where a young German soldier is turned into a dog-like beast and is spurned even by animals. During the Cold War, variety shows used dogs to illustrate American officials.

23. Other German villains often were made to look like Hitler, as does an interrogator in *Rainbow*, Lieutenant Hopp in *Lieutenant Hopp's Career*, and a sergeant in *Vanka*.

24. Werth, *Russia*, p. 367.

25. As Uvarova, *Estrada*, p. 101, explains, the circus sketch *Kak fashisty shli na Moskvu i obratno* (*How the Fascists Went to Moscow and Back*, 1942) "issued a death sentence to Hitler's war machine and to the garrulous propaganda of Goebbels." To the Soviets, Goebbels's propaganda was one of the two pillars of the Nazi regime. In *Pravda*, Feb. 1, 1945, 4, a poem entitled "Brandenburg" singles out Goebbels for a special venomous attack. *Estrada* artists and cartoonists took their topics from newspaper pieces, including reports of Goebbels's bulletins and speeches.

26. Even newspapers freely used language emphasizing German bestiality: see, for instance, "*Zverstvo nemetsko-fashistkikh liudoedov v Rostove-na-Donu*," in *Izvestiia*, March 13, 1943. The magazine *Ogonëk* contained realistic war stories and dwelt on the atrocities of the Germans, but its vocabulary was more restrained, closer to *Pravda*'s or *Izvestiia*'s, and not as comical as *Krokodil*'s. *Pioner*, the children's magazine of the Pioneer Youth, contained mostly stories of heroism and de-

monized the Germans, using the same vocabulary as posters and caricatures. Intended to instill a sense of duty, patriotism and obedience to the Soviet authorities, *Pioner* abounded with violent stories and poems that expose the enemy's complete disregard for human life: see, for instance, *Pioner*, 20 (June-Aug., 1943), 7–8; 23 (October, 1943), 9; 21 (May-June, 1944), 3. *Murzilka*, a publication for primary-school children, contained military adventures emphasizing patriotism, but very few violent scenes.

27. *Invasion*, a high-culture work by inspiration, contained enough anti-German messages to be apposite and popular during the war. See also Segel, this volume.

28. In *Rainbow*, all the Germans are demonized and deemed worthy of annihilation. In *She Defends the Motherland* the heroine says: "No sleep, no rest for the Germans, until they are all driven out or buried under the snow." *Estrada* couplets reveal a deep hatred for the enemy: "may white shrouds cover all German soldiers." See Nikolai Smirnov-Sokolskii, *Sorok piat' let na estrade: fel'etony, stat'i, vystuplenii* (Moscow, 1976), p. 90.

29. In posters, German women are depicted receiving clothes and other items that their husbands took from Russian children they had killed.

30. Terikov, *Kuplet*, p. 133; Uvarova, *Estradnyi teatr: miniatiury, obozreniia, miuzik-kholly, 1917–1945* (Moscow, 1983), p. 287.

31. Although the poster collection in question and other materials, including articles by Soviets in U.S. periodicals, letters of U.S. citizens concerned about the war and the alliance with the USSR to the State Department, and U.S. diplomatic reports from the Soviet Union to the State Department, do not belong to the original Smolensk Archives, they are housed and listed under the same title as the latter. The aforementioned materials can be found under the code numbers WKP-480 and WKP-482 in the Smolensk Archives, held at the National Archives in Washington, D.C. This collection of posters is not exhaustive of the Soviet wartime poster production, but is very representative thereof. Most posters were issued by Gosudarstvennoe Izdatel'stvo "Iskusstvo," and OKNO TASS (the latter issued over a thousand posters during the war). The average tirage of each poster was approximately 20,000 to 30,000 copies.

32. In an attempt to utilize the maximum of the productive resources of the nation, thirteen out of those twenty-eight posters (five percent of the total) address women specifically.

33. These instruct civilians to save electricity, to recycle materials, and to help defend their homes and cities.

34. Adolf Hitler, *Mein Kampf,* transl. & ed. John Chamberlain et al. (New York, 1940), pp. 75, 99, 314–15, 425, 826, 928. The notorious anti-Semitic film *Der ewige Jude* (Fritz Hippler, 1940) also compared Jews to rats by means of parallel montage.

35. See Eve Rosenhaft, *Beating the Fascists? The German Communists and Political Violence, 1929–1933* (Cambridge, Mass., 1983); Ulrike Linke, "Nazi Terminology and Left-Wing Political Violence in Contemporary Germany" (paper presented at the Symposium on Anthropology and Literary Studies: Analyzing Minority Cultures in Germany, Georgetown University, Washington, D.C., April 3, 1993).

36. V. I. Lenin, *Polnoe sobranie sochinenii*, vol. 35 (Moscow, 1969), p. 204: "*ochistki* zemli rossiiskoi ot vsiakikh vrednykh nasekomykh, ot blokh-zhulikov, ot klopov-bogatykh i prochee i prochee" (emphasis in the original).

37. Richard Pipes, *The Russian Revolution* (New York, 1990), pp. 345, 349–353.

38. Leon Trotskii, *How the Revolution Armed*, transl. Brian Pearce, (New York, 1979), pp. 237–39.

39. Karl Marx & Friedrich Engels, *The Communist Manifesto*, ed. Joseph Katz (New York, 1964), p. 75, refers to the *Lumpenproletariat* as "social scum," a "passively rotting mass. . . . "

40. Russians maintained a love-hate relation to Germans; see Werth, *Russia*, p. 367.

41. Ibid., p. 246.

42. The caption of a poster of 1945 reads: "We Russians, we won" (*My russkie, my pobedili*). For the deemphasis of Soviet and Communist and the emphasis of Russian in the theater, see Segel,

*Drama*, p. 318; Frederick Barghoorn, *Russian Soviet Nationalism* (New York, 1956), p. 27. The last phrase in *Alexander Nevskii* warns "Whoever comes against us with the sword, shall perish by the sword. Such is the law of the Russian land and it will always be." In the poem "Russkii chelovek" (*Pravda*, July 7, 1945, 2), Aleksandr Iashin exalts the Russians and praises the Ukrainians and Belorussians, but no non-Slavic peoples of the USSR. Stalin sealed this emphasis with his "toast to the Russian people." Announcing the German capitulation, on May 10, 1945, Stalin used the word *nemetskii* ten times, the word *vrag* three times, *gitlerovtsy* once and *fashisty* only once (*Pravda*, May 10, 1945, 1).

43. In the documentary *Walk Through the 20th Century: The Propaganda Battle* (1982) by Frank Capra.

44. Craig Cameron shows this in his paper "Clash of Cultures: Conquering the Superman Myth on Guadalcanal" (given at the "Conference on World War II: A Fifty-Year Perspective" at Siena College, Siena, N.Y., on June 4, 1992). The major work on the subject is John Dower, *War Without Mercy* (New York, 1986).

# 10

# Black and White

## The War on Film

### Peter Kenez

SOVIET CINEMA AT the outbreak of the war was already fully mobilized; only the propaganda themes needed to be changed.[1] The peculiar character of Soviet movies was the consequence of the extraordinarily repressive Stalinist political system. The Bolsheviks, even more than other politicians, believed in the malleability of the human mind; that is, they attributed great significance to propaganda. They were determined to convey their message, in which, of course, they deeply believed, to the common people. They were even more determined to suppress all competing views, and therefore spared no effort to ferret out the slightest evidence of heterodoxy. The Stalinists used all available propaganda vehicles, but they assigned a special role to the cinema. It is clear that they attributed great, perhaps excessively great, power to cinema: on the one hand, they lavished an amazing amount of attention on this medium of art; on the other hand, they were never satisfied with the results.

Already in the 1920s agencies of the state examined every scenario and finished product. As time went on the control mechanism became more and more fantastically elaborated. In the 1930s the studios contracted authors to write scripts on assigned topics. The finished scenarios were examined by departments within the studios in which the party and other mass organizations were represented. Then the scenarios were submitted for general discussion and for this purpose they were published in journals. At each stage, deletions were ordered and changes were made. The completed film was submitted to the Agitation and Propaganda Department of the Central Committee of the Party, which wrote a report. After that the entire Politburo, including, of course, I. V. Stalin, watched every Soviet film that was to be distributed. In almost every case so many changes were introduced that one could not talk about the film as the work of the scenarist—much less that of the director, who was kept on a short leash and whose work was held in low regard. (Soviet politicians naively imagined that

*157*

the director's contribution was small: they thought that he just held the camera.) The author and producer of every Soviet film was the state, which hired well-paid professionals to serve its needs. Andrei Zhdanov, a member of the Politburo and the man responsible for cultural life, explained to the filmmakers in May 1941 why the state had to take such a minute interest in the smallest details of every film. He said: "Since everyone knows that all our films are state-produced, I, a Soviet viewer, conclude when I see a film that the ideas expressed in it are recommended by the government. And if this film encourages a do-nothing attitude, I conclude that this is what the government recommends."[2]

The removal of Nikolai Ezhov from power was followed by a very modest decrease in terror. To use a term that only later came into usage, the period of Nazi-Soviet cooperation could be regarded as the first small-scale thaw in Soviet intellectual life. The slight relaxation in terror did not manifest itself in the kind of films that were made; however, the discussions concerning the problems facing the filmmakers became somewhat more open. In these circumstances not only could the politicians express their dissatisfaction, but the filmmakers also had an opportunity to respond. In September 1940 the Agitation and Propaganda Department of the Central Committee sent a report, signed by G. Aleksandrov and D. Polikarpov, to the Secretariat of the Central Committee concerning the unsatisfactory work of the film industry.[3] In it they complained that the studios made only half as many films as the plans had called for; that the industry did not produce enough profit; and, above all, that too many of those made could not be shown because they were ideologically unacceptable (*ideologicheskii brak*). In March 1941 Zhdanov himself raised the same issues mentioned in the Aleksandrov-Polikarpov report, and added some of his own complaints. In a speech to the Central Committee he pointed out that in spite of the attention given to films, too many of them could not be shown, for they contained "ideological errors."[4] (A film by Leonid Trauberg and Gregory Kozintsev on Marx could not be exhibited because Marx and Engels were not depicted with sufficient respect.)[5] Another could not be shown because in it Russians exhibited a too cavalier attitude toward Uzbeks;[6] and a third, made by Boris Barnet, was unacceptable because it showed kolkhoz life only as a series of festivities and "made fun of everything that characterized the new life in the collective farms, such as sports, radio and machines." Yet another was held back because it showed the enemy, a foreign agent, as smarter than the Russian border guards. This film, unlike the others, was remade and later exhibited under the title *Girl from the Other Side*.

In order to improve the situation, in May 1941, Zhdanov called together a conference of workers in the film industry. Since this was a closed conference, the participants spoke openly.[7] Zhdanov in particular, spoke with startling frankness about Soviet foreign policy:

You well understand that if circumstances allow we will further expand the socialist camp. You also well understand that this is connected with the need to educate our people in a spirit of hatred against the enemies of socialism and in the spirit of willingness to sacrifice. The people must be ready to deal a death blow against any bourgeois country and against any bourgeois coalition. It is one of the tasks of the filmmakers to educate our people in the spirit of attack. The filmmakers must understand, that, of course, the conflict between us and the bourgeois world is inevitable and that it must end with the victory of socialism.

In his remarks he admonished the filmmakers to get to know "Soviet reality" better, and for the first time advanced the controversial proposition which after the war became a basic principle of the Soviet film industry: Soviet studios should make only masterpieces. Even though the industry never came close to fulfilling the plan, it was better to make even fewer films but, from a political point of view, only first-rate ones.

The directors present, especially Gregory Aleksandrov, the maker of the best-loved comedies, and Mikhail Romm, the director of successful films about Lenin, made it clear in their remarks why it was difficult to make a film in the Soviet Union. Aleksandrov complained about the innumerable people and institutions which had the right to interfere. Bureaucrats afraid for their position always erred on the side of caution. He related an amusing story:

When Comrade Stalin saw *Volga-Volga*, he commented that the first kiss should be cut. Comrade Dukel'skii [at the time head of the Film Committee] decided that kissing is a dangerous business, and whenever kissing appeared he thought that there was no need to show it, but it definitely had to be cut. The Deputy of Dukel'skii, Comrade Burianov told me that it will be for the best if we cut all kissing. I asked him whose decision was it? He looked at me meaningfully and said that this was not his opinion. Ostensibly this is Comrade Stalin's opinion, Comrade Zhdanov's opinion, but I am sure that this is not your opinion, but Dukel'skii's.

Both Aleksandrov and Romm mentioned that it was impossible to depict convincing positive heroes, if people could not be shown with their faults. Aleksandrov in one of his films wanted to show a drunken sailor, but the navy would not let him. Romm remarked that it was better to deal with the intelligentsia because scientific establishments are weaker than others, "but it is impossible to touch agriculture, because there is Comrade Lysenko and then there will be serious trouble." Romm explained that completed films had to sit for months in various departments, each having the right to pass on them, and by the time they appeared in movie houses they were already out-dated. The politicians and the filmmakers obviously had different agendas.

The purest form of war propaganda was the newsreel. Lenin, who had a prescient appreciation of the indoctrination possibilities inherent in cinema, thought of feature films primarily as means of attracting an audience to the theaters in order to expose them to documentaries, the real vehicles for transmitting a message.[8]

Soviet documentary filmmaking had had a long and honorable tradition. The first films made after the Bolshevik Revolution were documentaries; the works of Dziga Vertov, and to a lesser extent of Esfir Shub, were known and admired beyond the borders of the Soviet Union. By the late 1930s, however, the period of innovation was over, and like many Soviet feature films, documentaries came to be boring and predictable. Although the technical level of documentaries had always been low, in the early days artistic virtuosity made up for backwardness. As this virtuosity disappeared, the technical backwardness of Soviet products became all the more glaring.

When the Second World War in Europe broke out in 1939, Soviet cameramen were not well prepared; they did not bequeath to posterity a good record of the military exploits of their country in the years of Soviet-Nazi collaboration. Since the invasion of Eastern Poland had been carried out in secrecy, no cameramen accompanied the Red Army when it crossed the Polish border on September 17th. There is only a spotty filmic record of the occupation of Eastern Poland, and the forced incorporation of Bessarabia and the Baltic states. About the four-months long Finnish-Soviet war there was only one film made; naturally, praising the accomplishments of the Red Army.[9]

Once the real war began, on June 22, 1941, the Soviet leadership carried out a complete mobilization. This was accomplished with impressive speed, a testimony to the ability of a totalitarian state to change directions at a moment's notice. The propaganda themes, of course, changed overnight. The war was not called an "imperialist" one any longer, one carried out entirely because of the wickedness of the British warmongers. The leadership, fully aware of the mobilizing value of moving pictures, concentrated all the available scarce resources and started to produce a large number of documentaries. The first wartime newsreel, amazingly, appeared in movie theaters as early as three days after the outbreak of the war, on June 25th. In the following months a new edition came out every three days.[10]

In this moment of extreme danger and confusion the leadership gave priority to documentary-making over all other films. The making of full-length films was suspended and prominent directors, such as Aleksandr Dovzhenko, Iulii Raizman, Sergei Iutkevich, I. Khaifitz, and A. Zarkhi gave their talent to editing documentaries. In the fall of 1941 the studios were evacuated from Moscow, but the documentary-makers remained; evidently, their work was considered too important to be interrupted. The films shot in different parts of the country were edited in Moscow. One can hardly exaggerate the technical difficulties that the documentarists had to overcome, and the dreadful material conditions in which they had to operate. During the blockade of Leningrad, for example, documentary-making continued in the besieged city.[11] A full-length documentary was made about the road on the frozen Lake Ladoga, that supplied besieged Leningrad.[12]

However great the dedication of the cameramen and editors was, and however clearly the government recognized the potential of documentary films in raising morale, the first newsreels neither were very good propaganda nor did they contain interesting historical material. First of all, there was an organizational problem: it took some time to set up special film groups at the headquarters of major army units, under the supervision of the political departments. In May 1944 the Central Committee of the Party created a council to oversee documentary-making, and named Sergei Gerasimov head of the documentary studio.[13] One suspects that, given the party's suspiciousness and excessive preoccupation with spies, the freedom of the cameramen, especially in the earliest stages, was strictly limited. Even during the second half of the war, at a time when the Red Army advanced victoriously westward, no foreign cameramen were ever allowed on the front. As a consequence, all film material taken on the Soviet side was the work of Soviet documentarists.

During the first months the cameramen rarely or never photographed actual military action, but used archival footage or photographed second- or third-echelon troops. Cheating, of course, was as old as documentary-making, but it was especially widely used at this time. Documentary-makers staged battle scenes, and filmed maneuvers pretending that their versions depicted actual battles.[14] During the great retreat of the summer and early fall of 1941, the newsreels never mentioned the specific locale of military actions, for the very place names would have revealed to the audience the desperateness of the military situation. The announcers instead talked vaguely about "southern front" or "northwestern front". The first time that the actual location of the battle was mentioned was the fighting for Kiev in September. Evidently, the bad news could no longer be hidden.[15]

The main problem the documentary-makers faced in producing propaganda, however, was neither organizational difficulties, nor technical backwardness, nor excessive suspiciousness on the part of the authorities. It was that documentaries, however remotely, ultimately depend on reality. Very little happened during the first months of the war that could be presented even to Soviet audiences, used to mercilessly distorted propaganda, that could both be made believable and at the same time uplifting. The situation was so desperate that it was impossible to present it, even in a distorted form, so as to raise morale. When the Soviet people most needed encouragement, documentaries were least able to provide it. In the early months the most interesting work depicted not the military situation, but the home front. Seeing the intent and anxious faces of Muscovites as they listen to Stalin's first wartime speech on July 3, 1941, is still a moving experience.[16] M. Ia. Slutskii, one of the best known documentarists, shot newsreels showing how Muscovites prepared for the siege. The film showed, of course, not the panic that had seized a part of the population, but citizens who heroically carried out their tasks while enduring extraordinary hardship.[17]

The turning point in the history of documentary-making coincided with the turning point in the history of the war. In early December 1941, the Red Army managed to bring in fresh troops from Siberia, and inflict a major defeat at the outskirts of Moscow on the overextended, tired, ill-equipped soldiers of the Wehrmacht. A collection of newsreels that was presented to the audiences in February 1942 as *The Defeat of the German Armies near Moscow*, made by L. V. Varlamov and I. P. Kopalin, became the most effective Soviet documentary of the war. The film did not intend to relate the actual course of the battle and showed not a single map. The most effective scenes, according to contemporary observers, were the ones that showed defeated, bedraggled, and obviously humiliated German soldiers led through the capital by their victorious captors. The audiences desperately wanted to be reassured that the Nazis could be defeated, and now here was visual evidence: the Germans were not supermen. The Soviet people—and also people in Allied countries—flocked to see the film. In Britain and in the United States this film, shown under the title *Moscow Strikes Back*, elicited favorable responses, and increased public support for the Soviet ally.[18]

The format of combining newsreels into full-length documentaries proved successful and in the following years thirty-four of these of these were made, each devoted to a major battle.[19] Once the liberation of Eastern Europe began, the fight for each country became the subject of a separate documentary. Slutskii made a very successful full length documentary, *A Day of the War*, that attempted to show the life of the peoples of the Soviet Union on June 13, 1942. He used the material shot by 160 cameramen working in different parts of the vast country, including the front.[20] Another full length documentary deserving special mention was the work of Dovzhenko, *The Battle for Our Soviet Ukraine*. In this work Dovzhenko, like many other filmmakers, contrasted the "peaceful and happy lives of the Soviet people before the the the war" with the difficult present. Dovzhenko's highly individual style, characterized by lyricism and attention to the beauties of the Ukrainian landscape, was very much in evidence. He was among the first to utilize captured German newsreels in order to make his points. He intercut smiling German faces and the depiction of the suffering of the conquered people.[21]

In the second half of the war the relative significance of the documentaries gradually declined. While at the beginning studios issued three newsreels a week, that was later reduced to two and ultimately to one. This development took place not because documentaries were no longer important, but because, as film makers got into their stride, they were able to provide the audiences with longer and relatively more sophisticated propaganda. Nevertheless, the overall achievements of documentarists in quantitative terms remain impressive. One hundred and fifty cameramen took 3.5 million meters of newsreel, presented in 460 editions.[22] Our view of the war on the eastern front is largely based on these film journals shot and assembled by Soviet documentarists.

The quality is harder to evaluate, for we cannot watch these films with the eyes of contemporaries. With the exception of the work of Dovzhenko, it is hard to recognize individual styles; the documentaries were similar to one another. Indeed, one might go further, and recognize that documentaries made in all the warring countries shared similar characteristics. One is impressed by the obvious bravery of the men who photographed front line action (forty Soviet cameramen lost their lives). War documentaries, wherever they were made, show tanks rolling in meadows; batteries firing followed by explosions that throw dirt into the air; and house-to-house fighting in dreadfully damaged buildings in which soldiers look through windows cautiously. But in spite of the obvious similarities, it is possible to talk about a particular Soviet-style documentary.

Soviet documentaries, unlike ones made elsewhere, did not shrink from showing misery and suffering. The willingness to depict the full horror of the war was not the consequence of mysterious qualities of the Russian soul, but followed from the specific situation of the country. In Allied countries the destruction was not comparable; and the Germans who did experience horror, after all, started the war; depicting their pain therefore could not possibly have served propaganda purposes. Goebbels's propagandists preferred to portray the fighting as victorious German armies marching forward. Pictures of bedraggled German soldiers encircled at Stalingrad obviously could not raise the morale of the home front. By contrast, showing devastation and pain increased the hatred of the peoples of the Soviet Union against the invader. As a consequence, Soviet newsreels have an air of reality today that is lacking in Nazi products.

A particular Soviet style was even more evident in the accompanying text than in the pictures themselves. The voice of the commentator was always solemn, bordering on the bombastic. The viewer was to feel that "History" was talking to him, rather than a mere mortal. There was no room here for understatement or flippancy. What would have been considered too much even for Soviet audiences in peacetime, was now allowed. No sentence was considered too flowery in praising Soviet heroism, and no word was considered too harsh in denouncing Nazi beastliness.

In the summer of 1941, quickly advancing German armies dealt devastating blows to Soviet forces. In the extraordinary conditions caused by the invasion, of course, filmmaking could not continue as before. The Kiev studio was lost within a few weeks, and by September it was impossible to continue work in Moscow and Leningrad. During the war the Central Asian cities, Tashkent, Ashkhabad, Stalinabad, and especially Alma-Ata, the new home of Mosfil'm and Lenfil'm, became the centers of Soviet film industry, and the already existing studios in Tbilisi, Baku and Erevan acquired new importance.

The leaders of the Soviet film industry dealt with the difficult situation according to the best of their abilities and mobilized the film industry with astonishing speed. They devoted most of their scarce resources to documentary-making, and prevailed on some of the best known and most talented directors to take on the editing of newsreels. Studios changed the scenarios of those feature films that were already in production by adding war themes. *Mashenka*, directed by Iu. Raizman, for example, though almost ready before the invasion, had to be remade. The film that was originally planned as a light comedy showing the happy lives of Soviet youth was substantially changed. In the new version, issued in 1942, the hero gets his girl by exhibiting heroism in volunteering for the front.[23] Some of the recently made films in circulation with anti-British and anti-Polish themes had to be recalled. *The Girl from the Other Side*, for example, a film that came out in April and which depicted an Iranian girl helping the Soviet authorities to unmask a British agent, not surprisingly disappeared from Soviet screens. *The Dream*, a film made by Romm, which showed the cruelty of the Polish ruling class, was held up for two years. (When finally shown, it was a sign of Stalin's determination to hold on to ex-Polish territories acquired in 1939.) Another film, *Hearts of Four*, directed by K. Iudin, was completed before the outbreak of the war, but was not publicly shown until 1945. Presumably the content of the film was regarded as too frivolous. Since the population needed feature films, prewar movies with patriotic themes, such as *Suvorov*, *Peter the Great*, and *Shchors*, were revived. Particularly important was Eisenstein's *Alexander Nevskii*, for it was a bitterly anti-German film that had to be taken out of circulation during the duration of the Molotov-Ribbentrop Pact.

The leaders of the Soviet film industry, well aware of the propaganda potential of cinema, innovated. Since it was impossible to make feature films with powerful propaganda content quickly, they made shorts and combined them into collections. The filmmakers returned to Soviet traditions: during the Civil War, another time of great hardships, the first products of the industry were short, rather primitive agitational films, suitable for showing in the countryside. These were called *agitki*, and were popular at the time. Immediately after the outbreak of the war anti-Nazi shorts were in production, and the first collection appeared in cinemas on August 2, followed by two other collections in the same month. The collections were called *Boevye kinosborniki*, fighting-film collections. Each consisted of several shorts—as few as two, or as many as six. Numbers 1–5 made up a series entitled *Victory Will be Ours*. In 1941 altogether seven collections appeared and in 1942, five more. The last one appeared in theaters in August; at that point they were discontinued, for by this time the relocated and reorganized industry could produce full-length feature films. The content of the *kinosborniki* was extremely heterogeneous, including Allied documentaries, such as one on the British Navy and another on the air war over London; and excerpts from previously successful films such as Liubov' Orlova as the singing mail carrier from *Volga, Volga* (1938).[24]

The segments of the first collection were introduced by the imaginary hero, Maxim, known to Soviet audiences from a series of successful films from the 1930s.[25] This collection included a short written by Leonid Leonov, *Three in a Shell Hole*. A wounded Soviet soldier, a wounded German and a Soviet nurse find themselves after a battle in the same shell hole. The nurse, a Soviet humanist, provides help to both of the wounded soldiers. The vicious German nevertheless is about to kill her, when the alert Soviet soldier prevents him by a well aimed and well timed bullet.

A segment in the second collection was called *The Meeting*. This short depicts the cruelties of the Germans in occupied territories, in this instance, in Poland. The Germans execute a group of people in 1939 because one peasant saved a bottle of milk for a sick child rather than handing it over to the occupiers. One of the peasants manages to escape into the Soviet Union, and two years later meets the same cruel German officer, but this time with weapon in hand as a Soviet soldier. He takes revenge for all the victims, Poles, White Russians, and Russians.[26] By common consent the best of these short dramas was *Feast in Zhirmunka* in no. 6. This sketch was also based on Leonov's scenario, and it was directed by Vsevolod Pudovkin. Praskov'ia, a Soviet kolkhoz woman, invites the occupying Germans to a meal in her house and poisons the food. In front of her guests she eats the poisoned food in order to allay their suspicions and encourage them to eat. When the partisans arrive they find everyone dead.[27]

Perhaps more effective than the dramas were the humorous shorts. The second collection, for example, included a vignette entitled *Incident at the Telegraph Office* made by Lev Arnshtam and Kozintsev. The entire film consists of one scene in which we see Napoleon at the telegraph office sending Hitler this message: "I have attempted it. I do not recommend it."[28] In the third collection appeared a short about Antosha Rybkin, a cook in the army, who aspires to be a hero. Soon the fighting gives him an opportunity to use his quick wit to fight the Nazis with weapons. The figure of Rybkin became so popular among the viewers that in 1942 director Iudin made a full-length picture about him, the first comedy of the war.[29] Iutkevich made a short about the new adventures of Schweik for the seventh collection. He turned the famous character of the Czech writer Jaroslav Hašek into an active fighter against fascism.[30] Schweik also became the hero of a full-length comedy in 1943.

People craved movies: they wanted to be taken away from their everyday miseries; they wanted hope; they wanted their faith in ultimate victory to be reinforced.

Going to movies was one of the few remaining forms of amusement. In wartime conditions, however, making and exhibiting films became extremely difficult. Theaters were destroyed. In 1940 the country possessed 17,600 projectors, but by January 1942 only about 8,000 were functioning, and a year later only 6,374. Even these numbers do not reflect the magnitude of the decline. The army took projectors from the villages for its own use, and many projectors stood idle for lack of electricity over long periods. There were few skilled mechanics in the villages who would have been able to repair malfunctioning equipment. As a consequence, the number of viewers declined from 436 million in 1940 to 292 million in 1942.[31] In the second half of the war the situation slowly improved: in early 1945, 7,325 projectors operated.

The directors faced extraordinary difficulties in making films in distant Central Asia. There were not enough writers and actors and the studios were miserably equipped. Mark Donskoi described how he made one of the most successful films of the war, *Rainbow*. Its story takes place in wintertime Ukraine, but it was made in heat of forty to fifty degrees centigrade in Ashkhabad. The snow was made of cotton, salt, and mothballs, and since the actors had to play their scenes in heavy overcoats, a doctor was constantly on duty to take care of those who collapsed.[32] When evaluating Soviet films made during the war, we must remember the conditions in which they were made. Fortunately, however, there is little connection between the quality of the equipment and the emotional power of the finished product.

Between 1942 and 1945 Soviet studios made seventy films (not including those for children and filmed concerts). Out of these, twenty-one were historical dramas. Let us first turn to the discussion of those forty-nine films that took place in the present, i.e., the war films. With the exception of one, a collective-farm musical, all of these were made with the explicit purpose of shoring up morale, and therefore can be considered propaganda films.

Surprisingly few dealt with the experiences of the soldiers at the front: *Front* (an adapted play with no combat action), *Two Warriors*, *Days and Nights*, *Malakhov Kurgan*, *Moscow Sky*, *Ivan Nikulin—Russian Sailor*. All of these, with the possible exception of *Front*, were undistinguished films that were attacked even at the time by critics for failing to show the face of battle.[33] Interestingly, the situation changed drastically after the end of the war. Then directors came to be preoccupied with the theme of heroism of individual soldiers; and audiences seemed to have an unquenchable thirst for these films.

It was one thing, however, to remember the war and another to live through it. As long as the fighting continued, there was little desire to romanticize it. Instead of depicting the war as a series of heroic exploits, the directors preferred to show the barbaric behavior of the Germans and the quiet heroism and loyalty of simple people in extraordinary circumstances. The most memorable films of the period, therefore, dealt with the home front and with partisan warfare in German-occupied territories.

Of course, it would be naive to imagine that Soviet directors consciously made such calculations. It was, however, films that dealt with the trials of the home front that depicted the most emotionalism and were ultimately the most moving.

One of the most powerful films made during the war was an extraordinarily simple one, made by Eisymont in 1944, *Once There Lived a Little Girl* (*Zhila, byla devochka*). Its almost unbearably bleak story takes place during the siege of Leningrad. Nastia, a little girl of seven or eight, takes care of her weakened and ill mother. She brings home water from the frozen Neva to make tea. There is no news from Father at the front. The mother dies, Nastia is taken to a home for orphans, and she herself is wounded while attempting to save a friend. The film, made almost a half century ago, has not lost its power to move, for its emotions are genuine, and it truthfully depicts a sad world.

A much better subject than battles was partisan warfare. Indeed, films about partisans turned out to be the most effective and also artistically the most satisfying ones. The three most memorable films dealing with this topic share so much with one another that they form a trilogy. The first of these, *She Defends the Motherland*, was made by Fridrikh Ermler and appeared in movie houses in May 1943. Like so many other wartime movies, it starts out by depicting the happy life of the Soviet people before the Nazi invasion. By recalling the wonderful past it sends the message that the people have much to fight for. Today these scenes appear rather ludicrous. Praskov'ia, a simple kolkhoz woman, is enjoying her life with her husband and son so much that she seems unable to suppress her giggles. On the first day of the war the invaders kill her husband and soon after, a German tank brutally squashes her son. Praskov'ia is transformed by the experience, and escapes into the forest where she becomes a partisan leader. She is accepted as leader presumably because her desire for vengeance is the greatest and her hatred of the occupiers the fiercest. She, rather improbably, not only succeeds in finding the murderous German tank commander, but also manages to get him out of his tank and ultimately kill him the same way her son was killed (see fig. 17). She returns to the village because she hears the rumor that Moscow has fallen to the enemy, and she wants to shore up the courage of the villagers by telling them the truth. The Nazis capture her and are about to execute her when her fellow partisans appear and liberate her and the village.

*She Defends the Motherland* is an artistically primitive film which has the simplest political message: the necessity of vengeance. Ermler gave few individual characteristics to his heroine. The picture obviously gave a vicarious satisfaction to Russians who had suffered so much. It could not appeal to foreign audiences. When it was shown in the United States with the title, *No Greater Love*, it was judged by critics as crude and stagey.[34]

A much more complex and successful work was Mark Donskoi's *Rainbow*, which came out in January 1944. It is about a woman partisan, Olena, who returns to her village to give birth. When captured, she is subjected to the most dreadful torture, but does not betray her comrades. The film has many characters who, unlike those in *She Defends the Motherland*, are endowed with individual traits with which the viewer can identify. *Rainbow* has a powerful effect even on today's audiences largely because of its unusually graphic and detailed depiction of Nazi barbarities. For example, the Germans kill a newborn babe and a young boy who tries to smuggle food to a prisoner (see fig. 18). Olena's torture is shown in naturalistic detail. A subsidiary theme is the punishment of collaborators. The director depicts a Red Army officer's wife, who co-habits with a German, with even greater loathing than he has for the Nazis themselves. When she is killed by her husband, who returns with the partisans, the audience read-ily accepts her death as just punishment. Similarly, the village elder who serves the Germans is punished by death.[35]

*Zoia*, directed by Lev Arnshtam, appeared on the screens only in September 1944. Its scenario was based on the martyrdom of the eighteen-year old partisan, Zoia Kos-modem'ianskaia (see Sartorti, this volume). She, like Olena in *Rainbow*, endures tor-ture and prefers death to betraying her comrades.[36]

The most obvious common feature of the three films is that the directors chose women as their protagonists. By showing the courage and suffering of women, these works could arouse hatred for the cruel enemy and at the same time teach that men could do no less than what these women had done. The basic message here, as in so many other wartime products, is the need for vengeance. Two of these films graphi-cally depict Germans killing children. No crime could be greater than that in the eyes of the Russians. The three protagonists are positive heroes without flaws, indeed with-out individual traits. They stand for an idealized image of Soviet womanhood and for patriotism. Artistically this is a source of weakness, for the viewer cannot recognize them as real human beings. By far the best of the three films is *Rainbow*, because it presents secondary characters who are better drawn and more believable than the central figure. *She Defends the Motherland* and *Rainbow* implicitly, and *Zoia* explic-itly, raise the question of what makes a hero. We see Zoia as a schoolgirl admiring the historical figure of Ivan Susanin, who had saved the Tsar. When tortured, Zoia says: "All through our lives we have thought about what happiness is. Now I know. Happi-ness is to be a fearless fighter for our country, for our Fatherland, for Stalin."[37]

The films show an interesting evolution. At the end of *She Defends the Mother-land* the partisans liberate the village and save the heroine from execution. In *Rainbow* the heroine is killed, but her death is avenged when the partisans liberate her village. *Zoia*, by contrast, concludes with our witnessing a martyr's death. The explanation for the differences is simple. In 1942, when the scenario of *She Defends the Motherland* was written, Soviet audiences would have found it too disheartening to watch an exe-cution. But by the summer of 1944 the people were confident of the ultimate victory and did not need the false consolation of a phony rescue.

Movies about partisans were effective, at least partially, because they showed most clearly the brutality and inhumanity of the Nazi occupiers. The depiction of Nazi behavior made a great impression on contemporary audiences, because the description was fundamentally truthful: the Nazis were beastly and Soviet citizens knew it. These films conveyed the essential propaganda point: the Germans had to be resisted because they left no alternative. Since German occupation was extraordinarily brutal, resistance to it was indeed heroic; the more vicious the enemy, the more attractive is the hero.

A strikingly high percentage of the memorable figures of Second World War movies were women. The themes that the directors emphasized—loyalty, constancy, endurance and self-sacrifice—could be best expressed by showing heroines. People craved not realism but consolation; at least in the cinema, if not in real life, constancy was always rewarded. In the film *Wait for Me*, inspired by the most famous wartime poem, Konstantin Simonov's *Zhdi menia*, the woman who remains faithful and waits for her man, even when she is told that he is dead, gets him back, but her friend who cannot wait ultimately destroys her own life and happiness. Films that dealt with the achievements of the home front usually also had heroines rather than heroes. In Gerasimov's *The Great Land*, we see the evolution of Anna. After her husband's departure for the front, she becomes an excellent worker in an evacuated factory, for she knows that this is the best contribution she can make to ultimate victory.

As in the case of other warring countries, vigilance was an important theme. At the time of the Great Purge Trials, Soviet films often dealt with the topic of ferreting out the hidden, internal enemy. Interestingly, in 1939 as the country was preparing for war, the figure of the internal enemy disappeared from the screen and his place was taken by the "foreign agent." When the real war began in June 1941, spy mania became obsessive. In the early films everyone, including children and old women, unmasked spies. A particularly amusing example of this genre was *In the Sentry Box*, a short that appeared on the screens in November 1941. The film is interesting inasmuch as it is an unconscious caricature. Red Army soldiers uncover a German spy who speaks flawless Russian and is dressed in a Soviet uniform. He gives himself away by not recognizing a baby picture of Stalin on the wall.[38] The movie is based on a perfectly realistic premise: no one who lived in the Soviet Union in the 1930s could possibly fail such a test. It is the subtext, however, that is important: Stalin protects his people even in the form of a picture, even as an icon. Most likely Soviet directors lost interest in making movies about spies as a result of an unconscious recognition that modern wars were won and lost, not as a consequence of subversion, but as a result of national mobilization.

Although directors truthfully depicted Nazi atrocities, they were not successful in making the character of individual Germans believable. Especially in the early films, the Nazis were not only bestially brutal—which of course they were—but also silly and cowardly. In a short sketch, for example *Elixir of Courage* (1941) the Germans dare to go into the attack only under the influence of alcohol.[39] In another, *Spiders* (1942) doctors murder their own severely wounded soldiers in a German hospital.[40]

Soviet opinion-makers consciously decided not to allow the depiction of decent Germans. In 1942 Pudovkin directed a film, *Murderers are on the Way*, based on stories by Brecht, that attempted to show German victims of Hitler's regime and fear among ordinary citizens.[41] The film was not allowed to be distributed. In Soviet films there was to be only one type of German: hateful. A characteristic example of this approach was Romm's *Human Being, No. 217* (1945), which was about the life of a Soviet slave laborer billeted with a German family. All Germans according to this film are cruel, stupid, money-grubbing and degenerate.[42] The movies even projected the wickedness of the Germans into the past. A particularly unattractive example of this tactic was *The Golden Road* (1945), which depicted Volga Germans in 1918 as smugglers of Russian gold.[43] This work implicitly justified the mass deportations of ethnic Germans that were carried out early in the war.

The soldiers of the Red Army and the partisans went into battle "for Motherland, for honor, for freedom and for Stalin." In this list, Motherland was first and most important: the Soviet people were to fight against a merciless foe not for communism, but in the name of patriotism. But what did patriotism mean in a multinational empire? The heterogeneity of the population clearly presented a danger, and Nazi propagandists—especially during the second half of the war, when the struggle was going badly for them—were ready to exploit national hostilities and jealousies. It was the task of Soviet propagandists to parry this danger. Studios turned out films showing the "friendship of peoples," meaning that the audiences would see, let us say, a Georgian and a Russian soldier going on a dangerous mission, the success of which would depend on their successful cooperation. At the end, either the Russian would save the Georgian or vice versa. In this respect, at least, the similarities with the film industry of that other multiethnic country, the United States, were striking.

The issue of Russian patriotism was a simple one: the more, the better. The turning from Marxist internationalism to old-fashioned patriotism began before the outbreak of the war; the spate of films about national heroes made in the late 1930s was an important part of this phenomenon. During the war the process accelerated. Films dealt with the great figures of the past, such as Marshal Kutuzov, the hero of 1812, and Ivan the Terrible, conveying the message that contemporaries had a high standard to live up to, and that the Russian people had always prevailed in the past and would, therefore, do so again.

The other side of the coin was that the communist nature of the regime was, for the time being at least, to be deemphasized. A conscious decision was made at the highest level: Moscow was no longer to be the capital of the international revolutionary movement. The allies of Soviet Russia were no longer the working people of the world, but the little Slav brothers, Czechs, Serbs, Croatians and Slovaks. Only rarely did communist functionaries appear in films, leading in the homefront or in the partisan movement. Ivan Pyr'ev's film, *The Secretary of the District Committee*, made in 1942, was remarkable because it was an exception. The deemphasis on the role of the party, however, did not mean a deemphasis on Stalin's role. At a time of increased hero worship, he was the greatest hero of all.

Minority nationalism was a ticklish issue. On the one hand, such nationalism had to be tolerated and even encouraged in order to gain the loyalty of the population, and therefore each major nationality was allowed to make one great national epic: the Ukrainians made *Bogdan Khmelnitskii*; the Georgians, *Georgii Saakadze*; the Armenians, *David Bek*; and the Azer, *Arshin-Mal-Alan*. Needless to say, the national heroes could never struggle against Russian oppressors, but on the contrary, the "friendship of peoples" had to be projected into the past.

On the other hand, too much nationalism threatened to undermine the system that was based on the "leading role" of the Russians. The Ukrainians presented a particular problem: the Germans hoped to turn those they did not kill or enslave against the Soviet regime and directed a special appeal to them. Stalinist leaders were concerned about the power of Ukrainian nationalism, and therefore Stalin personally banned a scenario by Dovzhenko that he considered too nationalistic. For this scenario, *Ukraine in Flames*, Dovzhenko was bitterly denounced, and all publishers were notified that none of his writings could be published without special permission. The director was blamed for implying that the party's policy was incorrect, that the party had not prepared the country for war.[44] Jews were conspicuously absent from Soviet films and even documentaries; the publicists almost never revealed that the Nazis had a "special policy" toward them. When the Red Army liberated some of the death camps during the last year of the war, the newsreels never pointed out the nationality of the victims. Evidently the propagandists did not want to give the Nazis an opportunity to depict them as philo-Semitic. Eisenstein wanted to use a Jewish actress, Faina Ranevskaia, in his film, *Ivan the Terrible*. He sent a photograph of her to Bol'shakov, the head of Soviet film industry. Bol'shakov wrote to Shcherbakov, a member of the Politburo: "It seems to me that because of the Semitic features of Ranevskaia, which are particularly visible in a close-up, we should not allow her to play the role."[45]

Most of the historical films were named after a single individual and aimed to show how a hero could change history. V. Petrov's film *Kutuzov* (1944) is a characteristic example, for his conception is diametrically opposed to that of Tolstoy's in *War and Peace*. According to this film, the old general was victorious not because he allowed his armies to lead him, but on the contrary, because he was a brilliant strategist. Cinema reflected reality: in the Stalinist Soviet Union it was the decisions of the wise leader that mattered.

Almost all historical films made anywhere and at any time are presentist, and aim to appeal to modern audiences by dealing with modern issues. It would be naive to expect that Soviet cinema in the middle of a bitter war would attempt to depict past events dispassionately, as it were, for their own sake. Nevertheless, it is extraordinary how brazenly directors distorted past events to make their points.

An entire series of films, for example, dealt with the German occupation of Ukraine in 1918: *Kotovskii, How the Steel Was Tempered, The Defense of Tsaritsyn,* and *Aleksandr Parkhomenko.* In these movies the directors wanted to show that the Germans had always been vicious, that the Red Army had always managed to defeat them, and that Stalin had always provided wise leadership. In order to make these points the directors faced some problems. In fact, the Red Army had not engaged the Germans, except for some minor skirmishes, let alone defeated them. Reality, however, did not deter the filmmakers. L. Lukov in *Aleksandr Parkhomenko* (1942) and the Vasilev "brothers" in *The Defense of Tsaritsyn* (1942) depict battles that never occurred, could not have occurred, and, if they had, would doubtless have resulted in resounding defeats for the Reds.[46]

Mark Donskoi brought to the screen the best-known Soviet novel of the 1930s, Nikolai Ostrovskii's *How the Steel was Tempered.* In that novel Pavel Korchagin's adventures in German-occupied Ukraine take up only a few pages. The film version, by contrast, concentrated entirely on this period. The scenarist, in order to fill the gap, had to rearrange some incidents and invent others. In the process, Korchagin is turned into a nationalist freedom fighter. Almost everyone in the audience knew that the director, to put it mildly, had not been faithful to the original, and yet none of the critics was disturbed enough to mention it in a review.[47]

The Second World War was the supreme test for the Soviet system: was the industrial base, created in the 1930s, strong enough to produce weapons in sufficient quantity and quality? Would the political system continue to function at times of extraordinary hardship? And, perhaps most significantly, did two decades of indoctrination produce a citizenry willing to fight for the existing Stalinist order? The war did not provide an unambiguous answer to the last question, for the Nazis behaved in such a beastly fashion that they left no choice to the Russian people but to resist. The answers to the first two questions, however, are affirmative: yes, Soviet industry produced weapons that enabled the Red Army to prevail, and the regime stood the test of time.

In order to stay in power the Stalinists, however, made concessions: they underemphasized the communist nature of their regime, compromised with the Orthodox Church, and attempted to tap the powerful current of Russian patriotism. During the closing phase of the war many Russians were euphoric; they not only defeated a dreadful foe, but believed that since the regime and the people fought on the same side, the leaders of their own country might relent and would not reintroduce repressive measures in their full severity.

During the war directors wanted to make propaganda movies and audiences wanted to see them. As Mark Donskoi, one of the best directors, put it: "We fought with our art."[48] People liked seeing the heroic exploits of the Red Army and of partisans against a beastly enemy; they needed and wanted faith in final victory.

The wartime Soviet film industry presents us with an irony. In every country cinema became more controlled by the state, and more heavily propagandistic. In the Soviet Union also, cinema was mobilized for the purpose of winning the war, and the films produced were obviously propaganda films. Nevertheless, given the immediate past and future of Soviet cinema, the period of the war appears as an oasis of freedom. The regime allowed a measure of artistic experimentation. It was only under these circumstances that Eisenstein managed to make his masterpiece, *Ivan the Terrible* (see fig. 19). In this film, the great director in full possession of his artistic creativity, succeeded in depicting a complex and interesting character, the troubled Tsar. Within a year after the end of the war, when the second part of the film was completed, the leaders of the regime used the opportunity to a signal a change in the cultural life of the country. Eisenstein's film was denounced and could not be shown until 1958.

During the war directors made films on subjects about which they themselves cared, expressing genuine and deeply felt emotions. After the passage of a half a century, at least some of these films have not lost their power to move us.

## Notes

1. Since I wrote my book *Cinema and Soviet Society, 1917–1953* (Cambridge University Press, 1992), the Party Archives have become accessible to scholars. On the basis of this material, I am able to describe in greater detail the nature and extent of intervention of party and state organs in filmmaking.

2. Party Archive (hereafter: P.A.) f. 77. o. 1 d. 919. May 15, 1941.

3. P.A. f. 17 o. 117. d. 174.

4. P.A. f. 77 o. 1 d. 98.

5. P.A. f. 77 o. 3. d. 23.

6. P.A. f 77 o. 1. d. 98.

7. At the time no mention was made in the press of this two-day conference. The protocols are to be found in P.A. f. 77 o. 1 d. 919.

8. Lenin expressed his thoughts on this topic in a letter he wrote in 1922 to E. A. Litkens, Lunacharskii's deputy at Narkompros. V. I. Lenin, *Polnoe sobranie sochinenii*, 5th ed., 55 vols. (Moscow: Gospolitizdat, 1960–1965), 44, 360–61. The Nazi approach to war propaganda, by the way, was similar to Lenin's.

9. Richard Raack examined the documentaries of the period: "Dark Side of the Moon: Soviet Actuality Film Sources of the Early Days of World War II," *Film & History*, 20, no. 1 (Feb. 1990), 3–16. Although I saw some of this material at the Hoover Archives Hermann Axelbank collection, I base my evaluation of the products of the 1939–41 period largely on Raack's work.

10. R. Katsman, "Frontovaia kinokhronika," *Novyi Mir*, 7 (1942), 109.

11. L. V. Maksakova, *Kul'tura Sovetskoi Rossii v gody Velikoi Otechestvennoi voiny* (Moscow: Nauka, 1977), pp. 189–90.

12. Zhdanov, in a letter to the Politburo, recommended wide distribution of this film. P.A. f. 77 0. 1 d. 949.

13. S. V. Drobashenko, "Dokumental'naia kinematografiia," *Ocherki istorii Sovetskogo kino, 1935–1945* (Moscow, 1959), 2, 562; A. A. Lebedev, "Frontovaia kinokhronika," in *Sovetskaia kul'tura v gody Velikoi Otechestvennoi voiny* (Moscow: Nauka, 1976), p. 256; and Maksakova, p. 199.

14. Some of the cheating was amusingly transparent. One newsreel, for example, showed a German truck driving into a Soviet ambush. The camera purportedly filmed the action from the cab of the German vehicle. Are we to believe that the Soviet cameraman was sitting behind the German driver? D. W. Spring, "Soviet Newsreel and the Great Patriotic War," in *Propaganda, Politics and Film, 1918–1945*, ed. N. Pronay and D. W. Spring (London: Macmillan, 1982), p. 277.

15. Raack, p. 13.

16. This early newsreel is in the Axelbank collection.

17. Katsman, p. 109.

18. Drobashenko, pp. 570–71; R. Katsman, "Perventsy kinopublitsistiki," *Literatura i iskusstvo* (Apr. 15, 1942), 3; *New York Times* (Aug. 17, 1942).

19. Lebedev, p. 258.

20. Slutskii had made a similar film before the war, *A Day of the New World*.

21. *Literatura i iskusstvo* (Feb. 12, 1944) and R. Sobolev, *A. Dovzhenko* (Moscow: Iskusstvo, 1980), pp. 214–22.

22. I. L. Repin, *Ekrannaia letopis' narodnogo podviga* (Ashkhabad: Turkmenskoe gos. Izd., 1975), p. 2 and Lebedev, p. 258. According to Drobashenko, p. 250, cameramen were working on the front. "Film Propaganda in the Soviet Union, 1941–1945," in *Film and Radio Propaganda in World War II*, ed. K. R. M. Short (London: Croom Helm, 1983), p. 96.

23. R. Iurenev, "Kinoiskusstvo voennykh let," *Sovetskaia kul'tura v gody Otechestvennoi voiny*, p. 235.

24. I. Bol'shakov, *Sovetskoe kinoiskusstvo v gody Velikoi Otechestvennoi voiny* (Moscow: Goskinoizdat, 1950), p. 13.

25. *Pravda* (Aug. 6, 1941) 4.

26. *Pravda* (Aug. 11, 1941) 5.

27. *Sovetskie khudozhestvennye fil'my: annotirovannyi katalog* (hereafter: S.kh.f.), 4 vols. (Moscow: Iskusstvo, 1961–68), 2, 259 and A. Karaganov, *Vsevolod Pudovkin* (Moscow, 1983), pp. 208–09.

28. *S.kh.f*, 2, 256.

29. *Literatura i iskusstvo* (Feb. 6, 1943) 3.

30. *Pravda* (Dec. 10, 1941) 3.

31. Maksakova, pp. 69–70.

32. *Sovetskii ekran* 4 (1969) 18.

33. See for example the review of *Malakhov Kurgan* in *Pravda* (Dec. 10, 1944).

34. *Literatura i iskusstvo* (May 22, 1943), 2; *The New York Times* (Feb. 5, 1944).

35. *Literatura i iskusstvo* (Jan. 29, 1944), 3.

36. *Literatura i iskusstvo* (Sept. 23, 1944), 2.

37. *Pravda* (Sept. 22, 1944).

38. *S.kh.f.*, 2, 262.

39. *S.kh.f.*, 2, 260.

40. *S.kh.f.*, 2, 294.

41. Karaganov, *Vsevolod Pudovkin*, pp. 209–10.

42. *S.kh.f.*, 2, 341.

43. *S.kh.f.*, 2, 352.

44. A. Shcherbakov wrote to the editor of *Novyi Mir* with copies to other journals. The virulence of the attack on Dovzhenko was extraordinary. He was held responsible even for lines that he put in the mouths of German soldiers. The explanation of this virulence must be the concern that the Soviet leadership felt about Ukrainian nationalism. None of the prominent directors during the war were subjected to comparable abuse. (P.A. f. 17. o. 125. d. 293.) As a consequence, the great Ukrainian director made no feature film during the war. See also Marco Carnyk, ed., *Alexander Dovzhenko: the Poet as Filmmaker—Selected Writings* (Cambridge, Mass.: M.I.T. Press 1973), pp. 30–31.

45. Bol'shakov to Shcherbakov, Oct. 24. 1942. P.A. f. 17. o. 125 d. 124. The letter shows not only the sensitivity of the issue of anti-Semitism, but also the extent of involvement of the top leadership in the minutiae of filmmaking.

46. *Pravda* (March 28, 1942), 3 and *Pravda* (July 22, 1942), 4.

47. *Literatura i iskusstvo* (Sep. 26, 1942), 2.

48. *Sovetskaia kul'tura v gody Velikoi Otechestvennoi voiny*, p. 246.

# 11

## On the Making of
## Heroes, Heroines, and Saints

### Rosalinde Sartorti

A TOUR OF the Museum of the Armed Forces in Moscow makes your head spin. A dazzling array of showcases, walls, and staircases resplendent with names, pictures, photographs, and the personal effects of countless numbers of Heroes of the Soviet Union pays homage to the glorious past of the illustrious Red Army. Wherever you turn your head you can marvel at relics of the victorious Red Army, the great Soviet people, and the momentous struggle which is known not as World War II, but as the Great Patriotic War.

The heroes and heroines come from all walks of life, from all branches of the armed forces—Army, Navy, Air Force. But there are also members of the partisan movement, young girls and boys, old men and women, underground fighters. Even entire cities bear the title "Hero." Nothing and no one seems to be omitted; all of them united in fighting the fascist aggressor. Golden letters on rich red cloth extend from wall to wall in one of the upper museum halls, proclaiming: "They will never be forgotten." But who can remember all these names? Who can possibly know them all?

By the end of the war, in May 1945, more than ten thousand citizens, among them some ninety women, had become "Heroes of the Soviet Union" (*Geroi Sovetskogo Soiuza*). They had been awarded—very often posthumously—the highest distinction one could achieve "for service to the state combined with a heroic deed (*podvig*)."[1] Enormous energy was invested over the years to preserve their memory for future generations. The country was flooded by a never-ending wave of novels, short stories, poems, films, biographical encyclopedias, and memoirs on the countless heroes of war. However, in contrast to the estimated twenty to twenty-eight million Soviet people (including both soldiers and civilians) who lost their lives during the war,[2] the 10,000 official heroes constitute less than 0.1 percent.

A closer look at Soviet war history enables us to distinguish different types of heroes and heroism. First there are the leading military men, honored and respected for their success in strategic planning, i.e., for their professional skills which finally led to the victory of the Red Army over Nazi Germany. Everyone knows the names of generals—like Timoshenko, Rokossovskii, or the renowned Marshal Zhukov—who became Heroes of the Soviet Union two, three, or even four times; not to mention Stalin, the Great Leader, the Generalissimo who, at least during wartime, was considered the greatest hero of all.

But the generals and their strategic planning needed the thousands and millions of enlisted men and women. What would they have done without the help of civilians working in partisan and underground movements? Here we find another category of heroes who excelled in extremely brave and courageous acts, more often than not sacrificing their own lives in combat or in otherwise fighting the enemy, and in doing so promoting the Red Army's victory. Every Soviet citizen knew the names of daring aviators like Maresev, Pokryshkin and Kozhedub, or the young bomber-pilot Gastello; everybody is familiar with Aleksandr Matrosov, member of a rifle regiment, who gave his life by covering the embrasure of a machine-gun nest with his body; the Young Pioneer Oleg Koshevoi and his friends who formed the Young Guard of Krasnodon to organize underground work against the occupying Nazis; or the twenty-eight Panfilov men who so heroically fought against a German tank division on the Volokolamsk highway and perished. Still another kind of heroism is shown by those who withstood the cruelest acts of torture by the enemy, the Soviet martyrs, loyal to their conviction in defending the Motherland (*Rodina*) to their last breath—as did the most famous of them: the Komsomol girl Zoia Kosmodem'ianskaia.

It is the two latter categories, the ones who died in combat or became martyrs for the good cause, and not the high-ranking army officers and generals, around whom myth, legend and hero cults evolved, which became deeply ingrained into popular consciousness and served as a strong bond of national identification. The heroism of the Soviet people in World War II remains unquestioned. Still, the apparent overabundance of heroes—not to mention the hundreds of thousands of military men decorated with stars, badges, medals, and orders of a lower category—is astonishing. Were the Soviet people more heroic than others? What made them fight so fiercely and bravely? Was it the confrontation with an extremely vile enemy, or was heroism a "natural" quality of theirs, as Soviet propaganda had always asserted?

## Russia—Land of Heroes

Every war produces its own heroes and at the same time requires heroes to populate the cultural battlefield of popular imagination.[3] The Soviet Union, however, officially declared itself a "Land of Heroes" (*strana geroev*), long before the country was attacked by foreign invaders. Lenin, in 1920, with reference to the manifold feats achieved during the Civil War, had praised Russia for its ability to give birth "not only to individual heroes . . . but to produce heroes by the hundreds and the thousands."[4]

During the Great War, the West had also known such collective forms of heroism, as for instance with the heroes of Verdun. Socialism, however, was to guarantee a rational relationship between individual and the collective, and promised a future in which self-sacrifice would become obsolete.

The specific Soviet type of hero was defined, first and foremost, as the heroic worker, the Hero of Labor (*Geroi truda*), shaped after the military example, bedecked with similar decorations, medals, and orders. The hyperactive industrialization program of the late 1920s created the prototype of the hard-working, diligent, energetic, and indefatigable model worker that populated the literature, films, and arts of the era. By the mid-thirties, at least as popular music of the time would have us believe, the country had truly turned into a "land of heroes." In the "March of the Enthusiasts," a popular song of those years, people happily chanted "Long Live the Land of Heroes," and the "Happy-Go-Lucky Guys" of Alexandrov's famous film even promised: "Anyone of us becomes a hero, if our country commands." Heroic behavior had become a "civic duty" not only for the few but for everybody. It was transformed into an "innate" characteristic of Soviets, as pronounced by official Soviet discourse. The feats of workers, Stakhanovites, scholars and scientists, and above all of aviators (transformed into Stalinist Falcons),[5] gave Soviet life the semblance of a fairy-tale world.[6]

The impression of a country that produced miracles in almost every field, of a people literally crossing all traditional boundaries, was overshadowed by the fact that for many years the population had truly been living in an atmosphere of internal warfare. The flourishing pantheon of Soviet heroes was accompanied by the ever-growing myth of the "parasite" and "saboteur" (*vreditel'*). The class warfare of the First Five-Year Plan was gradually replaced, in the mid-thirties, by a more patriotic rallying of the different nationalities of the Union, exposed to a common danger by the encirclement of menacing imperialistic powers. This amounted to the replacement of an internal enemy by an external one (invaders, spies, and infiltrators).

Paramilitary training for Pioneers and the Communist Youth was a required part of their education as loyal Soviet citizens. The salute of Young Pioneers and members of the Komsomol was a vigorous "Ready!" to be answered with an even more fervent "Always ready!" which implied the readiness to defend the country, the socialist Motherland.

## War and Heroism

Optimism and heroism in war are different than in peace-time. Being confronted with a "real" enemy and not an imaginary ideological one at the outbreak of the war in 1941 made the people almost forget the times of terror during the Great Purges. If Soviet heroes had thus far played the role of advancing Soviet society on the road to a distant, happy future, Soviet war heroes now had to fulfill a task far less utopian—to liberate the country from the German aggressors, to shorten the road to victory.

The German military attack on the Soviet Union in 1941 differs sharply from other wars. It was not simply a war between two armies or nations. The key Nazi leaders wanted to decimate and enslave the Slavic population and annihilate the Jews. The civilian population became a major target, subject to unusual indignities and utter cruelty. The Soviet people were confronted with a kind of warfare hitherto almost unknown in its racist excesses, vileness, and dreadful slaughter of defenseless people.

Given this situation, propaganda warfare took on as crucial a role as strategic planning on the battlefield. The official narrative, recounted by the media, had to shape the collective view of the events of war, to give sense and meaning to the manifold aspects of terror and despair, which would otherwise be beyond comprehension. Against this background, any news nourishing hope for an early victory was bound to fall on fertile ground, and be welcomed by people in despair.[7] Here we can locate the making of heroes and heroines as the official carriers of hope.

In the war years, short literary forms—the short story or the essay (*ocherk*) as well as lyrics and poetry—gained momentum over longer works like novels. Very often the public learned about exploits of future Heroes of the Soviet Union not by a simple and almost barren newspaper report on the facts, but in a literary form, by a warm and moving account written by professional novelists who worked as war correspondents—also called "literary scouts" (*razvedchiki*). The war also brought a tremendous joint effort on the part of writers, poets, artists, and composers, all engaged in building the legends and myths that were to surround those model men and women. Despite the enormous efforts invested in propagating the miraculous feats of almost every one of the thousands of official war heroes, only a few actually entered collective memory, and a still smaller number were truly beloved by the people. What distinguished these from their compatriots who also gave their lives in defending their country?

All the heroes were depicted more or less in the same way: their lives were stylized according to the pattern of socialist realism.[8] Only a few traits or, in some cases, a single deed was selected to shape the entire life of the hero according to those traits—in their structure as well as in their edifying and morale-raising function reminiscent of hagiographic tales. Such modeling accentuates the exemplary character of the specific hero or heroine and calls for identification and emulation. Their ability to commit heroic deeds was indiscriminately attributed to the fact, that "they were brought up by the Bolshevik Party, that they knew in whose name they entered battle, and in whose name they gave their own lives without regret",[9] and to their supposedly "Bolshevik qualities: intrepidity, daring, and fearlessness in battle . . . brought out in them by the Soviet Motherland."[10]

Given the great number of heroes and their similar treatment in the media, all depicted as following the prescribed road to communist perfection, it is interesting to examine what, beyond being imposed by propaganda, was necessary in order for a hero to become part of popular consciousness. There seems to be a considerable gap between the many officially concocted heroes and the few who were met with lasting enthusiasm or with great compassion. This is not to say that the people had "their own," i.e., unofficial heroes, but the popular ones demonstrate an almost accidental concurrence of certain elements of the canonized version with the needs and wants of the people, with popular imagination. Let us take a look at a few of the most popular heroes and their fate during and after the war.

## The Myth of the Aviator

It comes as no surprise that warfare in the air was followed with a different kind of attention than the movement of army units on the ground. The traditional admiration of the so-called chivalric qualities attributed to pilots imparted a greater significance to their deeds. The age-old dream of flying, freeing oneself from being bound to the earth, had finally come true and was personified by Valerii Chkalov and other daring Soviet pilots of international repute.[11] In the 1930s aviators were public celebrities in Soviet Russia.[12] They symbolized the extraordinary talent, courage and audacity of the Soviet people, and easily became a perfect object of identification and national pride. They figured not only as literary heroes of many a novel, but were also "real" men and women who could be looked up to as examples to be emulated. The great popular interest in aviation was also reflected in a growing number of amateur clubs in this field, heavily supported by the army and the government. Consequently, aviators figured among the most popular heroes also in wartime.

One of the most admired combat pilots was the legendary Aleksei Maresev. In April 1942 his plane was shot down in action, but he still managed to survive. After an eighteen-day crawl between the front lines, with both his feet very badly crushed, he was finally rescued by partisans and taken to a military hospital in Moscow where his feet had to be amputated. What had normally meant the end of a fighter pilot's career was, for Maresev, a challenge to overcome this severe handicap with absolutely superhuman strength and energy. Weeks after surgery, he not only learned to walk and even dance on his artificial limbs, but he actually succeeded in training himself to such perfection that, only a year later, he was allowed to return to active service and was awarded the title "Hero of the Soviet Union" in August 1943. He could fly again, fight the enemy and down many more planes—against all odds and expectations.[13] It was his heroic recovery, the enormous willpower with which he surmounted obstacles hitherto considered insurmountable, that most impressed the people. What was pictured as typically Soviet was merely the embodiment of universal and timeless qualities such as perseverance, strong will, and a strong sense of purpose.

Maresev belonged to the relatively small number of people who were awarded the title "Hero of the Soviet Union" during their lifetimes. And, as a hero, for many years after the war he publicly campaigned for peace. Yet his enormous popularity must be ascribed to the exceptional literary treatment he was given by Boris Polevoi in 1946. The biographical novel *The Story of a Real Man*[14] was a typical adventure story, translated into more than twenty languages, breaking all sales records.[15] Although his exploit had already become known during the war he is a typical example of successful postwar-heroization.

Another favorite among the war heroes was Nikolai Gastello, the young captain of a bomber group who, unlike Maresev, lost his life in the very first week of war. On June 26, 1941, after his plane was hit by a shell and caught fire, he did not try to save himself but directed his plane into the enemy forces and a column of tanks. The explosion caused great losses among the enemy. For this feat he was posthumously awarded the title "Hero of the Soviet Union." The list of pilots who committed similar deeds is endless, and yet it is Gastello who managed to enter collective memory and the hearts of the people. Why did the others fall into oblivion while he was immortalized? Was it his youthful charm and good looks, the fact that he was the first to commit this feat? Did such details really matter?

## Aleksandr Matrosov

The same question arises in connection with the heroic death of Aleksandr Matrosov, the young member of a rifle regiment who is reported to have pushed forward into an enemy machine-gun nest and covered the embrasure with his body. By sacrificing himself he enabled his comrades' unit to overcome the enemy. This took place on February 23, 1943. Several months later, in June 1943, the Presidium of the Supreme Soviet posthumously conferred upon him the title of "Hero of the Soviet Union," followed in September 1943 by an order of the People's Commissar of Defense, I. V. Stalin: "The great feat of Comrade Matrosov must serve as an example of military valor and heroism for all fighters of the Red Army."[16] Virtually every Russian knew and still knows Matrosov. But who has heard of the young *politruk* (political instructor) of the 28th Tank Division, A. K. Pankratov, who, in the battle at Novgorod, on 24 August 1941, also covered an embrasure with his own body and became "Hero of The Soviet Union"?[17] On the title page of *Pravda*, 2 December 1941, we learn about the "legendary exploit" of comrade Sosnovskii who decided the battle by his "exceptional heroism." By sacrificing himself in the same way as Pankratov before him he stopped the fire and "the Red fighters dealt a crushing defeat to the enemy fortification."

The names of Sosnovskii or Pankratov and the other two or three hundred who committed the very same act, repeatedly praised and honored in the press during the years of war, seem to have fallen into oblivion. Only Matrosov happened to enter popular consciousness as the model for this specific kind of self-sacrifice. A novel about his life by Pavel Zhurba and a forty page poem by Kirsanov,[18] meant to popularize his image, were written shortly after the war; but even during wartime, his name and feat had already become the topic of ritualized meetings in schools all over the country, telling the young ones of whom they had to be proud and to whom they had to be grateful for fighting the enemy and defending their Motherland.

However, even in those years, people with combat experience could and did comment that this kind of act was not one of exceptional personal courage or heroism but rather a result of extreme psychological stress in a deadlock situation. Faced with certain death, aware of its inevitability, they made use of their bodies to stop the fire, if only for minutes or seconds. Also, rumor had it that Matrosov did not sacrifice himself deliberately or voluntarily but, instead, was forced to do so on command. A homeless and parentless young hooligan brought up in a reeducation camp, he had to enter a punishment batallion, where he finally met his death.

What moved the people about this kind of heroism in despair must have been, first and foremost, pity over the fact that young men were forced into such extreme and hopeless situations that they could not but die, yet still applied their death to give the battle a decisive turn. If we follow Katerina Clark in her interpretation of socialist realist heroes,[19] then, for the ones who concocted the heroic myth of Aleksandr Matrosov, his being an orphan must have been an important element in making him a more convincing hero than the others who acted similarly. Reading the press of those years, we learn again and again that the most heroic of the Soviet people fighting the enemy were the ones who considered the Red Army their "second family," their homeland as their mother, and Stalin as their father. Would not an orphan be much more prone to accept Stalin, homeland, and army as his one and only family?

However, familiarity with a hero's name and feat is no proof of popularity. Even among the few whose model behavior was endlessly inculcated into the memory of all Soviet citizens, the people themselves selected their own favorites. But Aleksandr Matrosov probably never won the intimate admiration and affection that some others did. Perhaps the wrong writers and poets engaged in praising him, so that his type did not come across as very convincing. He might have lacked the sweetness and softness of a Gastello or the outstanding audacity and technical perfection in mastering a machine attributed to the renowned fighter pilots Kozhedub or Pokryshkin. It would seem that at least one of these attributes have to be present to make some heroes more admired or lovable than others: technical mastery and superhuman strength or exceptional personal qualities, gifts of nature, so to say, charm, beauty, sex appeal.

## Zoia Kosmodem'ianskaia—A Soviet Saint

The story of Zoia Kosmodem'ianskaia, the Soviet Joan of Arc, clearly the Number One heroine of war and postwar times alike, is a very fine example of how different media interacted in creating an image that met true popular response and compassion. Who was she? The biographical encyclopedia tells us that Zoia Kosmodem'ianskaia, also called Tanya, was a young member of the Moscow Komsomol (Communist Youth).[20] At the age of eighteen, upon the outbreak of the war, she volunteered for the partisan movement. In November 1941 she was sent behind the front line to carry out a military assignment in the rear of the enemy near Moscow. Early in December she was caught by the Germans red-handed while trying to set fire to a stable in the village of Petrishchevo where German soldiers were camping overnight. She was arrested, tortured, and finally hanged. Despite the cruel torments the Germans inflicted upon her, they could not break her resistance or extract any information from her.

This made Kosmodem'ianskaia a true heroine. In March 1943 she was posthumously awarded the title "Hero of the Soviet Union." Neither her fate nor her exceptional loyalty and steadfastness were unique. Many more were awarded the same title for the very same act. Yet, there must have been something special about Zoia that made her more admired and beloved than her fellows in fate. Her fame even spread abroad, into the Allied countries. And to this very day, every Russian knows her name and can recite her deed. Members of the older generation especially speak of her as of a true and dear friend, showing a closeness, an almost intimate relationship to her. How did her exemplary behavior and tragic fate become known to the public and what made people identify with her to an extent rarely met by other heroes or heroines?

The news about the life and death of Zoia was first spread to the Soviet people by the essayist Pëtr Lidov and his story "Tanya," published in *Pravda* on 25 January 1942. This story was rapidly followed by other, still more detailed and vivid accounts of her arrest and of the cruel methods applied by the Germans to torture her—bearing such titles as "We will not forget you, Tanya!" by S. Liubimov or "Our 'Tanya' " by B. Chernyshev.[21]

Her life as described in these brochures bears true hagiographic qualities. Zoia, also an orphan, a fatherless child, from early childhood on appears to embody a colorful mixture of communist and also traditional Christian traits and values: faithfulness, selflessness, diligence, love for her comrades, loyalty to authority—mother, party, country. With only minor variations, every story on Zoia followed the same pattern in praising her flawless model behavior, at times still fighting some weaknesses, but slowly growing into perfection. "Don't cry, mother. I shall either return home as a hero or die as a hero," she is supposed to have said to her mother on bidding her farewell. This presentiment of impending fate is also characteristic of the tales of many traditional heroes or saints.

Of equal, if not even greater, importance in this propaganda campaign was the radio address of Zoia's mother on 17 February 1942, published in *Pravda* a day later. The mother told of her immense grief and sorrow on the death of her only daughter, but also of her pride as the mother of such a truly exceptional and loyal daughter: "Zoia met death like a true man, a fighter, a communist."[22] At the same time, she appealed to the Soviet people to seek revenge. The suffering of a mother in such a situation was an image close to everyone and could not fail to arouse compassion and at the same time intensify hatred for the enemy. An equally moving impression was given by the personal appearance of Zoia's mother in various schools all across the country, telling the story of her daughter's fate.[23]

The call for revenge as expressed by her mother was also pronounced by the young poet Margarita Aliger in her long poem "Zoia," first published in September 1942.[24] The young woman writer was so touched and moved on hearing of the fate of the Komsomol girl that she began her own investigations and finally gave an account of them in her renowned poem. Aliger had gained particular fame and popularity by reading her poetry on the radio.[25] "Zoia" was only one of her many works dealing with the war[26] but, according to all recollections of the war, it became the most famous one. In the same year, M. Kremker wrote the lyrics for a song about "Tanya,"[27] learned by heart in pioneer groups and in schools all over the country. The young pioneers then visited the military hospitals and sang the song about the admired partisan to the wounded soldiers.

Many other feats were achieved, but the reports on Zoia, her childhood, her youth, her short life, and her long death, never ceased. Up to 1945 we can count at least twenty different publications on Zoia, occasionally presented with the life of several other heroes or heroines of the partisan movement. They were mostly issued as small brochures in pocket format, easily carried as a steady companion, followed by new or revised editions, even in English,[28] all through the years of war. But it was not prose and poetry alone that guaranteed her such a prominent place in popular consciousness.

There was also the publication of several photographs of Zoia taken before and after her execution that were supposedly confiscated from German prisoners of war.[29] They gave documentary proof of the beastly and brutal acts committed by members of the Hitler army and probably did not fail to intensify the hatred felt for the enemy. These pictures also served as a model for many a painting on the same topic produced by Soviet artists in postwar times.[30]

Yet one picture taken by the frontline-photographer Sergei Strunnikov moved the public more than all the rest. It showed Zoia's frozen body lying in the snow, bare-breasted, with the noose still tied around her neck (see fig. 21). This picture was unusual indeed in several respects: not only did it document the result of a cruel death, its lasting impression must have been a strongly erotic one, especially viewed against the traditional iconographic context of those times, when women were depicted as either martial or maternal figures,[31] i.e., either themselves fighting to defend their country or representing the "Motherland" that the others had to protect. There was no room for eroticism. Zoia's remarkable beauty, unflawed by any sign of suffering, the tranquillity of her expression as if blissfully asleep, the absolute serenity radiating from her, comes close to an artistic transfiguration of death. Other elements of the picture though—the bare breast for example—suggest depictions of the French Liberty. In Stalinist culture, only a picture of death could contain such a strong erotic component.

"It is happiness to die for my people" and "Stalin is with us"—are reported to have been the last words of Zoia before being executed. Bearing this in mind, one could interpret the picture such that this kind of happiness, her belief, her faith in the righteousness of her death, having given her life for a good and noble cause, were written on her face. The portrayal's uniqueness, though, derives first and foremost from a symbolism that transcends definite space and time and the given political context. Her expression and poise compare only to depictions of saints, not to Soviet heroines. As such it acquires a quality that has no equivalent in Soviet photography of this period. All later representations, as for instance the statue of Zoia by the Soviet sculptor Manizer, erected in 1950 in Petrishchevo where she was hanged (see fig. 22), returned to the official iconographic code and gave her a martial appearance.

## Zoia—the Film

The impression Zoia had left in people's minds through Strunnikov's photograph was to be intensified once more. In 1943 the director Lev Arnshtam decided to make a film on the life of Zoia (see Kenez, this volume). It had its premiere in the summer of 1944, with music by Shostakovich. As for the story we are told about Zoia in this film, it is based on the poem by Margarita Aliger and the many other publications preceding it. With the beautiful young actress Galina Vodianitskaia in the role of the young partisan, we can now follow on screen the different stages of her development into an exemplary member of the Communist Youth: striving to excel in every activity, faithful, filled with the insatiable desire to learn and study, caring for others. Once again, we learn about her intense desire to make other people happy, to serve her people. The question "What is happiness" is exemplified by three Soviet aviators who died on a test flight with a balloon into the stratosphere.[32] Shaken by the news about this catastrophe, Zoia is told by her mother that they died for the happiness of others.[33] Their sacrificial death becomes Zoia's model: to give one's own life for the happiness of others. This already foreshadows her own destiny.

It is in this film that we learn about the long heroic tradition of the Russian people. We learn the names of victorious Tsarist commanders, Russian war heroes like the peasant Ivan Susanin who fought against the Polish invasion in the early seventeenth century, of daring Soviet pilots and explorers like Chkalov, all serving as models of identification for the young Komsomol girl, people she will emulate. It was these very names and feats that had become exemplary for all Soviet citizens.

The film only echoes and reflects what can be considered for that time common knowledge and conviction, common ideals propagated and depicted in literature, the arts, and in history books. Yet, it was the beauty and the performance of Vodianitskaia in the role of Zoia that makes the lesson of the film come across so convincingly. She imparts a very special kind of beauty to the heroine. Her strongly androgynous looks, not to be found in any other depiction of Soviet heroines of that time, may have lent an element of "identification" for young soldiers at the front. In addition to the immaculate beauty of the actress, another reason for the lasting impression Zoia left in popular consciousness through this film was its unique poetic, impressionist qualities "that distinguished it from all other films of the period."[34]

> When Zoia is shown on her last road, at night, walking through the snow, spectators first see her bare feet and slender legs, then her whole figure in vague outline against a background of whirling snow, and then her radiant and inspired face, seeming lit from within by the flame of her thoughts and emotions.[35]

This is especially remarkable, as the whole film otherwise fits perfectly into the framework of socialist realism. Arnshtam's film is a brilliant visualization of a Soviet saint's road to paradise. Zoia attains eternal life by entering into collective memory. In the concluding scene of the film, we see her smiling face, high up in the wintry sky above the deadly combat fire of the front lines (see fig. 20). Death cannot touch her. If we had not believed it before, now we know for sure; Zoia is alive. Zoia lives. And the voice-over tells us: "Zoia is with us." If her own courageous and unwavering behavior had been inspired by Stalin, repeatedly expressed in her words "Stalin is with us" (*Stalin s nami*) it is now Zoia who will inspire us forever: *Zoia s nami*.

Immortality had not been attributed to Zoia alone but to all the heroes of the Soviet Union. Great suffering and ordeals, martyrdom, and the ultimate sacrifice, the hero's life, are a prerequisite for heroism and they guarantee immortality. Despite the pain felt over the loss of young lives, all reports on heroes conclude with the conviction that they will never be forgotten, which almost automatically transforms mourning into pride, almost ecstasy.

As for the visualization of eternal life, the film *Zoia* was not the first to depict deceased Soviet heroes in "heaven" (the sky). Lenin, for instance, had been portrayed as a steady companion of the people or the children in film and photography, a godlike figure looking down from celestial heights, keeping watch over his flock. And the same techniques were later used for the depiction of the living Stalin. The weightless body of a woman commissar, floating in the air as an eternal companion for her comrades left behind, could already be seen in the 1930s in a film based on Vsevolod Vishnevskii's *Optimistic Tragedy*. Is this the depiction of Soviet angels or saints?

## The Effects of Heroism

Most of the military heroes were enrolled forever as members of units that were often named after them; thus the 254th Guard's Rifle Regiment where Aleksandr Matrosov had served was named after him, and his name was inscribed for all eternity into the first company of this regiment.[36] From then on "the Matrosov Guardsmen pledged their oath to the flag in front of the new silken banner on which the name of their comrade was embroidered with golden thread, and they pledged to fight just as Matrosov did," says P. Zhurba's literary biography.[37]

What was written in retrospect about the comrades of Matrosov and their will to fight like him was not just wishful thinking. His act was indeed emulated nearly three hundred times.[38] Yet heroic deeds and their legends did not just serve as model behavior to strive toward, they also caused a closer link to the party and its ideology. This is evident in the repeated waves of applications for membership in the Komsomol or the Communist Party immediately following the news of some self-sacrifice in action or of someone who had withstood extremely vile treatment by the aggressor, for example, Zoia Kosmodem'ianskaia. As brave, daring and fearless behavior was always attributed to faithful Communists, their belief in socialist ideas, which was more often than not tantamount to their unwavering belief in Stalin, could only be interpreted as an inexhaustible source of inspiration. This suggests a parallel to a phenomenon characteristic of the early times of the persecution of Christians: nonbelievers were moved to convert after having witnessed the public torturing and execution of believers whose stalwart courage convinced them of their divine inspiration.

## Legend and Reality

The relationship of Soviet citizens to their officially sanctioned heroes was impaired long before the dawn of glasnost and perestroika. At least for the last three decades, Soviet heroes have undergone a continued process of demystification. The "power of the model man" began to crumble. Almost all categories of heroes and feats became the target of biting anecdotes and underground songs. Given the experience of everyday life, the glorification of Soviet reality and the heroism of their people was no longer plausible. Belief in the imminent "radiant future" propagated for all those years had been overstrained. Through the years, long before 1986, heroism had become a tedious and tiresome topic, starting to lose its appeal. With glasnost, however, it was publicly discussed for the first time in the press and, in August 1991, finally led to an iconoclastic eruption.

The abortive coup d'état of 1991 marked the turning point in the relationship of the Soviet people to their official heroes, the symbolic representatives of the Soviet system. As we all know, their statues were pulled down from their pedestals. Even the heroes of the Great Patriotic War were "dismantled," but not, in contrast to the others, in the literal sense. Their statues have, so far, been left untouched. At the same time, journalists and other individuals (represented by letters to the editor of various newspapers) started to engage in meticulous research on the biographies of individual heroes. Ever since the archives began to open up they have collected data and facts about particular exploits and presented new knowledge to the public, more often than not in sharp contrast to the official canonized version of some Soviet heroes and heroines. In the media, the citizens of the former Soviet Union are now confronted with the painful "truths" about the war, presented with the fact that many lives could have been saved with a different kind of policy, and that the deaths of hundreds of thousands of Soviet citizens could not all be blamed on the enemy but, instead, were the responsibility of the political leader, of Stalin. Can historical truth diminish the heroism of the Soviet people in defending their Father- and Motherland, their home country?

How does the public react to the new documentary reports on the heroic deeds of their once treasured idols? Some openly and vehemently protest against the attempt to demolish publicly an almost sacred image. This not only shows the importance still attached to those model men and women by former Soviet citizens, but also expresses the pain and the fear felt by the threat of losing an important part of one's own history and orientation, of being deprived of one's own identity. The pressure to admit that they have hailed the wrong heroes, that they were continuously deceived, was naturally met with resentment. Others relentlessly continue to "defend the truth." After long decades of being lied to, they call for truth at any cost, regarding the dismantling of an old identity as a prerequisite for a new beginning.

## Zoia Kosmodem'ianskaia—Deconstructed

The rewriting of Soviet history has also involved the concomitant rewriting of the lives of Soviet heroes. Personal recollections combined with archival documents shed new light on some heroic deeds and make them appear a mere concoction of official propaganda.

Amazingly, Zoia Kosmodem'ianskaia again best illustrates the recent debate on legend and reality of Soviet war heroes, of the "holy" heroes of a "holy" war—as the official wording puts it. Some people already knew alternate versions of the Zoia story even during the war. Yet, in those years, it did not yet result in a general process of demystification. A woman remembers her husband, a war correspondent, coming home from the front in March 1942, shortly after Zoia had been posthumously awarded the title "Hero of the Soviet Union" and the public had been made familiar with all the details of her tragic death. He told her that Zoia had neither been tortured nor hanged by the Nazis. Instead, some of the villagers had been shot by the Nazis who suspected them of having set fire to the stables. When Zoia was seen by those who survived the "punishment" of the German military, they, in a blind rage, took revenge on her and stoned her to death.

In 1991, this version was publicly affirmed in the new Moscow weekly, *Argumenty i fakty*.[39] On the basis of his private investigations among the members of Zoia's partisan unit and in the village in which she was captured, another former war correspondent reported that, according to those villagers, no German troops had been in town at the time Zoia was supposed to have been caught and tortured. This account was buttressed in one of the next issues of the same paper[40] with reference to official documents. We read that Zoia did not set fire to a stable where German soldiers were staying overnight. Instead, she was sent to the rear of the enemy, like many other partisans by order of the Supreme Commander,[41] to burn down all settlements within a radius of forty to sixty kilometers behind the front line. In this new version, Zoia, previously admired for having heroically defended her country against the fascist aggressor, is transformed into a henchman of Stalin's operative plan of "scorched earth." Not only the enemy, but also the unrecruitable Soviet population, women, children, and the elderly fell victim to this policy.

According to a letter by a retired Moscow colonel,[42] the story about Zoia's death is complemented by still another detail: Zoia had not been alone, either on her mission or on the day of her execution. Another girl of the same partisan unit as Zoia, Vera Voloshina, was hanged together with her. Supposedly she was also caught and most cruelly tortured by the Germans, behaved like a heroine, but was never awarded the title "Hero of the Soviet Union." Is the colonel right in suggesting "that the frontline command worked according to a notorious plan, afraid that there could be too many heroes?"

Still another interesting detail emerges in an open letter to the paper by the chief doctors of the psychiatric children's ward at the Medical Diagnostical Center in Moscow.[43] Four years before the outbreak of the war, Zoia Kosmodem'ianskaia, at the age of fourteen, had repeatedly been treated in the clinic for "schizophrenia." Immediately after the war, the NKVD came to the clinic and confiscated her medical file. Some degree of madness, cured in Christian times not in a hospital but in a monastery or convent, had often had a place in the lives of saints and heroes. Obviously, the authors do not expect anybody to associate this schizophrenia with the classical Soviet schizophrenia, attributed to almost all Soviet dissidents.

The painstaking search for truth does not end with Zoia's deed. Even her identity is in question. If we are right in assuming that Strunnikov's photographic portrait of the dead Zoia left the greatest impression on the popular imagination, then even this image is now in danger of being destroyed. Some claimed that the legendary photograph of the hanged Zoia did not in fact represent her but some girl named Lilia Azolina.[44] This most serious iconoclastic attempt led the Central Archive of the All-Union Leninist

Communist Youth League (Komsomol) to try to dissipate those doubts in order to save Zoia from deconstruction. They asked the Research Institute for Legal Evidence at the Ministry of Justice to produce expert evidence on the identity of the deceased, on the basis of a total of nine photographs, including one of Lilia Azolina. The experts ruled that the photograph of the hanged girl's body was indeed that of Kosmodem'ianskaia.[45] Whom are we to follow? Whom are we to trust? To what extent can empirical data affect the myth? Have not myths always been independent of time and space?

## Historiography vs. Hagiography

Does this debate lead us to the conclusion that "historical truth" will destroy heroes and heroines who have become legends in their times? Or can legend be superior to historical facts? Lev Arnshtam, director of the film *Zoia*, claims that it is. When one of his war correspondent friends came home from the front with other than the official news and hinted to Arnshtam that the "real" story of Zoia was quite a different one, the film director, not upset in the least, answered: "I would have made the film just the same. The story is more important than the actual details." Margarita Aliger also insisted almost thirty years later that her depiction of Zoia was not invented, but "reflected the truth we believed in."[46]

A true myth does not lend itself to empirical verification. The notion of historical truth does not apply to a legend, while, at the same time, doubts as to its authenticity already foretell its fragility and decline. In the making of a hero, popular imagination is just as selective as is official propaganda. It might not emphasize the same traits, but as long as the official presentation offers a broad enough spectrum to choose from for the purpose of identification, then both sides might meet in favoring one and the same person. Thus, the popular hero is born.

In a system where all social endeavor is supposed to serve a political purpose, it is most revealing to note that the most beloved and cherished heroes and heroines seem to have gained their high rank in popularity first and foremost by their human qualitites, more often than not by their good looks, their pleasant smile, or sex appeal. One could even say that the most popular ones were those whose behavior or deeds— in the imagination of the large majority—were literally stripped of their ideological connotation. It is beyond doubt that all the Zoias, Matrosovs, Koshevois, Panfilovs— authentic or not—played an important if not a decisive part in propaganda warfare, enabling the Soviet people to stop Hitlerism.

The devastation, slaughter, and brutality inflicted on the Soviet people in the years 1941–45, the millions of lives lost, not by the impact of a natural catastrophe but by the most brutal attack of the German Army, were unequalled in history. To withstand extreme suffering requires extreme strength. Without the heroic deeds and model behavior of Soviet heroes and heroines during those years, fascism might have known a different history.

Zoia's true fate may well remain a mystery forever. Nevertheless, those who re-write Soviet history, and not just Soviet war history, should try to embrace the popular component in the shaping of reality. There seems a vital element of "self-will" (*Eigensinn*)[47] contained in popular imagery constituting the human factor that might not decide events but, in any case, survives in history. It represents the universal wants and needs of the people to create a world not necessarily "larger" but "smaller than life," irrespective of, or despite, the system or society in which they live.

Victims of post-Stalinist society who almost lost their lives in fighting the falseness of official Soviet heroism, opposing the system as anti-heroes, as for instance the writer Venedikt Erofeev,[48] were right in denouncing "the irreproachable Zoia, the martyr Zoia" as the symbol of the particular brand of communist stoicism which he perceived as the root of all evil and the cause of hundreds of thousands of deaths in Soviet society.[49]

Veterans of the Great Patriotic War must be excused for trying to save "their Zoia" from being dethroned and deconstructed. "Once, they destroyed churches, now they destroy monuments," said an advocate of the canonized Soviet war heroes.[50] Yet the fact that a whole generation believed in her cannot be attributed to a unique and perfect achievement of communist image-making but, quite the contrary, can only be explained by some lapse in canonization, by accidental impurities in its official representation that leave room for a somehow subconscious attachment to unofficial values and qualities. Therein lies the hope contained in Zoia.

## Notes

1. This honorary title could be considered analogous to the American Congressional Medal of Honor.

2. For the latest figure, see John Barber and Mark Harrison, *The Soviet Home Front, 1941–1945: A Social and Economic History of the USSR in World War II* (London, 1991).

3. See the remarkable analysis of Paul Fussell on the literary treatment of traditional and modern warfare, *The Great War and Modern Memory* (London, 1975); and his *Wartime: Understanding and Behavior in the Second World War* (New York, 1989).

4. V. I. Lenin, *Polnoe sobranie sochinenii*, 5th ed., 42 (1963), 4.

5. See Hans Günther, "Stalinskie sokoly: analiz mifa tridtsatyikh godov," *Voprosy literatury* 11/12 (1991), 122–41.

6. Katerina Clark refers to the conversion of "reality" into "fiction" as characteristic of the heroic age of Stalinism: *The Soviet Novel: History as Ritual* (Chicago, 1985).

7. Clausewitz, in his famous treatise *On War* (1832), had already alluded to the relevance of information in war to counteract "the timidity of man" and his being "inclined to lend credence to

the bad rather than the good." For him, success in warfare depended largely on the ability to incline "from the side of fear to that of hope." See Brooks, McReynolds, this volume.

8. See the outstanding analysis of the structure of the socialist realist novel in Clark, *Soviet Novel*.

9. *Pravda* (Dec. 1, 1941) and the same wording in reports on the heroism of the Soviet people in almost every number.

10. *Pravda* (Dec. 23, 1941) and many other instances.

11. The first Soviet woman awarded the title Hero of the Soviet Union in 1938, Valentina Gribodubova, was also a pilot who had broken the record in long-distance flight.

12. On the socialist superman, see Hans Günther, *Der sozialistische Übermensch: Gorkij und der sowjetische Heldenmythos* (Stuttgart, 1993).

13. He was supposedly inspired by two other heroes: the Russian pilot Karpovich, who had lost a leg in an air battle in World War I and also managed to reenter active service; and Pavel Korchagin, the hero of Nikolai Ostrovkii's novel *How the Steel Was Tempered* (1934).

14. *Povest' o nastoiashchem cheloveke* (Moscow, 1946), English trans. E. Manning in *Soviet Literature* 4/5 (1947) and Joe Fineberg as *A Story about a Real Man* (1949; Moscow, 1986). In the novel, Maresev's name is changed to "Meresev." The 1948 film by A. Stolper remained popular for decades.

15. In German alone, the book on Maresev saw at least a dozen editions within the first ten years after the war.

16. Prikaz No. 269, Sept. 8, 1943, quoted in an appendix to the novel by Pavel Zhurba, *Aleksandr Matrosov* (Moscow, 1949).

17. *Pamiat' o podvige: po zalam Tsentral'nogo ordena Krasnoi Zvezdy Muzeia Vooruzhënnykh Sil SSSR* (Moscow, 1985), p. 140.

18. First published in *Oktiabr'* 5 (1946) 3–49.

19. See Clark on "The Stalinist Myth of the 'Great Family,' " in *Soviet Novel*, pp. 134 ff.

20. *Geroi Sovetskogo Soiuza: entsiklopedicheskii slovar'* (Moscow, 1984).

21. Both in *Besstrashnaia partizanka Zoia Kosmodem'ianskaia* (Piatigorsk, 1942).

22. "Vystuplenie po radio L. T. Kosmodem'ianskoi—materi geroia Sovetskogo Soiuza Z. A. Kosmodem'ianskoi," in Pëtr Lidov, *Tania: geroi Sovetskogo Soiuza Zoia Anatol'evna Kosmodem'ianskaia* (Moscow, 1942).

23. She continued to tour the country in the years after the war, reporting then also on the tragic death of her son Shura. See also her *Povest' o Zoe i Shure* (Moscow, 1950).

24. Aliger was awarded the Stalin Prize in December 1942 for her poem.

25. See Richard Stites, *Russian Popular Culture: Entertainment and Society since 1900* (Cambridge, 1992), p. 110.

26. A year later she finished a play about Zoia, *Skazka o pravde (dramaticheskaia poema v 4-kh deistviiakh)* (Moscow, 1947).

27. Valerii Zhelobinskii, *Pesnia o Tane partizanke, dlia golosa, khora, i f.-piano* (Tambov, 1943).

28. Liubov' Kosmodem'ianskaia, *My Daughter Zoya* (Moscow, 1942).

29. *Narodnaia geroinia: sbornik materialov o Zoe Kosmodem'ianskoi* (Moscow, 1942).

30. Paintings by N. N. Zhukov, "The Heroine Zoia Being Interrogated" (1950) and by Sergei Grigorev, "Arsonist" (n.d.).

31. Stites, *Russian Popular Culture*, p. 83.

32. The balloon test-pilots Fedoseenko, Vasenko, and Usyskin, sailing at an altitude of 90,000 feet, perished on January 20, 1934. To a certain generation of Russians, this is as well remembered as is the explosion of the airship *Graf Hindenburg* in New Jersey in 1937 to Americans.

33. See Clark on "Patterns of Ritual Sacrifice" in *Soviet Novel*, pp. 178ff.

34. Jay Leyda, *Kino: a History of the Russian and Soviet Film* (New York, 1960), p. 379.

35. *Cinema Chronicle* (Aug. 1944), quoted in Leyda, *Kino*, p. 379.

36. Prikaz No. 269 of the People's Commissariat for Defense, Sept. 8, 1943.

37. Zhurba, *Aleksandr Matrosov*, p. 321.

38. Figures vary from 250 to 350, depending on the source.

39. A. Zhovtis, "Utocheniia k kanonicheskoi versii," *Argumenty i fakty* (to be cited as *AiF*) 38 (1991).

40. "Istoriia Tani v dokumentakh," ibid. 7 (1992), 8.

41. Prikaz No. 0428, Nov. 17, 1941, cited in ibid.

42. N. V. Anokhin, "O podvige sibiriachki Very Voloshinoi," *Sovetskaia Rossiia* (Nov. 23, 1991), 2.

43. "Zoia Kosmodem'ianskaia: geroinia ili simvol?" *AiF* 43 (1991), 3.

44. Ibid.

45. "Lozh' oprovergnuta," *Sovetskaia Rossiia* (Jan. 29, 1992).

46. M. Aliger, *Stikhi i proza*, 2 vols. (Moscow, 1975), 1, p. 431.

47. Oskar Negt and Alexander Kluge, *Geschichte und Eigensinn* (Frankfurt, 1981).

48. Venedikt Erofeev (1938–1990), one of the most brilliant and sarcastic critics of the Soviet system who—during his lifetime and more so after his death—became a cult figure for a new generation of Russians strongly opposed to official heroism.

49. Ol'ga Sedakova, "Venedikt Erofeev (1938–1990)," *Teatr* 9 (Dec. 23, 1991).

50. Vladimir Ivanov, "Kogo oplakivala mat' Olega Koshevogo," *Pravda* (Dec. 23, 1991).

# 12

# The War of Remembrance

## Nina Tumarkin

O NE SATURDAY NIGHT in the summer of 1986, in the polar region of northern Russia, six young men on motorcycles who were going fishing happened to pass by the "Valley of Glory," where repose the remains of thousands of Soviet fighters who died in the three-year effort to prevent the Nazis from taking Murmansk. During the war it was called "Valley of Death," but now flowers surround the pedestal of an obelisk in what has turned into a modest war memorial. The youths downed a case of beer, then one of them produced a rifle, and, for sport, they began to take turns shooting at empty beer bottles which they ranged along the pedestal. Then, evidently bored with those pedestrian targets, they opened fire on the monument itself. They set their sights on the date "1941," and on the words:

THE MOTHERLAND REMEMBERS HER SONS

The shooting spree lasted almost three hours. Most of the youths were between eighteen and twenty-three, and they all got off with light sentences—three to five years in the reformatory. *Iunost'*, a periodical for young people, carried an article about the incident containing a brief interview with Andrei Kulikov, the first of the youths to open fire:

> "Andrei, is it difficult to kill a person?"
> "Of course it is difficult."
> "And is it possible to kill memory?"
> "What memory?"
> "Human memory."
> Kulikov remained silent.[1]

Operation Barbarossa was launched well over a half century ago. Yet so traumatic were the invasion and war—affecting virtually every family in the Soviet Union—that they left a profound imprint on the deep structure of the country's body politic and psyche. Memories and legendary recollections about the war years created a cosmology that informed Soviet political culture, providing generations of Soviet citizens and

*194*

their leaders with the fundamental lexicon that they drew upon to explain themselves to the world.

Today, some fifty years after the war's end, glasnost, perestroika, and the demise of the Soviet Union have demolished that combination of self-pity and self-congratulation that for so long had characterized the official memorialization of the war. The enshrined, idealized saga of the Great Patriotic War is being replaced with raw human memory. "Our understanding of the war," historian Mikhail Gefter remarked to me in the summer of 1989 as we sat on little wooden chairs in the lush, Russianly overgrown garden of his small rented dacha, "is being transformed from a heroic farce to the tragedy that it really was."

When Andrei Kulikov and his pals went on their tipsy, gun-toting fling at the "Valley of Glory," they were surely not out to kill memory. At best, their choice of location for target practice was entirely random; at worst, theirs was an act of iconoclasm, of sacrilege—the desecration of a sacred object in a civil religion. Indeed if anyone sought to kill the real human memory of World War II in the Soviet Union, it was not the vandals, but rather the designers who had labored to concoct out of the Valley of Death a contrived "Valley of Glory," with its predictable obelisks and ritual slogans. The tens of thousands of war memorials that still dot the landscape of the former Soviet Union are the most visible, central embodiments of a decades-long effort on the part of Soviet authorities to eradicate historical memory and replace it in the popular consciousness with a sacred saga that sang the praises of the Communist Party as the guiding force behind the Victory of Light over the Forces of Darkness.

In June 1989, in a discussion with members of the USSR Academy of Sciences' Institute of Ethnography, I asked the members to plumb the real meaning of the rituals and myths celebrating the Great Patriotic War. Immediately a young man in his late twenties or early thirties stood up. He was tall, pale, and mustachioed, and neatly attired in a light-blue shirt and navy trousers. "The Great Patriotic War was the greatest catastrophe in the history of Soviet foreign policy," he said. "And so to cover up the disgrace, our authorities canonized it and called it a victory. But what kind of victory was it if we lost twenty or thirty million people and the Germans lost two or three million?" After a stunned silence I called on a middle-aged man who, in a bold voice, said that "ours was a victory because even though the costs were enormous, we did save the world from fascism."

"*Save* the world from fascism?" shouted the young man, jumping up again. "On the contrary, we *brought* fascism to Eastern Europe and enslaved our own people as well. What kind of salvation was that?"

Then a stout elderly woman in a blue and white flowered dress slowly stood up. Her thin white hair was pulled back in an old-fashioned knot. She looked directly at the young man and in a quivering but determined voice said, "We Russians have always had in our hearts a special place for *victims*. You are right in saying that the war was an incomparable catastrophe. But the victims of that catastrophe—the millions and millions of war dead, the countless orphans and widows—shall always, yes, always merit our compassion, and our love."

The old woman was right, of course. No matter who is to blame, the victims' sufferings were real. Indeed, the pathos of their deaths surely is not diminished, but rather heightened by the fact that so many succumbed to the blunders and evils of their own leaders. Self-inflicted wounds on the body politic are always the most painful.

Wrenching as it is, the revival of posttraumatic real memory may be a sign of mental health. Societies—like individuals—may gain strength and eventual wisdom from repeated intensive recollections of traumatizing experiences. And they are emotionally crippled by successful efforts to keep those recollections below the surface of consciousness.

"During the first twenty years after the war's end there was a decided effort to forget about the war, to push it into the background," observed Lazar Lazarev, an elderly literary critic with a specialty in war literature, and editor of *Voprosy Literatury* (*Problems of Literature*). "Undoubtedly my life-long interest in the war is autobiographical, since I belong to that generation of people who in 1941 went to war directly from high school. In 1941 I was seventeen. At eighteen I already commanded a reconnaissance detachment and fought for two years until I was wounded in August 1943." The fourth and fifth fingers of his right hand were missing—a legacy of the war.

"In school we had all believed the myths about the all-powerful Supreme Leader. The military catastrophe of 1941–42 forced us for the first time to question Stalin, and threw us back onto our own resources. So for many of us, those first two years of the war coincided with a spontaneous de-Stalinization. We felt that everything depended on us personally, and that gave us an extraordinary feeling of freedom."

Lazarev's strained smoker's voice provided a dramatic dissonance to his palpable passion for the war and its legacy. "Even before the war's end Stalin knew very well that truth had eroded the illusions on which his rule was based, and he moved swiftly to suppress my generation, which had matured in the terrible freedom wrought by the shock of war. In May 1945, at a Kremlin banquet celebrating the victory, Stalin made a famous toast in which he said 'Let us drink to the patient endurance of the Russian people, because under these circumstances any other people would have long ago toppled their government.' What he meant was that the war was over and best forgotten, lest the truth about his conduct of the war erode some of his total authority."

Lazarev then mused about Leonid Brezhnev's decision to resurrect the Great Patriotic War, exploiting it to serve political ends. "Those of us who had fought in the war thought at first that at last the war was getting the attention it merited," he said. "But in fact that attention was purely an official attempt to turn the war into a show made up of concocted legends."

Lazarev was right. In the quarter century that began with Leonid Brezhnev's accession to party rule in 1964 and ended at the close of the 1980s with the devastating collapse of the system that Brezhnev had inherited from Stalin, the Communist Party created nothing less than a cult of the Great Patriotic War, including a panoply of saints, sacred relics, and phony sagas of the war which were endured by millions of tired tourists held hostage by their Intourist guides at the most famous of the USSR's thousands upon thousands of war memorials.

The saga's basic plot was a kind of post-hoc messianism: collectivization and rapid industrialization under the First and Second Five-Year Plans prepared our country for war, and despite an overpowering surprise attack by the Fascist Beast and its inhuman wartime practices, despite the loss of twenty million valiant martyrs to the Cause, our country, under the leadership of the Communist Party headed by Comrade Stalin, arose as one united front and expelled the enemy from our own territory and that of Eastern Europe, thus saving Europe—and the world—from fascist enslavement.

The cult narrative fixed the number of wartime losses at twenty million. Like world Jewry's six million Holocaust victims, the Soviet Union's purported twenty million war dead came to represent a store of redemptive suffering that the Brezhnev regime called upon again and again as evidence of the country's unique position in world history.

The organized cult of the Great Patriotic War was an effective system of political symbols and rituals. It celebrated the great legitimizing myth of the party and the government, helped inspire respect for the armed forces even during the demoralizing Afghanistan war, bolstered pride in the USSR and its socialist economy, and served to justify foreign policy positions. It also provided a vision of a powerfully united nation as a counterweight to the tensions straining the nation's periphery. At the same time it was genuinely popular: the war cult supplied legions of moral exemplars to inspire the increasingly cynical and apathetic populace; it shored up the self-esteem of elderly war veterans, provided a source of nostalgia for their wearily disillusioned ranks, and helped resolve intergenerational discord in favor of the fathers.

The frequently trumpeted motto of the Great Patriotic War cult—"No one is forgotten, and nothing is forgotten"—is the last line of a poem by Ol'ga Berggol'ts engraved on the rear wall of St. Peterburg's Piskarevskoe Cemetery, the resting place of some half-million of Leningrad's wartime siege victims. The motto, however, was fundamentally mendacious. So much was forgotten: the Nazi-Soviet Pact and its secret protocol; Stalin's 1940 massacre of thousands of Polish officers in the Katyn forest; the Holocaust; the real extent of lend lease; Soviet prisoners-of-war who were later incarcerated for the purported treason of surrendering to the enemy; and the millions of

Soviet citizens whose wartime deaths were caused, directly or indirectly, by Stalin's brutal rule.

May 9, 1985 was the fortieth anniversary of the victory, and turned out to be the USSR's final flamboyant, tastelessly orchestrated megaholiday celebration, replete with billboards splattered with self-congratulatory slogans, posters of idealized soldiers with Candide's innocent eyes and Dick Tracy's chin, a military parade in Red Square—the first held on Victory Day since 1945—and thousands of bemedaled veterans strutting proudly before their respectful younger compatriots.

Victory Day was both the tool of propagandists touting its triumphs, and a memorial day for millions of relatives and friends of the war dead—a time for an inescapable barrage of self-serving hype, and a day for families to lay flowers on the graves of their loved ones, or to leave a bouquet at their local war memorial. I spent the morning leaning out of my hotel room window as a formidable display of military hardware rolled down Gorky Street and into Red Square, emitting deafening noises and belching smelly puffs of smoke.

Four years later, in June 1989, Nikolai Volkov, an official at the All-Union Committee of Veterans, assured me that the forty-fifth anniversary of the victory in 1990 would be commemorated with great fanfare. "At the fortieth anniversary our country had seven and one-half million veterans. There are now about five million left, and our numbers are rapidly dwindling. How many of us will be around in 1995 to enjoy the fiftieth?" For most Soviet veterans, the forty-fifth would be their last hurrah.

In early May 1990 I came to Moscow for the forty-fifth anniversary of the victory. The city felt solemn and hard-edged, with none of the ready-for-a-party feel of the 1985 jubilee. Moscow buildings and streets sported few of the usual megaholiday slogans, gargantuan posters, and red bunting. The old, roseate version of the war experience had been a carefully orchestrated symphony in a major key, promoting an image of national harmony and unity. But now that symphony was drowned out by a cacaphonous clamor of dissonant voices, memories, passions. The remembrance of the war had become a prism refracting an entire spectrum of emotions unleashed by five years of perestroika and the most fundamental kind of social disintegration.

The bankruptcy of the official celebration of Victory Day was poignantly palpable in School No. 110, one of downtown Moscow's better schools. In its muddy courtyard rests the only successful war memorial I have ever seen in the Soviet Union. It shows five thin, vacant boys going off to the front; they had all attended School No. 110, and none of them ever returned from the war. Every year on the day before Victory Day, the students used to proceed, class by class, to lay flowers on the monument's pedestal. And on Victory Day itself, it was traditional for them to meet with veterans, mostly alumni of their school, and present them with the small bouquets of flowers that are, always and everywhere in the Soviet Union, the prime symbol of respect.

On the forty-fifth, the children were not buying into any part of those rituals. During the flower-laying in the courtyard not even the older ones could muster up a few moments of respectful silence following the teacher's little canned speech about "that generation to whom we owe so much." When one boy made believe he was going to eat his flower instead of placing it at the foot of the monument, the teacher slapped him across the face. After witnessing this most unsatisfying ritual, I managed to spend an hour in charge of a class of seventh-graders. At the beginning of the hour a teacher came into the classroom and reminded the children to show up the next day at the designated meeting with veterans. "I don't want to see a repeat of last year's sorry performance, when not a single one of you turned up!" she warned in a nasty tone of voice. After she left, the children told me they would not spend their holiday putting on school uniforms and going out to greet the veterans. "It's not a pleasant thing to do and besides, why should our parents have to pay for the flowers?" said one intelligent-looking boy with big glasses. (Two years later, on the eve of Victory Day, 1992, the monument in the courtyard of School No. 110 was badly vandalized and had to be moved into the school for security.)

On May 9, 1990, brilliant spring sunshine added dazzle to the military parade, which was doubtless held to placate the disgruntled army leadership. The parade was short, and, by the standards of totalitarian kitsch, decidedly modest, quite unlike the extravaganza of five years earlier. As I tried to get the best view of the proceedings, teetering on a stone ledge to the left of the mausoleum and only a few feet from a line of elegantly uniformed KGB guards, I knew I was witnessing the swan song of the cult of the Great Patriotic War. The swagger, the self-congratulation, and the hyperbole about socialism having defeated imperialism were no longer there. Indeed, in view of its subsequent painful collapse, any of the old hype about socialism's superiority being proven by the victory would have been laughable.

The informal meetings of veterans in front of the Bolshoi Theater and in Gorky Park were subdued and only partly focused on the Great Patriotic War. For the first time in anyone's memory, uniformed *afgantsy*, young veterans of the decade-long embroilment in Afghanistan, some of them in wheelchairs, made their appearance at a Victory Day celebration. According to tradition, old folks sang war songs on the steps of the Bolshoi; only fifty yards away, young adults danced in graceful pairs while others belted out the ancient Russian folk songs that are so popular in today's spirit of revived nationalism. In Gorky Park I threw a ten-ruble note into an enormous plastic bowl half-filled with money being collected for a planned *kniga pamiati*, a book of memory listing the names of every single victim of the Great Patriotic War. No mention here of the victory. Just an effort to pay respects to the war dead.

At six-fifty I clicked on the television set, expecting to see the familiar flickering flame of the Unknown Soldier Tomb and hear the unseen, unctuous voice of the high priest of the war cult exalt the glory of the victory and its bitter costs in the annual Victory Day television service. What I saw instead was a collage of scenes depicting wartime horrors. The narrator called upon his viewers to find in the memory of the war a source of healing and reconciliation. He urged people to seek mutual forgiveness at the common graves of the millions who died in the war. Astonishingly, the text included references to the Jewish contribution to the war effort, and refrained from singling out the Communist Party as the most valued segment of wartime society. The cult of the Great Patriotic War was over, replaced by an admixture of passion, regret, nostalgia, rage and remembrance.

A few days before Victory Day, the newspaper *Komsomol'skaia pravda* published an article entitled "Stolen Victory" which brought into high relief some of the most sensitive questions tugging at the war myth.[2] It began with a conversation that had recently taken place between two elderly veterans: "We've given away Germany, we've given away Europe—for what, then, did we lay down so many lives during the war?" "What's there to discuss?" responded the other veteran, "they've stolen our victory, and that's the whole story."

Did those veterans really believe that their country had defeated fascism in order to take over half of Europe? Gennadii Bordiugov, a scholarly commentator interviewed in the article, was not surprised at this reaction to the recent liberation of Europe: "Our sea of spilled blood was too vast, our wounds too deep to expect our people, especially those who fought, to respond to the events in Eastern Europe without pain." But he went on to assert that in fact the victory *had* been stolen from the people—by Stalin and his system—on the very day of the victory, May 9, 1945. In the 1930s Stalinism had bled the populace, driven the peasantry onto collective farms, instituted a reign of terror that stripped the nation's soul of its energy, spunk, and self-confidence, and purged the armed forces of its officer corps—all in the name of preparing for a future war. The *Komsomol'skaia pravda* interviewer, Aleksandr Afanasev, remarked that it was "as though Roosevelt, with the aim of strengthening his position on the eve of war, had taken the farmers and 'collectivized' them, driven them onto reservations, and had locked up all potentially discontented individuals into concentration camps. . . . " When war did come, the Stalinist system proved singularly incapable of waging it.

"Stolen Victory" revealed that in 1941 and 1942 groups of factory workers rebelled against their bosses, complaining of their ineptitude in meeting wartime needs, and, even more frequently, protesting that party officers and NKVD men were taking care of themselves, evacuating their wives and families, and doing nothing for the people. For Stalin, the imperative to rein in the anti-Stalinist and anti-party sentiments in the country at large was at least as important as defeating fascism. In the end, "Who was victorious and who was conquered, who won the war against whom, if the vanquished are now sending food to the victors?"

A united Germany supplying an impoverished Soviet Union with food! Who would have predicted it five, or even three years earlier? Who was victorious indeed? More than once I have heard young people (including Jews) assert that it would have been better had Hitler won the war, contending that a fascist regime would have been no worse, and probably better, than the Soviet system that has provided them with nothing but frustration and grief. Such inanities are not common, but many members of the intelligentsia have, in fact, come to equate communism and fascism, Stalin and Hitler.

By the end of the 1980s, many had come to blame Stalin for much of the war's destructiveness. Stalin's collectivization drive and First and Second Five-Year Plans resulted in millions of deaths and—as the recent collapse has shown—dislocated the economy beyond repair. The party purge and mass terror of the thirties took many more millions of lives and broke the morale of the people. "And then, bled white, unimaginably weakened," wrote *Komsomol'skaia pravda* reporter Aleksandr Afanasev, " 'with naked hands,' as my father used to say, this people was thrown against a steel wall"—the German army.[3]

Recent publications and films about the war have been relentless in their drive to reveal the ugliest aspects of the war, and in particular, Stalin's brutality toward his own populace. The Soviet high command under Stalin never hesitated to use its own citizens as hostages or cannon fodder. In 1990 *Shtrafniki*, a documentary film, created a major stir. It graphically detailed the wartime fates of some of the notorious *shtrafbataliony*, punishment battalions of former prisoners, including political ones, who were sent on the most dangerous, often suicidal missions, followed by commissars pointing guns at their backs to make sure they followed orders.[4]

In 1941 the Red Army had few officers to lead it: "We used to think that some forty thousand army and navy officers died in the 1937–39 purge of the military," said Professor Georgii Kumanëv, an historian of the Great Patriotic War.

Now we know that figure to be more than fifty thousand. By 1939, in effect, our armed forces had no commanders. Stalin had destroyed the army. The military purge gave Hitler the certainty that the USSR would be incapable of military action against the Reich in the event of a German attack on Poland in 1939. Moreover, Stalin's senseless Finnish war of 1939–40 demonstrated to Hitler our utter weakness and without a doubt brought about the June 1941 invasion. Of course, when the invasion came, our forces were totally unprepared because Stalin was terrified of arousing Hitler's wrath by mobilizing our defenses, despite repeated warnings of the planned attack from credible sources. And then, did our whole country rise up to fight? No, because millions of able-bodied men who could have helped save civilian lives were languishing in Stalin's jails and labor camps.

Kumanëv, whom I interviewed in his Moscow office, was especially concerned about getting straight the numbers of Soviet war dead. He assured me that the legendary twenty million figure ought to be hiked up to somewhere between twenty-seven and twenty-nine million. Twenty-seven million was the figure Gorbachëv quoted in his 1990 Victory Day speech. The assessment of these figures today seems thoroughly politicized, a gruesome numbers game in which the more radical, anti-Stalinist, anti-Soviet critics estimate ever-higher losses and point to them as a reflection both of the system's incompetence at waging war, and of Stalin's direct and indirect role in those millions of deaths. Some estimates run as high as almost fifty million wartime losses.[5]

This raises the inevitable explosive question: how many of the tens of millions of Soviet lives lost in the war must be blamed on the Supreme Leader of the Soviet People? Some might argue that the numbers are unimportant, that "war is war," and that inevitably any belligerent power needlessly destroys many of its finest youth through error or the chaotic circumstances of war. But such an assertion leads willy-nilly to the troubling question of numbers. What if it turned out that in fact the Soviet Union had been directly or indirectly responsible for the deaths of two million of its own citizens, or four million or fifteen million? Should one say that two million self-inflicted losses properly can fall under the rubric of "war is war," but fifteen cannot? And if it could indeed be determined that Stalin and his compatriots must be blamed for fifteen million, or one-half of all wartime losses, do we accord the Soviet Union fifty percent less respect and sympathy than if the Germans had in fact killed the entire thirty million?

That way lies madness. It spills over into the whole bedeviled question of the quantification of suffering. Did the Soviet people suffer five times as much as the Jews because they lost more than five times the number of people? The answer to that question is clearly no. Victims of terrible ordeals, such as enslaved African-Americans, the Jews in the Holocaust, the Soviet people in World War II, become aggregates of national suffering on behalf of which future generations make compensatory claims. Few would dispute the legitimacy of such claims in principle. However, fewer still would be prepared to rationalize numerically the intensity of a nation's ordeal and the assessment of its demand for recompense.

And yet, on some level numbers do matter. It does in fact matter if indeed a significant portion of the Soviet war deaths cannot be blamed on the Germans; not because we need to know just how much to temper our sympathy for the Soviet side, but because in that case the decades-long Soviet mourning for their twenty million martyrs was in part a cover-up for the past sins of Stalin, his system, and the Soviet people.

In 1990 Ales Adamovich, a renowned Belarusian novelist and political activist, published an article about Stalinism and the war, which he called "the war with Hitler." The term, "Great Patriotic War" had become so loaded that by 1990 its very usage identified the user as a conservative, a traditionalist, or an old fogy. In the article, published in *Literaturnaia gazeta*, Adamovich reiterated an argument that had come to represent the revisionist interpretation of the 1945 victory: "In paying an immense price for the victory over Hitler, the people facilitated the complete victory of Stalin's absolutist tyranny." Of course it was necessary to defeat Hitler, Adamovich wrote. The big challenge during the war was to remain human while being squeezed by two inhumane tyrannies. Hitler and Stalin were each other's doubles. "How to distinguish between those Hitler killed and those Stalin killed, if they killed our people the same way—one entering the country from the outside, the other—from within." Hitler had his Khatyn, and Stalin his Kuropaty. Kuropaty is a wooded area in Belarus containing recently discovered mass graves from 1937–1938. Khatyn was a Belarusian village. In 1943, with the help of the *Polizei*, collaborators from the local population, the Germans rounded up all the residents of the village of Khatyn—including the children—into a wooden barn and burned them to death, a fate they meted out to more than six hundred villages in Belarus (see fig. 24).

Stalin and Hitler did each other's work, wrote Adamovich. Stalin served Hitler's cause when he shot those tens of thousands of experienced Soviet military commanders in the purge of the army and navy. And Hitler did Stalin's work, killing off the bespectacled members of the intelligentsia, only he wasn't thorough enough about the Jews to satisfy the Georgian leader.

Adamovich, himself a former partisan, exploded the war cult's "Glory to our partisans!" myth. He recalled that in 1944, in the Vitebsk region, the high command of the army managed to pull together most of Belarus's partisans, tens of thousands of them, to await reinforcements from the regular army—but these never came, and thousands of partisans were mowed down by German tanks. Adamovich suggests that this all happened according to plan, that Stalin feared partisans as potential postwar terrorists and arranged to have them taken care of before the war's end. " 'Glory to our partisans!' but it is better, easier, safer, if they have first died a heroic death!"

Adamovich also dismantled the legend about the wartime unity of the Soviet people. Quite the contrary, for him the war was in many ways a continuation of the 1918–21 Civil War—virulently divisive, conflicted, strife-filled. Gentiles against Jews, collaborators against noncollaborators, Stalinists versus anti-Stalinists—these were just some of the wars being waged on Soviet territory in 1941–45 during the war with Germany.[6]

But not all memories are so negative. Other survivors of the war—particularly women—recall those years as a positive experience in which the national divisiveness that has lacerated the USSR in recent years was nowhere in evidence. "I was a participant in the war and from 1941 until 1945 I helped the wounded," wrote a woman with a Ukrainian name in a letter published in *Izvestiia*. "They were all dear to me. I was with the 223rd Azerbaijani Division defending the Caucasus. And it never came into my head to think about which of my friends were Azerbaijani, and which ones were Armenian or Georgian. . . . Let the memory of the war, the friendship of peoples tempered in its fires, be an example for our conscience today."[7]

In 1989 I spoke with two Muscovite women in their early seventies. Their voices breaking with emotion, they recalled their wartime years as navy nurses as the most satisfying period of their lives. "Never again did we feel so absolutely needed," explained Tamara, a cheerful, athletic-looking woman with close-cropped gray hair and a youthful complexion. "Of course the work was horrible. I spent most of the war in a makeshift hospital along the Ladoga lifeline that supported Leningrad during the blockade. There was bombing all the time. And I will never forget the incredible stench in the separate tent we had for victims of gangrene. When after the war I had a son, I already knew how to feed him after all those years of feeding paraplegics."

"But those were our finest hours, the most brilliant time of our lives," added her old friend Lela, a small but vigorous woman with a melancholy face. "I know that the regime here has for years exploited the memory of the war to militarize the youth and so on, but nonetheless, for our generation the memory of the war is a holy memory."

During the war they were young, energetic, selfless. They knew what was right and what was wrong. Moral questions seemed easy and clear, unlike the terrible confusion of today's chaotic times.

The "Great Patriotic War" was neither consistently great, nor consistently patriotic. Ales Adamovich called it the "war with Hitler," but that is not right either, since he himself points out that during the war Stalin was no less an enemy to the Soviet people than was Hitler. It was just a war that, like all wars, revealed the extremes in human behavior—bravery, self-sacrifice, sadism, treachery, cowardice.

Out of the rubble of the Soviet Union, painfully, insistently, real memories of the 1941–45 war have been coming out, from the bottom and the edges of society. Descendants of the war's hidden heroes—members of punishment battalions, prisoners of war—are demanding that their loved ones be rehabilitated and given at the very least the same honors as other veterans. The *shtrafniki*, of course, will need to receive their honors posthumously; almost none of them returned from the war and those who did, did not last long. Many of the war prisoners ended up in Soviet labor camps for the crime of having surrendered to the enemy, victims first of Hitler then of Stalin. Now a few survivors of this fate and their children have been demanding—and receiving—rehabilitation and veterans' benefits. With the recent compulsion to honor the war's real victims, even the Vlasovites—an anti-Stalinist collaborationist army that fought alongside the Germans in 1944—are now, in some quarters, considered heroes who sacrificed themselves in a courageous effort to rid Russia of its hated tyrant.

A number of television documentaries in the past three years have taken up the cause of those many participants in the war who disappeared without a trace, missing in action. Volunteers have been combing forests and slogging through swamps in former battle zones where an untold number of war victims—probably two to three million of them—lie unburied and unidentified.

At informal Victory Day gatherings people still bear placards pleading for information about their missing fathers, brothers, grandfathers, front buddies. In 1990 at the forty-fifth, I saw a man no longer young, with a face utterly devoid of emotion, stand-ing stock-still in the Bolshoi Theater park and holding a sign asking for information about his father, whose wartime photograph showed a handsome young soldier with the same vacant face. A passer-by told me in a whisper that every year, for as long as he could remember, that soldier's widow had held up that same photograph in exactly the same spot in the park; as now the son had taken over, the old woman was presum-ably infirm, or dead.

The one prime—even primal—act of respect that any army owes its soldiers is to bury those killed in action and notify their loved ones. The young volunteers who are now doing the grisly work of sorting out the war dead may well deride their former government for having constructed tens of thousands of war memorials, while leaving millions of carcasses to rot in the forests and swamps of the Motherland to whom those unnamed unfortunates gave their lives.

Many surviving veterans complain that the regime has been no less callous toward them, denying them necessary medical care, decent housing, the most basic amenities of life. On Victory Day 1991, the progressive newspaper *Kuranty* published an article entitled "I Was Needed While I Fought," written by a veteran who lashed out in rage about his tiny pension. The sentiment was very familiar, but his argument had a dis-tinctly modern twist: "In *Argumenty* [*i fakty*] they wrote that in America after only ten years of service a soldier is fully supported for the rest of his life."[8] From the very first days after the war's end, veterans, particularly invalids, were neglected, until a little over a decade ago, when the Brezhnev regime granted them a few privileges accom-panied by the specious organized homage to those who had fought in the war.

The veterans' license to some few coveted goods and conveniences has exacer-bated an already troublesome tension between the generations which gained freer expression when by the end of the decade—like so much else—glasnost and a grow-ing disdain for the military combined with almost unprecedented shortages of con-sumer goods to make tempers short. "My mother was never at the front, and she didn't work in war industry," a taxi driver explained to me in June 1991. "But," he continued, "she ran herself ragged trying to feed her children in our Urals-region evacuation, where there was far less food than at the front. She worked and suffered as much as any veteran. Why shouldn't she be entitled to privileges too?"

In the late Gorbachëv era, the press published many letters from indignant veter-ans, complaining of shabby treatment by their compatriots. "I walked, limping (my wounded leg was hurting) and hesitantly placed myself at the head of a taxi queue at the Kiev Railroad Station [in Moscow]," began one such letter. " 'Look at the *Vova*,' curtly remarked a woman holding a string bag." [The derisive term *vova* comes from the acronym for the words *Velikaia Otechestvennaia voina*, or Great Patriotic War.] "As a rule, I almost never avail myself of my insignificant privileges," continued the author, "since they elicit only humiliation and insults. '*Vovy*' indeed! Like mammoths we are disappearing from the face of the earth. We limp, get sick, forget things, repeat ourselves. We cling to our battle stripes, our wounds and medals, only because they dare to demean us with pitiful privileges, pitiful pensions, vacant glances."[9]

The fiftieth anniversary of the invasion was but the first of many half-century commemorations connected with the war that Russians have marked and surely will continue to mark until Victory Day, May 9, 1995. Characteristically, on December 5, 1991 the Soviet army newspaper, *Krasnaia zvezda*, hailed the fiftieth anniversary of the Red Army's first victory in the war—the Battle of Moscow—with a classic coverage, including the front-page publication of a self-congratulatory *prikaz* (order) by USSR Minister of Defense Shaposhnikov directing that the capital mark the event with fireworks. At the same time, some articles in the more liberal newspapers made it a point to parallel the ordeal of the war with the collapse of the Soviet economy and the Soviet Union. For example, a piece in *Izvestiia* about a reunion of veterans of the Ladoga "lifeline" on the fiftieth anniversary of its inauguration, ended with an ominous warning: "Today we need to rescue from hunger those people who in an earlier day saved Leningraders from death."[10] Surely one of the most despairing cries was uttered by one O. Golubeva, an invalid of the Great Patriotic War residing in Saratov, whose letter was published in *Literaturnaia gazeta*. After a bitter lament about the outrageously high prices of goods (and this was some months before the momentous price rises of January 2, 1992) and an utter condemnation of an uncaring government, she concluded: "I envy my friends who died in the war. I envy the fact that they left this life without having lost their faith, without becoming disillusioned."[11]

On the afternoon of June 22, 1991, the fiftieth anniversary of the German invasion of the Soviet Union, I went to Moscow's Poklonnaia Hill, the site of a planned central museum and monument to the "Victory of the Soviet People in the Great Patriotic War." Accompanied by a bushy-haired philologist with the Gogolian name of Flavius who worked on the staff of the not-yet-completed Central Museum of the Great Patriotic War, I ascended a grassy mound not far from the museum construction site and joined a crowd of some two hundred people assembled near a large, rough-hewn, wooden cross. Like most everyone else, Flavius and I each bought a tan candle from a kerchiefed woman who was selling them out of a worn tote bag. To the tolling of bells suspended from a wooden frame, a Russian Orthodox priest and church choir appeared, followed by parishioners bearing icons. When he reached the cross the priest, an enormous man in golden robes, performed a requiem mass in memory of the victims of the Great Patriotic War.

This was a fitting, affecting memorial to the Soviet people who fought and died in the war with Germany. The priest chanted out the names of the war dead given to him by the crowd, and also invited the congregation to pronounce out loud the names of their loved ones who had died in the war. Women and men called out those names simultaneously in a cacaphonous cry of mourning followed by a stream of mellifluous *Alleluia*'s that wafted out into the warm gray summer air. For me, the event was only slightly soured by the fact that it was evidently inspired by the Russian nationalism of the early nineties—at once prideful and xenophobic. Prominently displayed in front of the cross was a large icon of St. George the Dragon-Slayer, patron saint of the ultranationalistic organization, *Pamiat'*.

The monument to the victory of the Soviet people in the Great Patriotic War may or may not be constructed. The museum may or may not be completed. But it is certain that, year in and year out, no matter what form of government they have, Russians and other peoples of the former Soviet Union will remember to pray for the souls of those millions and millions of children, women, and men who perished in the war between their country and Nazi Germany.

## Notes

1. Leonid Gurevich, "Ostanovite puliu," *Iunost'* 7 ( July 1987), 11.
2. *Komsomol'skaia pravda* (May 5, 1990).
3. Ibid.
4. *Literaturnaia gazeta* (March 7, 1990). For a moving review of the film, see Viacheslav Kondratev, "*Parii voiny*," ibid. ( Jan. 31, 1990).
5. Iurii Geller, "Nevernoe ekho bylogo," *Druzhba narodov* 9 (1989), 229–44.
6. "Kuropaty, Khatyn, Chernobyl," *Literaturnaia gazeta* (Aug. 15, 1990).
7. *Izvestiia* (April 28, 1990).
8. *Kuranty* (May 9, 1991).
9. *Sovetskaia kul'tura* (April 14, 1990).
10. *Izvestiia* (Nov. 25, 1991).
11. *Literaturnaia gazeta* (Oct. 30, 1991).

# Contributors

Jeffrey Brooks is Professor of History at The Johns Hopkins University and author of *When Russia Learned to Read.*

Peter Kenez is Professor of History at the University of California at Santa Cruz and author of *Civil War in South Russia, Birth of the Propaganda State,* and *Cinema in Soviet Society.*

Louise McReynolds is Associate Professor of History at the University of Hawaii and author of *News Under Russia's Old Regime.*

Argyrios K. Pisiotis is a Doctoral Candidate in Russian History and German and East European Studies at Georgetown University who has published on Balkan and European affairs.

Harlow Robinson is Associate Professor of Russian at SUNY-Albany and author of *Sergei Prokofiev* and *The Last Impresario.*

Robert A. Rothstein is a Professor in the Department of Slavic Languages and Literatures at the University of Massachusetts, Amherst.

Rosalinde Sartorti teaches Cultural History at Freie Universität Berlin and is author of *Pressefotographie und Industrialisierung in der Sowjetunion.*

Harold Segel is Professor of Literature at Columbia University and author of *Turn-of-the-Century Cabaret* and *Twentieth Century Russian Drama.*

Richard Stites is Professor of History at Georgetown University and author of *Women's Liberation Movement in Russia, Revolutionary Dreams,* and *Russian Popular Culture.*

Nina Tumarkin is Professor of History at Wellesley College and author of *Lenin Lives!* and *The Living and the Dead.*

James von Geldern is Associate Professor of Russian at Macalester College. He is author of *Bolshevik Festivals* and coeditor (with Richard Stites) of *Mass Culture in Soviet Society.*

# Index